Romantic Vision, Ethical Context

Romantic Vision,

Ethical Context

Novalis and

Artistic Autonomy

Géza von Molnár

Theory and History of Literature, Volume 39

University of Minnesota Press, Minneapolis

Published by the University of Minnesota Press
2037 University Avenue Southeast, Minneapolis MN 55414.
Published simultaneously in Canada
by Fitzhenry & Whiteside Limited, Markham.
Printed in the United States of America.

Library of Congress Cataloging-in-Publication Data

Molnár, Géza von, 1932-
    Romantic vision, ethical context.

    (Theory and history of literature; v. 39)
    Bibliography: p.
    Includes index.
    1. Novalis, 1772-1801 — Criticism and interpretation.
2. Romanticism — Germany.   3. Romanticism.   I. Title.
II. Series.
PT2291.Z5M64   1986   831'.6   86-11229
ISBN 0-8166-1496-2
ISBN 0-8166-1497-0 (pbk.)

The University of Minnesota is an
equal-opportunity educator and employer.

For Barbara, Karen, and Anina,
and for M and B

Theory and History of Literature
Edited by Wlad Godzich and Jochen Schulte-Sasse

The kind words, "amiable enthusiast," "poetic dreamer," or the unkind ones, "German mystic," "crackbrained rhapsodist," are easily spoken and written; but would avail little in this instance. If we are not altogether mistaken, Novalis cannot be ranged under any one of these noted categories; but belongs to a higher and much less known one, the significance of which is perhaps also worth studying, at all events will not till after long study become clear to us.

Thomas Carlyle ("Novalis")

Novalis a romantika egyetlen igazi poétája, az egyetlen, akiben dallá vált a romantika egész lelke és akiben csak ez vált dallá. A többiek, ha költők voltak is, csak romantikus költők voltak, akiknek csak költők motivumokat adott a romantika, módosította, gazdagította fejlődésüket, de költők voltak már, mielőtt az új érzést magukban felismerték volna és azok maradtak megváltozott látással is. Novalis élete és költészete — nem tehetek róla, itt nincs más igazság, mint ez a banalitás — elválaszthatatlanul egy és a maga egységében symboluma az egész romantikának.

Novalis is the only true poet of the Romantic school. In him alone the whole soul of Romanticism turned to song, and only he expressed nothing but that soul. The others, if they were poets at all, were merely Romantic poets; Romanticism supplied them with new motifs, if altered the direction of their development or enriched it, but they were poets before they recognized Romantic feelings in themselves and remained poets after they had completely abandoned Romanticism. Novalis' life and work — there is no help for it, it is a platitude but it is the only way of saying it — form an indivisible whole, and as such they are a symbol of the whole of Romanticism.

György Lukács (Soul and Form)

Contents

Acknowledgments

Many people have known about my work on this book and have helped generously in word and deed to sustain me in my efforts. Friends in Vermont, New Hampshire, California, Washington, in Wisconsin's Spring Green and Chicago's North Shore, in Melbourne, Amsterdam, London, Kiel, and Heidelberg, my thanks to you all and to my family on whose patient and steady support I relied most heavily.

A fellowship from the American Council of Learned Societies and leaves of absence granted by Northwestern University assisted me in pursuing my studies; I gratefully acknowledge my debt to both institutions.

I also wish to thank the editors and publishers of *Studia Mystica, Erkennen und Deuten* (Berlin: Erich Schmidt Verlag, 1983), and *Versuche zu Goethe* (Heidelberg: Lothar Stiehm Verlag, 1976) for permission to include passages from articles previously published. Furthermore, Frederick Ungar Publishing Co. graciously allowed me to rely on Palmer Hilty's English text of *Heinrich von Ofterdingen* for my translations of excerpts from this work.

Finally, I wish to extend my heartfelt gratitude to Jochen Schulte-Sasse for joining me in this enterprise.

Foreword
Do We Need a Revival of Transcendental Philosophy?
Jochen Schulte-Sasse

I

The series in which Géza von Molnár's relatively specialized study of the early German romantic thinker and poet Novalis is appearing has, in the past, garnered the unintended image that it deals primarily with general and theoretical concerns. Yet, besides seeking to bridge the gap between theory and history so often perceived as adverse to one another, it has always been part of our intellectual project to promote specialized studies that are narrow and traditional in the best sense, but which also contribute to a larger project and relate directly or indirectly to broader aspects of ongoing debates. To mention a few examples: we find Jay Caplan's study of Diderot, Daniel Cottom's study of George Eliot, and the present book to be excellent examples of how specialized studies can relate to more general issues. Not only do all three authors refuse to take the canon of their respective fields for granted, but they also reflect on connections between their own subject matter and contemporary debates while simultaneously addressing the research interests of specialists.

Von Molnár expresses his intentions in relation to current debates very clearly in the last chapter of his book. By reconstructing abandoned stages in the history of transcendental philosophy — i.e., the transcendentalism of Novalis, who was next to Friedrich Schlegel *the* major thinker and poet of early German romanticism, and, via Novalis, of Fichte and Kant — von Molnár argues for the relevance and necessity of a revival of that philosophical tradition. He insists, for example, that Fichte's arguments against the realists' concept of reality are still valid and that they can be turned against the more recent ''and equally misconceived point of view — actually the same one reversed — that assigns reality to language or *écriture* exclusively.'' He states provocatively that ''the prison wall of things has merely been exchanged for one of words, and the only difference is that the former makes the world into a prison, whereas the latter pretends to make the prison into a world.'' Furthermore, he believes ''the transcendental approach offers a possibility for avoiding the mutual exclusion of the consciously real and the reality referred to, because it provides a perspective that can account for both spheres of reality'' (p. 195 below).

Is there indeed a need for a revival of transcendental philosophy? And if so, which of the many varieties of transcendentalism? Any contemporary attempt to reconstruct and appropriate the tradition of transcendental philosophy has to be assessed in the context of the best known and most influential of such attempts; that is, in the context of Jürgen Habermas's work. In this foreword, I first discuss the similarities and, more important, the differences between the two attempts at reviving transcendental philosophy represented by von Molnár's book on Novalis and by Habermas' *Knowledge and Human Interests*. Both books invite such a comparison because both regard Fichte's philosophy as the starting point for a rethinking of contemporary intellectual issues. Second, toward the end of my foreword, I discuss the mutual interests underlying such reconstructions of self-reflective reason and how they compare with another, competing tradition, one not guided by a concept of self-reflective reason but rather by one of deconstructive imagination or fancy and its conceptual derivations. Paradoxically, it will turn out that both traditions have their roots in the very same historical juncture in which thinkers first tried to grasp the features of emerging modern societies and the impact of modernization on culture. Afraid of the effect of instrumental reason on intellectual life in general, they reflected on cultural modes of resistance capable of preventing linguistic and cognitive atrophy. In a sense, the critique expressed by von Molnár in his last chapter points to a rift in the family.

II

In *Knowledge and Human Interests*, his first major philosophic work, Habermas made his ''way over abandoned stages of reflection'' in order ''to recover the forgotten experience of reflection.''[1] It is no mere coincidence that Habermas develops his notion of self-reflective reason in the context of a historical reconstruction of the philosophical achievements of Johann Gottlieb Fichte, the same thinker who had such an important influence on Novalis and who plays an equally important role in von Molnár's book. According to Habermas, Kant solved the problem of the unity or synthesis of representations, i.e., the unity of human consciousness, by assuming that unity is brought about by self-consciousness, that is, "by my representing to myself the identity of consciousness in these representations" (p. 37). Kant's answer, though, is insufficient since it only enables us to think of self-consciousness as the representation "I think," which accompanies "identically all other representations, without this representation itself being able to be accompanied by and reflected by a further one" (p. 37). In other words, Kant solved the problem of individual identity on the basis of a basic and unsublatable duplicity, the difference between the synthesis of all individual representations and the accompanying one of "I think." Precisely in overcoming this simultaneity of sameness and otherness lies the importance of Fichte, according to Habermas, who introduces his own notion of reflective reason by proceeding, out of historical sequence, in his reconstruction of the abandoned stages of reflection: from Kant to Hegel to Marx to Fichte, showing that each of these philosophers achieved something that can and should be recovered. What Fichte achieved, what makes him a more pivotal thinker to Habermas than Marx, whose materialist accomplishments Habermas also wants to preserve, is a notion of reflection "that goes one step further than self-consciousness" (p. 37). Fichte, according to Habermas, insists

that whoever wants radically to think himself must depart from the dimension of mere thinking and representing. . . . Self-consciousness is not an ultimate *representation* that must be able to accompany all other representations: it is an *action* that goes back inside itself and thus in its own accomplishment simultaneously makes itself transparent — an act that becomes transparent to itself in the course of its own achievement. (pp. 37-38)

This precisely is the starting point for a reconstruction from which Habermas can unfold his own concept of self-reflective reason. Social interaction in every society is determined by a form of consciousness that is a complex conjunction of habits, norms and values, historically grown dispositions, and so on. Under normal, unreflected circumstances, such forms of consciousness operate with the force of unquestioned, involuntary transcendental rules. Trying to recover Fichte's concept of activity (*Tathandlung*) within a materialistic philosophy as an act of conscious apprehension of such rules, as an act of release from a state of bondage, and, hence, of self-generation, Habermas argues that Marx limited his investigations "to historical formations of the ego and the non-ego, to societal subjects and their material environment" (p. 43) without investigating the possibility of self-reflexivity which Fichte discussed along with his concept of the absolute ego. When Marx conceived of human interaction merely in terms of instrumental action and reduced reflection to labor, he deluded himself, according to Habermas, about the nature of reflection (see p. 43) and, in effect, concealed the difference between science and criticism. In short, Marx is, in Habermas's view, a victim of the very positivistic epistemology prevalent in most nineteenth-century writings.

From this perspective, Marx — at least in one aspect of his thinking — has fallen prey to a central feature of the culture-political project of social modernity, the instrumentalization of the human mind for the economic well-being of all. But, on one level, Habermas' notion of reflective reason can also be seen as a rather instrumentalized notion. Reflective reason cannot take effect without appropriating language as a medium. For Habermas, though, this does not pose a serious problem since he conceives of language, the basis of communication, as an instrument rather than an agency in its own right. In other words, language viewed as an unproblematic means of communication can only be distorted from without, through mechanisms of social repression; it cannot itself be a distorting force. This assessment of Habermas's concept of language is only contradicted at first glance by statements like the following.

> The grammatical relations of communication, once distorted by force, exert force themselves. . . . The distortion of the dialogic relation is subject to the causality of split-off symbols and reified grammatical relations: that is, relations that are removed from public communication, prevail only behind the backs of subjects, and are thus also empirically coercive. (pp. 58-59)

Habermas, though, insists that ideology-critical reflection, by making the context of the genesis of prevailing ideologies transparent, can in principle always dissolve such distortions by applying the nonlinguistic means of rational argumentation. To be sure, an ideology critique informed by semiotics can often make us cognizant of "the causality of split-off symbols and reified grammatical relations" and can thus help us in overcoming the effect of such symbols and grammatical relations. The question remains whether such "distortions" can be completely overcome by interpretative moves that stay within an established semantic order. As far as I can see, Habermas never doubts that *all* such "distortions" can be dissolved through communicative strategies that remain external to linguistic considerations. This becomes most evident when he explicitly speaks of the linguistic dimension of a social practice of self-reflective reason:

> Once the interpreter is socialized in his mother tongue and has been instructed in interpreting as such, he does not proceed *subject* to transcendental rules [as is the case in the behavioral system of instrumental action], but *at the level* of transcendental structures themselves. He can decipher the experiential content of a historical text only in relation to the transcendental structure of the world to which he himself belongs. Here theory and experience are not divorced, as they are in the empirical-analytical sciences. When a disturbance occurs in a communicative experience that is reliable according to common schemata of world-interpretation and of action, the interpretation that must be made immediately is directed simultaneously at the experiences acquired in a

world constituted through ordinary language and at the very grammatical rules that constitute this world. Such interpretation is linguistic analysis and experience at once. (p. 193)

That is to say, interpretation is supposedly capable of changing the level of transcendental structures *themselves*, i.e., the rules according to which individuals and societies reproduce themselves ideologically or normatively or morally, even if interpretation proceeds from a starting point *within* an existing semantic (ideological) system. (For Habermas, that is the only starting point possible.) In this case, linguistic analysis can only mean relating linguistic structures to strictures that not only *exist* outside, i.e., independent of linguistic structures, but that can be *comprehended* independent of those structures. Whereas the normative rules constituting communicative action are transcendental, the differential linguistic system as such is not. The rules which reason is supposed to examine self-reflectively are allegedly autonomous in relation to language. Had Habermas ascribed transcendental status to language, he would have had to grant rhetorical strategies capable of deconstructing differential linguistic systems a systematic function in his thinking. In effect, this would have bridged the gap between the two philosophical traditions I mentioned above, the traditions of self-reflective reason and of deconstructive imagination. Therefore, the status Habermas ascribes to language is all the more important with regard to differences between the two traditions.

This is exactly the point where the transcendentalism of the early romantics, including that of Novalis in particular, can offer an awareness of problems that is lacking in Habermas' attempt to reconstruct a transcendental philosophy *after* the historical achievements of materialism. Depending on which of the various features of the early romantics' thinking is chosen for emphasis, one can merge the tradition of transcendentalism represented in Novalis's writings with the tradition of transcendental philosophy in general, including Habermas's version of critical philosophy — thus collapsing differences in that tradition — or one can uncover a rift in this very tradition, which paradoxically would move Novalis closer to that other tradition I mentioned, the tradition of deconstructive fancy. But Novalis' thinking is as relevant as it is because it cannot be merged fully with either one.

III

In his *Wissenschaftslehre*, Fichte had assumed that the positing of the nonego (that is, of objects, whether material or spiritual) precedes all individual thought and provides the foundation for identity and for thinking in identities (in the context I am concerned with here we can say: in semantically defined entities). This means concretely that the ego exists only as something always already filled up with perceptions and that the always already existing division between subject and object, ego and nonego cannot be eliminated or sublated *within* the framework of that division. In other words, within that always already established realm, we cannot trace our perceptions to their origins thus making them transparent and dissolving their force in developing a consciousness of their own genesis, as the critique of ideologies proposed by critical philosophy attempts to do. On the level of established divisions we can only compare perceptions with one another and favor the one over the other according to accepted rules of logic. For a theory of literature and literary criticism, this means that we can criticize, favor, or reject norms and values portrayed in literature in an open-ended discussion if we choose to do so, but we can only discuss that which is compatible with and mediated by existing cognitive forms — at least if we are committed to the accepted rules of rational argumentation. Starting from the level of existing divisions, we cannot transcend the realm of established norms and values in a radical sense, i.e., in a way that would eliminate our epistemological dependency on existing differential systems of language and ideology.

Fichte's introduction of the "absolute ego" as a horizon transcending the division of ego and nonego has to be understood as an effort to inquire into the conditions for the possibility of overcoming the determining effect of existing structures. It attempts to locate that moment of reflection that enables a sublation (*Aufhebung*) of the always already unfolded system in which we find ourselves. Habermas, as we have seen, did not address language's role as a constitutive medium of existing structures; he did not pursue the question whether language too must be included in our self-reflective efforts to overcome the delimitations of the existing orders.

This is exactly the point where Novalis tries to expand and radicalize Fichte's project, and where his philosophical awareness advances that of Habermas. The early romantics saw themselves confronted with the social process of modernization, which they comprehended as the increasingly universal domination of society by exchange value.[2] Simultaneously, they recognized that as society was progressively becoming a totalized and totalizing structure, subjectivity, the very precondition for a practice of self-reflective reason, had become problematic. On the basis of their analysis of the historical changes society had undergone, the early romantics no longer considered it legitimate to conceive of human beings as agents, who as socially active beings are juxtaposed with the social totality in the way a subject, as a free center of cognition, juxtaposes itself with an object, according to the model of positivistic epistemology. Consequently early romantic thought addressed the basic question: can subjectivity constitute itself in a manner free of domination when the constricted social context has inevitably engraved itself on that subject, both in material and in linguistic terms?

In contrast to the kind of transcendentalism represented by Habermas, Novalis assumes that language and self-reflective reason are intertwined in a mode that cannot remain external to either. Art, which in Habermas' thinking never retained a constitutive function except as a compensatory counterbalance to the one-sided demands of modern life,[3] takes on an irrevocable and unrelinquishable role within Novalis's attempt to think a praxis of self-reflective reason. In his view, artistic praxis is the only available linguistic practice that employs rhetorical strategies capable of preventing everyday language from atrophying. The artist's production of signs amounts to a suspension of the existing divisions of subject and object, ego and nonego, in the self's agency. Novalis calls the state in which such sign production becomes possible "freedom," which in turn is the effect of "suspended [and suspending] imagination" (N II, 188).[4]

As a result, the concept of "imagination" plays a central role in Novalis's thinking. Functionally, it occupies a place equivalent to the one self-reflective reason occupies in Habermas's thinking. This functional equivalence becomes evident when Novalis identifies "practical reason" with "pure imagination" (N II, 258; see p. 51 below). The big difference is that Novalis attaches the possibility of progress to art as an institutionalized medium of suspension or chaos that can halt the effectiveness of the existing order temporarily. In Novalis's view, transcendental rules guiding social interaction can only be reflected productively, and then changed, in a state of suspended imagination ("Gesetz muß Produkt der Freyheit seyn," N II, 188), in which the usual political as well as epistemological dependency of humankind on the differential system of language and ideology has become indeterminate. This, in my opinion, is the context in which Novalis's often discussed statement "In each poetic statement, chaos must shimmer through the veil of regular order" (see p. 157 below) has to be understood.

With this newly defined social potential of art in modernized societies in mind, Novalis can logically state: "The artist is thoroughly transcendental. . . . Literature is the high art of constructing transcendental health. Thus the poet is the transcendental physician. . . . Literature merges everything toward its end of all ends — *the elevation of man above himself*." ("Der Künstler ist durchaus transscendental. . . . Poesie ist die große Kunst der Construction der transscendentalen Gesundheit. Der Poet ist also der transscendentale Arzt. . . . Die Poesie . . . mischt alles zu ihrem großen Zweck der Zwecke — der *Erhebung des Menschen über sich selbst*.") (N II, 534-35) Taking advantage of the artist as transcendental physician is, of course, no more than an opportunity offered to modern societies that want to overcome ideological atrophy. Art cannot, in and of itself, and from a position of historical necessity, "construct transcendental health." As a matter of fact, Novalis included a scene in his unfinished novel *Heinrich von Ofterdingen* that illustrates very well how art can and will be integrated into society affirmatively if one accepts uncritically the project of modernity, in which the differentiation of social totality into functionally differentiated subsystems is a constitutive part.[5] (Von Molnár deals with this scene on p. 131 below.) The merchants who usually obey "the continued demand of mercantile interests," i.e., who normally live according to the rules of instrumental reason, are elevated by art to a state of "enjoyment" and "ecstasy." In moments of aesthetic pleasure they can free themselves from the strictures imposed on them by the division of labor. Art here assumes a compensatory, counterbalancing function, which is the prevailing function of aesthetic enjoyment in modernity.

It is, of course, not enough to simply state that art could "construct transcendental health" without further justifying the necessity of such a project. Novalis holds that any reflective move against false forms of consciousness, i.e., any human self-realization, is only possible on the basis of self-representation. To assume, however, that representing our being to ourselves is possible is, in his eyes, one of the most problematic assumptions of idealist philosophy. Von Molnár shows convincingly how important the following statement is within Novalis's philosophy: "The nature of identity can be demonstrated only by a *pseudo-sentence* of identity [since the formula $A = A$ expresses a simultaneity of sameness and otherness]. . . . We leave the *identical* in order to represent it" (See 30 below). Representation undermines any metaphysics of presence.

Novalis nevertheless sees self-representation as both absolutely necessary and principally impossible. Starting from this paradox, he develops a rather revolutionary, modern concept of self-representation. He emphasizes the "re" in representation, that is, the duplicity of being and representation which can never be sublated or conflated. As von Molnár puts it: "The self is on an unending path to itself along which it can only recognize itself negatively, as that which it is not, or, one might add, only in representation," (p. 52 below). What interests me here is the importance of Novalis's ideas for a theory of experience and for the possibility of representing our experiences to ourselves. Novalis conceived of self-representation, despite the constant failure of its final attainment, as a necessary, although Sisyphian, activity that leads humans to an ever clearer understanding of themselves. However, complete awareness of one's self would presuppose, first, a representation of that awareness in signs since we can only understand ourselves if we represent that understanding to ourselves in language; and, second, the identity of the self with its representation. This is, as Novalis sees very clearly, impossible. Yet the paradox of self-representation being both imperative and impossible ensures that we do not fall prey to atrophy; it is a precondition for a state of constant activity, and as such, it is a condition for the potential of art to "construct mental health."

It is in this context that the romantic concept of irony gains importance. Romantic irony is a hermeneutic strategy grounded in the fact that humans are incapable of collapsing the discrepancy between representation and being. In pointing to a basic contradiction between Lukács's notions of irony and of the imitation of reality in his *Theory of the Novel*, Paul de Man expressed this very cogently: "Irony steadily undermines this claim at imitation and substitutes for it a conscious, interpreted awareness of the distance that separates an actual experience from the understanding of this experience."[6]

All of this should demonstrate sufficiently that the transcendentalism of early German romanticism and of Novalis in particular articulates a surprisingly pertinent theory of interpretation, representation, and self-realization that was, at least in some respects, more advanced than the theory of self-interpretation suggested by Habermas. Paradoxically, the idealist Novalis put forward a theory of self-representation that can be read as a more genuinely materialistic theory of self-interpretation than the one proposed by the materialist Habermas.

The idealistic notion inherent in Habermas's concept of self-reflection is particularly evident in his assessment of psychoanalysis as a practice of self-reflective reason. The practice of psychoanalysis becomes relevant for him "as the only tangible example of a science incorporating methodological self-reflection," (p. 214). Although he insists that psychoanalysis did not realize this potential because of its "scientific self-misunderstanding" (p. 214), the potentialities Habermas ascribes to a psychoanalysis not subject to such misunderstandings document his theory of self-representation rather clearly. In regard to this theory it is most telling that he concurs with those (alleged) aspects of Freud's psychoanalytic model that hold that "all habitual interactions and all interpretations relevant to life conduct are accessible at all times" and that psychoanalytic interpretation "works toward the critical dissolution [!] of resistance" (p. 231) and, if successful, "undoes processes of splitting-off" (p. 232). The realm of psychoanalysis, Habermas holds, is "wrong" behavior, i.e., "every *deviation from the model of the language game of communicative action* in which motives of action and linguistically expressed intentions coincide" (p. 226). Habermas, of course, sees that "right" behavior in this sense would be possible "only under the conditions of a non-repressive society" p. 226). But he never doubts the assumption that human intentions can fully coincide with their linguistic expression and that both can coincide just as fully with motives for actions — an assumption that can only be held on the basis of an unproblematized concept of self-representation.

Novalis's grounding of his theory of interpretation and of self-representation is, to be sure, idealistic. But it is easy enough to reverse that grounding in a materialistic context in which we still would have to deal with the conditions under which a representation to ourselves of the text engraved on our minds and bodies by social interaction might be possible. Rational argumentation on the basis of accepted rules and accepted semantic and ideological definitions, no matter how deeply we have comprehended these rules intellectually, would surely not allow for a working-through of such inscriptions. Self-reflection, which does not ascribe transcendental status to language, necessarily remains within the delimitations of accepted functional divisions. Within those delimitations only a chance occurrence of art, as Althusser has suggested, would be able to create moments of suspension which allow for fundamental change. If humankind were incapable of producing and apprehending "transcendental art" consciously, we all would be confined to the state in which Novalis's merchants find themselves. When they feel the effect a new, poetic language has on their self-representations, the merchants — being at home in the realm of established definitions and divisions — can only react with surprise: "one hears a foreign language and is able to understand it nonetheless" (N I, 210, see p. 130 below). The project of modernity as advanced by Habermas relates art to the mental well-being of people like the merchants in *Heinrich von Ofterdingen* — surely honorable and valuable people, as Novalis's novel makes clear.

IV

To be sure, the early romantics' transcendentalism grew out of the same fear that led Habermas to reconstruct the abandoned stages of reflection — namely the fear that the mode of rationality promoted by the natural sciences would be unable to justify rules guiding social interaction, and that in a state dominated by scientific rationality political discourse must turn into disguised mass manipulation. Where scientific reason becomes the only accepted mode of reason, it necessarily displaces public discussions of norms and values into the irrational "no-place" of selfish needs, without ever being able to uncover the motivational power of those needs in a critique of society. Habermas thus emphasized that "where a concept of knowing that transcends the prevailing sciences is totally lacking, the critique of knowledge resigns itself to the function of a philosophy of science, which restricts itself to the pseudo-normative regulation of established research" (p. 4). This runs absolutely parallel to the early romantics' project. Witness Friedrich Schlegel's accusation, in a review of Fichte from the year 1808, that contemporary philosophy has accommodated itself to "that vulgar mathematical-dialectical scientism," which is one of the "fundamental mistakes of the age," and whose influence "surfeits and oppresses the speculative spirit more than it enriches it." Opposed to this, he demanded a "higher form of knowledge" that would abandon the "vulgar objectivity" and not just "prefabricate the history of the self-annihilation of reflection out of the principle of splitting and separating."[7] In a similar vein, he contrasts the merely analytical with the reflective-practical use of reason and blames the atrophy of the latter on the instrumentalization of thought in the course of economic development.

But differences emerge where the reach of self-reflective rationality has to be assessed. Logical argumentation can certainly help free people from those instances of control sanctified only by tradition (the Enlightenment's successful critique of feudal absolutism can serve as an example); no romantic would doubt this. However, since rationality, whether instrumental or self-reflective, merely *dissects* problems, it cannot prevent humanity from falling into the snare of logical advances of thought, which ultimately means that the rules of instrumental

reason and quantifying exchange penetrate thinking as a whole, erasing an aware-
ness of the transcendental status of language. This is inevitable once capitalism
and instrumental reason have established themselves in society and made logical
argumentation the only valid form of intellectual achievement. To put it still
differently, can the very process of forming and discussing opinions be guided
by a form of reason that is not dependent on a gesture of force and that is not
always enmeshed in the interests of a society based on exchange value? The
early romantics answered this question with an emphatic "no." They recognized
that the approaches of both Kant and Fichte were incapable of providing and
justifying a praxis of writing and reading with whose help individuals could
erase the inscription of social totality from the individual's mind and body. They
saw that this approach elevates logocentric thought to the *only* form of thinking.
Yet the specific goal of the romantic project was to destroy the universal power
of "petrifying and petrified reason" (Novalis) so that a freely reflecting subjec-
tivity could be constituted despite social totality.

Here is the precise point where the romantics felt compelled to develop a
concept of imagination or fancy that would institutionalize the praxis of self-re-
flective reason as a rhetorical practice. Kant had already called the imagination
"a productive faculty of cognition," in whose use "we feel our freedom from
the law [!] of association (which attaches to the empirical employment of imag-
ination)."[8] Kant had already defined imagination as a state of mind and mental
force characterized by freedom from logic. For Kant, though, acts of emancipation
instigated by the mental force of imagination were only sporadically necessary,
so that the individual could, when necessary, momentarily overcome instrumental
reason. In other words, he derived its necessity in functional terms. For the early
romantics, on the other hand, anarchistic-deconstructive acts of imagination in
the poet's commerce with language were the basic condition necessary for the
recovery of subjectivity; they were supposed to lead to a *fundamental* emancipa-
tion from instrumentality. According to Novalis, the language of literature should
not "be inspired by a corresponding object but [should originate] outside of
so-called mechanical laws. . . . Fancy is such an extramechanical force" (N
III, 430). Fanciful art thus dislodges, in the words of Friedrich Schlegel, "deadly
generalizations. . . . For all poetry begins by sublating the process and the
laws of logically thinking reason and by transporting us again to the beautiful
confusion of fancy, to the original chaos of human nature."[9]

The role ascribed to fancy in the romantic project and the socio-critical,
epistemological, and rhetorical foundation allotted that role place the romantic
project somewhere between the currents of critical transcendentalism and decon-
structive antimetaphysicism. This is one of many reasons why von Molnár's
thorough investigation of such a major thinker in that project as Novalis should
appeal not only to specialists but to a general academic public interested in the
archaeology of current theoretical debates.

Preface

The term "romanticism" invariably elicits such a variety of conceptual associations that its usefulness for designating certain intellectual and literary trends in European cultural history has become increasingly problematic. Whatever difference of opinion might prevail regarding the term's connotations, the list of authors that comes to mind at its mention meets with a far more uniform consensus. Among those whose names present themselves, Novalis is as certain to be counted as would be Coleridge or Wordsworth, yet information about him available to an English-speaking public is disproportionately scarce. There are, to be sure, a number of specialized studies in which individual products of his literary endeavors or isolated aspects of his work are discussed, but none of them furnish a comprehensive analysis of this pivotal thinker's unique attempt at a fusion of art and life in a synthesis that succumbs neither to the simplistic reduction of mimesis nor to the absolutist claims of creative representation.[1] The primary aim of this book, therefore, is to establish Novalis's intellectual identity outside the boundaries of his native land, in a manner that would acquaint the reader with the full dimensions of his ideology's range and depth.

Since general background accounts regarding his life and his circle of friends are readily accessible in standard compendia, familiarity with the most fundamental historical data can be presupposed, which makes an introductory reiteration of it unnecessary. Biographical details are introduced, occasionally at some length, in several chapters, but they serve only as pertinent complements to the stages of Novalis's philosophical and artistic development, in order to indicate the lived reality that nurtures and reflects his spiritual progress. Thus, the continuity of this presentation draws its pace from the inner chronology of the mind and not from the uninterrupted succession of external events. To insist on such an arrangement is no matter of arbitrary choice; it will become clear, later on, that it is most appropriate to the manner in which Novalis came to understand himself and his world.

There are also secondary aims that arise from the primary one just stated. First, some insight is to be offered into the nature of the relationship between philosophy and literature; both are inextricably linked for Novalis, so that any discussion of his work must necessarily shed light on this crucial relationship as well, a relationship that is never absent for any artist, even though few are as consciously aware of it. Consequently, rather detailed expositions of Novalis's interpretations of Kantian and Fichtean philosophy had to be included, which some readers might find trying. I can merely apologize in the hope that their efforts may ultimately prove to have been rewarding since an acquaintance with these speculative efforts becomes essential if romanticism is to be understood in its wider, theoretical context. The German version is characterized by its conscious origin from these schools of thought, and no one succeeded better than Novalis in integrating the abstractions of critical philosophy[2] into an aesthetic and existential reality.

My other and ultimate aim is to redirect attention to a crucial factor in the conceptual matrix of critical philosophy that has largely been neglected in the burgeoning contemporary discussion on the philosophy of literature. In all the diversity of opinion that characterizes that discussion, there seems to be agreement in crediting, or blaming, critical philosophy for setting us on the path to literary autonomy with its attendant schools of theory and criticism, which prevail and proliferate to this day. This line of argument has become so established that it is no longer questioned, and it invariably refers to the epistemological shift effected in the eighteenth century, which Kant fittingly designated a "Copernican Revolution."

If it were merely a matter of epistemology, there would be no refuting the contention that critical philosophy furnishes the ideological basis from which it becomes possible not only to cut off artistic expression from its mimetic bonds but also to deny its relevance to any context external to it. Once this possibility is realized, the result is an artistic or rather literary solipsism that spans the field between a panliterary universe arising from the "deconstruction" of the old one and an infinitesimally relativistic indeterminacy, which might very well move one to ask whether there is "a text in this class," or anywhere else.[3]

However, it is not merely a matter of epistemology; it certainly was not that for Kant, as a closer examination of his philosophy would show, because his epistemological position makes sense only if it is viewed from the perspective of his moral philosophy. In other words, he can only sever the ties between the self's conceptual realm and the world in the *Critique of Pure Reason* because they are confirmed in the *Critique of Practical Reason*. Without the principles enunciated in the second *Critique*, he would indeed have laid the foundation for an inescapable solipsism.

Fichte was fully aware of the linkage between ''practical'' and ''theoretical'' reason and formulated his philosophy accordingly. Novalis, the Fichtean, was equally aware of the same relationship and, unlike those who currently cite critical or romantic philosophy in their deliberations on literary theory and criticism, he never lost sight of it.

I very much hope that this study will aid in regaining sight of this crucial element in early romantic literary theory and practice, not so much in order to justify the philosophical standing of the past but to furnish a corrective that might serve to point out a possible avenue of deliberation in the present.

Introductory Remarks

Since Friedrich von Hardenberg's untimely death in 1801, the name "Novalis," the name under which he had entered the arena of public authorship, has been the password that would initiate outpourings of emotional commentary as vehement as it was diverse. Hordes of young admirers soon began flocking to his grave, according to the wrath-inflated report by the elder Goethe, and his friends did much to imply his canonization as the first saint of the new church that was then emerging from the romantic admixture of aesthetics, metaphysics, and nationalist nostalgia; but only much later did he take hold in the popular imagination as "The Poet of the Blue Flower," by which name, with its attendant ethereal connotations, he is still known to most Germans. Until recently, the history of his fame was essentially the history of a cultic myth that originated with his love for Sophie von Kühn, assumed its doctrine as well as some of its mystery from arbitrary editors like Tieck and Bülow, and derived its substance from all the ardent acclaim and virulent censure it inspired over the years. With the advent of more reliable texts, the accumulated layers of misconception could finally be dispelled and the Novalis unencumbered by the precast mold of a stereotype arch-romantic proved far more fascinating than the revered idol.[1]

Ever more sober and ever more insightful investigations into the many facets of Novalis's endeavors and interests have been conducted these last decades, particularly recently in conjunction with the new critical edition of his works.[2] The notebooks and fragments have drawn more extensive and closer scrutiny,[3] his early attempts at literary expression have found unprecedented exposure,[4] later accomplishments in lyric poetry have been the subject of careful analyses,[5] his historical essay and the great prose works have received a good deal of attention,[6] and much effort has been expended to arrive at an objective determination of Novalis's place in the history of politics and letters.[7] These individual achievements in current research, together with the new availability of primary sources expertly edited as never before, make a comprehensive study on Novalis not only possible but necessary.

Friedrich Hiebel sensed this obvious need and revised his book, which had been standard since 1951, to accommodate the findings and changes in Novalis scholarship that had caused the urgency for revision to arise. He brings a great deal of information, an extensive biography, a new section on the poet's philosophical interests, and thoughtful interpretations of his works; he has also eliminated the previous subtitle "Der Dichter der blauen Blume," and modified it to "Deutscher Dichter: Europäischer Denker: Christlicher Seher," but the basic tenor of the book remains unchanged and its expanded version again serves only to buttress the image of a Christian visionary. Christianity, however, is not the chief concern in Novalis's writings, nor does their sum total culminate in its acclamation. No single topic of the many that comprise Novalis's literary estate, be it mineralogy, poetics, chemistry, religion, geology, politics, history, love, philosophy, nor even his artistic productivity itself, can be said to hold the distinction of such superiority that it subsumes all others under its conclusive importance. The objective categories of his interests simply do not suffice to define his person, because the philosopher is quickly replaced by the poet, the poet by the scientist, the scientist by the lover, the lover by the Christian, the Christian by assorted other religious tendencies, and so on until the round can be recited over again. Needless to say, much of the strife among his adherents and the comparative unison of his disparagers stem from this seeming indeterminateness of personality that defies circumscription by labels coined from recognized accomplishments. This difficulty is easily overcome, once the perspective is reversed and external classifications are no longer considered potential sources for a criterion of evaluation; Novalis's achievements and activities do not define him: he defines them. Nothing he encounters becomes his in the usual sense of transitory ownership that leaves its objects essentially intact; he reformulates everything into his expression and in this manner imparts meaning to the world as he gains an evergrowing awareness of self. All he attains in any walk of life ultimately stands in the service of self-discovery, which does not imply subjectivist isolation in the tradition of Goethe's Werther but rather purposeful activity and engagement with objective reality in an effort to fathom its true relationship to himself. The student, lover, philosopher, poet, Christian, scientist, even the state official, each represent way stations along the road that leads away from the perennial strife between subjective license and objective determinism to the vantage point of freedom, the point of unity that is the self in its function of determining the realms of subject and object as one fundamental reality. Since the theme of this search underlies the profusion of Novalis's recorded thoughts and poetic images, it also supplies the uniform base from which they may be examined.

Amid the variance of scholarly opinion, there has been general agreement for some time that the concept of unity is the single most characteristic concern for Novalis and that he considers the self capable of initiating the process toward realizing it. Even though his terminology may differ according to the topic under discussion, his reflections never cease to probe the possibility of overcoming the primary dualism that underlies all human experience, the schism between subject and object. It is less clear, however, how Novalis envisions this process to take place, what his concept of self entails, or, for that matter, which formulation he deems most appropriate for the ultimate state of harmony. Is it a version of Fichte's Ego, fountainhead of the nonego and the moral imperative for its annihilation? Is it the timeless dream of a new "Golden Age?" Is it chiliastic prophecy, the promise of utopia, a program for the world's aesthetic transformation, or an unrealizable ideal? Are the creative powers of the artist the guarantors of the spirit's oneness with nature? Or is it God? Is God to be approached through any of His creatures, or directly, or by stages along a *via negativa*, or in bursts of ecstasy, or within the confines of formalized religion? These questions and more can be and have been asked concerning Novalis's vision of ultimate unity; aside from reasons of personal prejudice, the answers differ very much in accordance with the respective topological or chronological limits of their authors' research interests.

Surprisingly, none of the numerous studies on Novalis pursue his admittedly central concern persistently throughout his work, which would alleviate some of the confusion. My purpose is to furnish such a study. As unity is the theme common to the entire range of Novalis's preoccupations, his awareness of self and its powers to bridge the gap between subject and object is his consistent point of departure and return. The self marks the division into the basic dichotomy from which all other divisiveness stems and, in this capacity, the self also holds the key to its resolution. The path toward that resolution consists of progressive stages at which the self becomes ever more conscious of its freedom, a freedom characterized neither by the common tendency to absolutize the subject nor by the more esoteric subterfuge of idolatry, of self-denial in order to gain identification with an absolutized objectivity. For Novalis, freedom entails synthesis rather than exclusion and he finds it to be evident whenever the outer and inner realms of reality interpenetrate, from the mind's fleeting consciousness of any given object to the free agency of ethical self-realization which is complemented by the highest form of consciousness, that of "poetic" apperception. As the subsequent chapters will show, Novalis arrives at the conclusion that poetic receptivity and practice are not only the communicative exercise of the self's freedom but also the highest form of recognizing the transcendental horizon of communality within which object and self derive their respective conceptio-linguistic and moral validity. And again, or rather, even more so, art springs neither from an absolute mind nor does it ''mirror'' an absolute nature and, in a corollary sense, the artist is neither the high priest of an esoteric elite with apolitical pretentions nor must his place be sought among those who lose themselves in service to a deified concept of society.

I. Beginnings: 1772-94

Noch war ich blind, doch schwankten lichte Sterne
Durch meines Wesens wunderbare Ferne,
Nichts war noch nah, ich fand mich nur von weiten,
Ein Anklang alter, so wie künftger Zeiten.

I was still blind, but twinkling stars did dance
Throughout my being's limitless expanse,
Nothing had yet drawn close, only at distant stages
I found myself, a mere suggestion sensed in past and future ages.

Novalis

Chapter 1
Early Years

Georg Friedrich Philipp von Hardenberg was the second of eleven children born to Heinrich Ulrich Erasmus and Auguste Bernhardine, his second wife; when she died in 1818, only her son Georg Anton was to survive her by seven years. Short-lived as individual members of the family may have been, its documented history dates back to the twelfth century and the ruins of the ancestral home at Nörten, near Göttingen, add further testimony to its longevity. The background, however, is more impressive than the average circumstances at Oberwiederstedt into which Friedrich entered on 2 May 1772. Very little, other than the name and the social contacts it ensured, lent an aristocratic aura to this household. The father seems to have been of rather narrow financial and intellectual means, shortcomings for which he compensated with a career in the service of the state and a tendency toward righteous overbearance; what openness he had entertained for the world at large had vanished with the death of his first wife, so that the restrictions of country living were further enhanced by the studied and religiously inspired provincialism of his attitude. The rigors of this unpromising setting were supposedly softened by the mother, whose devotion to her husband and children invariably merits special mention in all biographical sketches on the poet, just as the father's character never escapes criticism. This juxtaposition, founded on passages from the family's correspondence and, occasionally, on remarks made by outsiders, can be presented in drab or lighter colors; the inescapable conclusion is that social, cultural, and intellectual stimulation did not abound where the elder Hardenberg held sway. Yet his son's early records indicate that he suffered little from these restrictions. The general impression they convey is one of a

lively youth with a keen appreciation of female companionship and the happy
disposition to be very much at home in his world. Whatever conflict existed
between the generations was comparatively mild and moved along the time-hon-
ored topos of the son's floundering in his preparation for a career or entertaining
disadvantageous matrimonial plans, which tested the father's patience to the
point of threats. There were undoubtedly great, even forbidding differences
between the two, as Friedrich's brother, Erasmus, points out in harsh terms when
he counsels against the advisability of seeking an administrative position under
paternal supervision:

> Gesetzt aber auch, Du erhieltest die Stelle noch bei Lebzeiten des Vaters,
> so müßtest Du doch vorher eine ganze Zeitlang unter ihm und, wenn Du
> sie erhalten hättest, vielleicht mehrere Jahre mit ihm arbeiten und daher
> fast immer um ihn sein! Nun dächte ich doch, müßte Dich eine 22 jährige
> Erfahrung hinlänglich belehrt haben, daß Ihr beide euch nicht
> zusammenpaßt, daß die unendliche Verschiedenheit Eurer Denkings- und
> Handlungsart und weise eine ungeheure Kluft zwischen Euch
> befestigt hat, so daß, wenn Du auch nach den Grundsätzen: daß man mit
> allen Menschen müsse leben und auskommen können, zu einem Vergleiche
> die Hand bötest, der Alte doch niemals ihn annehmen, sondern vielmehr
> mit Unwillen von sich weisen würde! — — — —
> Blinder Religionseifer und wütende Feindschaft gegen alles, was
> Neuerung heißt, haben eine ewige Scheidewand zwischen Euch
> aufgerichtet, die weder Toleranz von der einen Seite noch Belehrungseifer
> von der andern je einreißen werden! Wenn ich Dich sehe, welches
> vielleicht bald geschehen kann, werde ich Dir Erdmannsdorf des Älteren
> seine Geschichte erzählen, die muß einem die sächsischen Dienste vollends
> verleiden! — — —

> Let us even assume you were to be granted the position at some future
> date while father is still alive, then this would mean that you would have
> to apprentice yourself to him for quite some time and, possibly, work
> alongside him for several years thereafter; in other words, you would have
> to be around him almost constantly. Now, I should think that twenty-two
> years of experience ought to have taught you sufficiently that the two of
> you are just not the ideal match, that the immeasurable difference in your
> ways of thinking and acting has established an immense gap between you.
> Even if you were to act according to the principle that one ought to be
> able to live and get along with all people and offered him your hand in
> this spirit, the old man would never accept it and reject your offer with
> indignation! — — — —
> Blind religious zealotry and furious enmity against everything that could
> be considered a change or innovation have erected an eternal wall of
> separation between you and cannot ever be torn down, neither by tolerance
> on your part nor by his zeal to give you advice. When I see you, which

may be soon, I shall tell you the elder Erdmannsdorf's story, which is enough of a tale to cure anyone of the desire to enter public service in the state of Saxony altogether. — — —

(IV, 371, ll. 12–29)

There is no reason to doubt this indictment's substance, although the degree of passion is far more indicative of the younger brother's personal feelings. Under these circumstances, it is all the more surprising that these difficulties find such a weak echo in Friedrich's letters, have no obvious bearing on his artistic production, and are without consequence for the actual collaboration between father and son, which began fourteen months after Erasmus's warning. Obviously, Novalis[1] did not permit himself to be drawn into a state of paralyzing frustration nor did he perpetuate the differences between himself and his parent by exhausting his life in useless confrontation; instead, he followed the maxim to seek out grounds of mutual interest that would allow for cooperation without requiring the submission of either partner to the other and leave each his respective integrity. He tends to overcome obstacles rather than relish the suffering and despair they may occasion. Friedrich Schlegel, in contrast to his friend Hardenberg, seems more prone to do just that when, for example, both engaged in unhappy love affairs with the sisters Laura and Julie during their student days at Leipzig. Schlegel strikes a far more pathetic pose, rallying his friends around him to bask in their reaction to his solemn pronouncement that his beloved, by whom he felt betrayed, must die, and later in the stormy relationship he seems to have gone through a period of suicidal inclination, unfailingly eliciting comparison with Werther from those who knew him.[2] Novalis, on the other hand, is not so much interested in dramatizing his plight as he is in coming to terms with it; he takes steps to seek his family's support in obtaining an officer's commission,[3] and after the impossibility of realizing this plan becomes evident, he agrees to complete his studies at Wittenberg, where he remolds his life into a new cast of serious and disciplined effort, at the same time finding new friends and pleasant social diversion to strike an appropriate balance.[4] Schlegel himself sees this difference but does not, as might be expected, fault Novalis for lacking intensity of feeling. On the contrary, Schlegel credits Novalis with showing a capacity for love that surpasses his own and foresees, already at this time, the decisive role this capacity will play in his friend's life:

Lieber Freund! Du wirst sicher noch glücklich werden; übersieh nur die schönen Kräfte Deiner Seele, die Fülle Deiner Einbildungskraft, die Schnellkraft Deines Herzens, die Leichtigkeit Deines Verstandes; und was weit mehr ist, alles das, was zum edlen Manne reifen wird — der Glauben, die schuldlose Zuversicht auf Dich und die Natur, die warme Ehrfurcht für alles Große . . . Ja! Du bist itzt schon glücklich — wenn Du Dich und uns nicht täuschest! Wenn Du wirklich *so* liebst! Du lebst, die andern atmen nur. Was kann das Schicksal gegen dies Gefühl? Trennen, zerstören, des Irrtums zeihen? O! darüber hat die Natur keine Gewalt, denn was bedarf eine solche Liebe? Ist sie nicht in sich selbst alles? und niemand kann sie Dir rauben. — Wie viel glücklicher Du, als ich! Ich wäre, auch glücklich, arm geblieben, denn meine Liebe war kleiner, als ich.

Und zudem bist Du nicht itzt, und mußt Du es nicht sein, zufrieden mit Dir selbst? Du hast Dich selbst nicht verloren — das ist genung. Wenn Du auch nicht fühltest, daß sich die Männlichkeit in Deiner Brust anmeldet — ich würde es sehen an Deinen Handlungen. Sie nahet sich Dir ernst, aber doch milde. Mir nahte sie schrecklich — der erste Gedanke des jungen Mannes war Selbstmord, der zweite ein andrer schrecklicherer Mord.

Dear friend! Rest assured you will be happy one day; just take stock of your soul's beautiful powers: your imagination's abundance, your heart's ever-ready generosity, your intellect's effortless grasp; and — far more important — take stock of those traits that will help you mature into noble manhood: your faith, your innocent trust in yourself and nature, your heart-felt reverence for all greatness. . . . Indeed! You are happy even now, provided you do not deceive yourself and the rest of us, provided your love is *really* that deep and consuming. You are alive, whereas everyone else is merely breathing. What powers has fate over this emotion? At most it can separate, destroy, prove the lover to be in error; over that feeling itself, however, nature has no power because what, after all, does such love require? Is it not perfectly self-sufficient? No one may take it away from you. — How much more fortunate you than I! Even if I had been fortunate enough to be granted my love's desire, I should have remained poor, because my love was smaller than I.

And furthermore, are you not now satisfied with yourself and are you not compelled to be? You have not lost yourself — that is enough. Even if you did not notice that you were about to make the difficult transition into full manhood, I would see it reflected in your actions. Manhood approaches you in all seriousness yet gently. My fate was more terrible: the first thought occasioned in the young man was of suicide, the second of an even more terrible murder.[5]

According to the available documentation, of which this letter is a representative sample, the relative absence of divisive struggle that characterizes Friedrich von Hardenberg's growth into manhood cannot be construed as originating from weakness, submissive adaptability, shallowness of feeling or any other privation of the kind. One gains the impression that his is the very opposite of an impoverished personality, one that owes its remarkable stability to strength rather than circumscribed means.

Hardenberg seems to have had an unusually strong sense of identity that manifested itself not only in his ability to regain his internal balance when confronted by trying situations but also in his eschewal of having to establish his sense of self at the expense of others. His life appears curiously free from those personal antagonisms and rivalries that season the histories of most contemporaries who are to share the stage of intellectual fame with him. Again, Friedrich Schlegel serves to illustrate the point in immediate contrast since some of his rivalries, with Schiller and Woltmann in particular,[6] could easily have involved his friend. Novalis refuses, however, to become embroiled in such clashes and does not follow the all too common practice of establishing his own right and worth by insisting on open triumph over others; even his later objections to Goethe's *Wilhem Meister* do not stem from this desire, as Hans-Joachim Mähl's careful investigations have pointed out.[7] In his dealings with people, Novalis shows varying degrees of cordiality from the ecstatic to cool withdrawal and rarely, if ever, assumes the negative attitude of pronounced and active hostility. He reportedly told Schlegel when they first met that there was no evil in the world,[8] an opinion that sounds childish or saintly in its naivety but actually may be understood as one more expression of a personality that places more trust in its own integrity than in the powers that stand ready to destroy it.

From his ninth year on, after a serious illness had worked a miraculous quickening of the boy's previously sluggish intellect, Friedrich von Hardenberg demonstrated an astounding ability to gather an immense array of knowledge. Here, too, his inclination to assimilate that which lies outside is as evident as it is in his social conduct. Just as Hardenberg seems to group people around himself in a hierarchy of affinity so that others function as an extension rather than abridgment of his person, his self expands in unceasing intellectual and experiential forays. This impression is not only conveyed by the young man whose notebooks are filled with a bewildering wealth of material but also by the boy about to enter his teens, of whom Karl C. E. Schmid, his tutor at the time, reports:

Zuerst lernte ich den schönen, leben- und geistvollen, für Alles regen und Aller Hersen gewinnenden Knaben in seinem zehnten Lebensjahre [1782] kennen. Sein ehrwürdiger, trefflicher Vater nahm ihn damals mit auf eine Reise nach Niedersachsen, wobey mir die besondere Aufsicht über diesen Knaben, dessen übrige Geschwister ihres Hofmeisters nicht beraubt werden sollten, vorzüglich während des Aufenthalts in Luklum, dem Wohnsitz seines Onkels, anvertraut wurde. Es war von meiner Seite der erste Versuch eines Jünglings im Geschäfte der Erziehung, und ich will es offen bekennen, daß ich der zweckmäßigen Leitung eines so empfänglichen, selbstthätigen, originellen und Phantasiereichen Knaben mich nicht gewachsen fand; doch war es vielleicht das mir einzig mögliche negative Verdienst, welches ich mir dadurch erwarb, daß ich mehr den Begleiter, den aufmerksamen Beobachter, den unmerklichen Leiter und Beschützer vor physischer und sittlicher Gefahr, als den bestimmten Lehrer und strengen Führer meines Zöglings machte.

When he was in his tenth year [1782], I first made the acquaintance of the handsome, vital, and intelligent boy, who was responsive to everything around him and charmed everyone's heart. His venerable and excellent father had taken him at that time on a journey to Lower Saxony, and I was entrusted with this boy's care during his stay at Lucklum, the residence of his uncle, because his siblings were not to be left without their regular tutor. On my part, it was a young man's first venture into the business of pedagogy, and I have no qualms admitting that I was but ill equipped to offer purposeful direction to a boy of such intelligence, motivation, originality, and imagination; however, it may have been my only, if negative, merit that I was more of a companion, a careful observer, an unobtrusive guide and a guardian against physical and moral danger than a purposive teacher and strict superior to my charge.

(IV, 567, l. 31–568, l. 9)

Very little else is known concerning his education and development during those early stages; except for a brief stay at the Pietist community in Neudietendorf and a longer one with his uncle in Lucklum, where he seems to have made his only contact with a worldlier atmosphere, his education took place within the territorial and intellectual confines of his home. Given these circumstances, his earliest exercises in poetry show an amazing familiarity with most of the literature available in his day. Even a cursory reading leads to the realization that, at eighteen, he had fully explored this area to which he felt drawn, and Richard Samuel's editorial commentary adds the assurance of detailed proof; Samuel's introduction (I, 439–58) and individual explications in the appendix (I, 630–53) leave no doubt as to the volume and depth of study that must have preceded or accompanied the writing of these poems. In summary:

Hardenbergs fast unglaubliche Aufnahmefähigkeit fremden Dichtungs- und Gedankenguts in seiner Frühzeit — seine Belesenheit schon als Schüler war fabelhaft, wie die unzähligen Bücher- und Namensaufzeichnungen im Jugendnachlaß und die Bibliothek des 18 jährigen erweisen — machen solche Versuche [eine genaue Einordnung nach Einflüssen zu treffen] illusorisch. In Hardenbergs Jugendversuchen macht sich nicht nur der Einfluß der Antike, des französischen, englischen und italienischen Schrifttums geltend — sie spiegeln fast alle Dichtungsströmungen seiner Zeit wider: die Aufklärung und das Rokoko, die Empfindsamkeit und den Pietismus, den Göttinger Hain und den Ossianismus. Dieses Mosaik chronologisch zu ordnen ist nicht möglich.

Hardenberg's almost unbelievable receptivity to literary and intellectual traditions in his early years make any attempt illusory, that would order his own early poems according to a chronology of dominant influences. It is amazing how much he had read, as the library of the eighteen year old and the innumerable recorded names and titles attesting to his activity prove. In his poems one can detect not only the influence of Greco-Roman antiquity, of French, English, and Italian literature but, more than that,

almost all the trends of his own time: Enlightenment and Rococo,
Sentimentalism and Pietism, the style introduced by the poets of the
"Göttinger Hain," and Ossianism. To order this mosaic chronologically
is impossible. (I, 441)

It would be unreal to ascribe independent literary merit to this collection;
Novalis's obvious dependence on models for his astonishing versatility in mood,
style, meter, and topic is too pronounced to permit it. Yet, it is equally impossible
to think of his work simply as imitation because, in his characteristic manner,
he is not satisfied with mere acquaintance but transforms what he finds into his
own. The vast scope of this enterprise quite clearly represents an extremely
ambitious attempt to acquire citizenship in the realm where sovereignty over
language rules supreme.

The two years during which these efforts were concentrated end in the summer
of 1790; Novalis was then under the tutelage of Christian David Jani, a renowned
classicist and head of the Luthergymnasium at Eisleben. According to his younger
brother, Karl, Friedrich had mastered Latin and Greek at age twelve (IV, 531,
ll. 21–23), so that six years later his German renditions of passages from Homer,
Horace, Virgil, and others are sufficiently sophisticated to let these authors come
alive in a foreign tongue. Friedrich's translations mirror quite fittingly the entirety
of this particular phase in his development because all his literary accomplish-
ments at that time can actually be considered translations of the works of others
into his personal sphere of reference. This true form of translating from the
language of one person into that of another is based on the same demanding
level of linguistic craftsmanship that is a prerequisite to any poetic expression
at all, and Novalis furnishes ample evidence of his having attained membership
in the guild by the fall of 1790, when he begins his university studies at Jena.

These early poems show little originality that would attract critical attention;
however, they do convey to the reader certain indications of their author's
inclinations and preoccupations, even though the conventions of form may hide
such individual concerns. For example, the Anacreontic mood that makes itself
felt throughout the collection is not merely a study in style; all available informa-
tion points to the young man's very real interests in matters that furnish the
themes of Anacreontic poetry. In a similar fashion, it may be supposed that
repeated references to content containment, as in the phrase "Philosophie des
Lebens" ("philosophy of life"),[9] are not merely verbal reflexes of popular
Enlightenment doctrine or religious platitudes. Novalis is undoubtedly serious in
his desire to experience in a positive manner whatever limitations life may impose
on him, as containment rather than confinement. If this were not the case, he
would not have been left as unconcerned by the Storm and Stress parole against
all shackles that curb the spirit's freedom; as it is, he hardly acknowledges the
topic. Here is the first indication that his expansive, assimilative drive is com-
plemented by a tendency to observe formal limits.

From the balance of these two directions he would seem to derive the strength, growth, and independence of his personality, because the self needs both — the restrictive moment, to prevent it from becoming lost to the potential infinity of objects that attract its interest, and the outgoing moment, to avoid stagnation within the confines of circumstance and utilitarian concern. It is a balance not easily gained or maintained, but Novalis instinctively recognized its central importance to himself from the very beginning and never loses sight of it. Very early, he becomes aware of this field of stress; it assumes concrete reality for him both in his love for literature, which harnessed the almost limitless power of the imagination to his intellectual sojourn, and also in the limits imposed by his being confined to a pragmatic world. Already at Lucklum, his uncle must have tried to foster an imbalance in favor of the latter, a service the boy rejected and the man still remembers with apparent appreciation of his own good judgment when Novalis writes to Oppel in January of 1800:

Mein Onkel hatte mir oft schon vergebens das Ridicule eines Schöngeistes gezeigt und wenn ich auch im Gefühl dieser Lächerlichkeit mich wohl in Acht nahm meine Vorliebe blicken zu lassen, so konnte ich doch im Stillen nicht unterlassen diese reitzenden Beschäftigungen zu verfolgen.

My uncle had already often pointed out to me how ridiculous those are who dally in the arts, and even though I was careful to hide my predilection because I knew myself to be ridiculous in his eyes, I could not but continue these charming pursuits in private.

(IV, 309, ll. 32-36)

Later on, his poems occasionally dwell on the same theme, at times even from the opposite perspective; "To Lycidas" ("An Lycidas"), for example, written between the autumn of 1788 and the spring of 1789, treats the artist's dilemma with an irony that anticipates the tone set by Heine (1797–1856). After seven stanzas, in which Novalis describes the glorious world of the imagination that must, unhappily, be purchased at the expense of the less splendid but physically far more sustaining gifts proffered by mundane reality, he concludes:

> Von nun an dichte, wer da kann,
> Ich will das Grabscheit nehmen
> Und durch den Schweiß, der mir entrann,
> Die Dichterwut mir zähmen.

> Let him, who can, write poems at will,
> A spade is far more handy,
> And with my sweat I'll surely kill
> All my poetic frenzy.

(I, 494)

Chapter 2
Apprenticeship to Schiller

The same confrontation between life and art, without the benefit of ironic distance, fashions the history of his years at the universities of Jena (1790–91), Leipzig (1791–93), and Wittenberg (1793–94), where he finally brought his studies in jurisprudence to a successful conclusion. Repeatedly, he resolves to restrain the inclination that draws him on in the pursuit of the "fine arts" (*schöne Wissenschaften*) and concentrate his efforts on those studies to which filial and civic duty would commit him in preparation for the realities of gainful employment. In the person of Schiller, that very struggle between duty and inclination reaches its ideal resolution, and for this reason Hardenberg, who comes to know Schiller quite well at Jena, reveres him all his life. Here was someone who could encompass the manifold limitations of corporeal existence and the boundless claims of the spirit in mutual support of each other, who used every privation that would hold him in bondage as one more occasion to make freedom manifest, who stood firmly rooted in the equilibrium between self-abandonment to the limitless possibilities of fantasy and self-elimination in unresisting submission to the demands of physical reality, who had succeeded in uniting artistic ambition and pragmatic necessity into a career that satisfied both without compromise. The impact of Schiller's personality on Novalis was decisive in its stabilizing effect; under its influence he begins to recognize criteria that give direction to his conduct and continue to guide his views on ethics and aesthetics long after those memorable months of their association.

It is Schiller who persuades Novalis that the narrow straights of a useful profession are only stifling for spirits of equal limitation. Armed with this assurance, full of good intentions to remain in the service of his "duty" if only occasional allowances are made for his "inclinations" to the muses, Novalis is about to leave for Leipzig and openly acknowledges great indebtedness to his mentor at Jena along with a deep affection for him:

Ihnen größestentheils werde ich es zuschreiben, wenn diesen Winter mein eifrigster Wille meine Kräfte unterstützt, um die gefährlichste Klippe eines jungen, lebendigen Kopfs die sauren und anhaltenden Vorarbeiten zu einem künftigen, bestimmten Beruf glücklich zu übersteigen, denn Sie machten mich auf den mehr als alltäglichen Zweck aufmerksam, den ein gesunder Kopf sich hier wählen könne und müsse und gaben mir damit den lezten, entscheidenden Stoß, der wenigstens meinen Willen sogleich festbestimmte und meiner herumirrenden Thätigkeit eine zu allen meinen Verhältnissen leichtbezogne und passende Richtung gab. Ich kann Ihnen zwar nicht verheelen, daß ich fest glaube, daß meine *Neigung* zu den süßen Künsten der Musen nie erlöschen und meine liebe, freundliche Begleiterinn durchs Leben seyn wird, daß immer die Werke der Lieblinge Apolls einen unnennbaren Zauber für meine Seele behalten werden, und ich nie ungeneigt seyn werde dem Wunsche des Königs von Preußen beyzupflichten, wenn gleich auf eine ganz verschiedne Art, der die Zaÿre Voltairs lieber gemacht haben wollte als Sieger in so vielen Schlachten gewesen zu seyn; daß ich endlich selbst in manchen süßen, heimlichen Augenblicken Funken vom heiligen Altar der Kunst zu entwenden mir nicht entbrechen werde und selbst an der Seite der strengen Göttin, zu deren Priester ich mich an Kopf und Herzen combabisiren lassen soll, noch manchen verstohlnen Blick und manchen liebeathmenden Seufzer den glücklicheren Lieblingen der Grazien und Musen und ihren Schutzgöttinnen zuzuwerfen, aber demohngeachtet hoffe ich auch zu Gunsten meines bessern aber vielleicht kleinsten Selbsts, der Vernunft meinem gefaßten Vorsatz und dem mir am fernen Ziel winkenden Genius der höhern *Pflicht* treu zu bleiben und dem Rufe des Schicksals gehorsam zu seyn, das aus meinen Verhältnissen unverkennbar deutlich zu mir spricht. Aber zuseufzen werde ich Ihnen doch noch wol zuweilen: ora pro nobis.

I shall owe it to you, for the most part, that the highest concentration of will-power is going to support my intellectual and physical faculties this winter in a persistent effort at successfully overcoming the most threatening obstacle confronting a young and intelligent person, which consists of those unpleasant and drawn-out labors in preparation for a future profession; you were the one who called my attention to the more than utilitarian purpose a clear mind could, and would have to choose in this situation, and in doing so you gave me the final, decisive push that instantly decided my will and at least gave my unfocused activities a sense of direction to which I can easily and fittingly accommodate the demands of my circumstances. To be sure, I cannot hide from you my firm belief that my *inclination* toward the sweet arts of the Muses will never expire and remain my companion through life, that the works of Apollo's favorites will always retain a mysterious spell over my soul and that I shall never be disinclined to agree in principle, if not specifics, with the king of Prussia [Frederick the Great (1712–86)], who would rather have been the author of Voltaire's *Zaire* than victor in so many battles; and, finally, that I shall not refrain from snatching sparks off art's sacred altar in some sweet secret moments. Even at the side of the strict goddess, whose priestly castrate in mind and heart I am to become, I shall still direct many a hidden glance and lovelorn sigh at those more fortunate favorites of the Graces and Muses, and at their patron goddesses as well. All this notwithstanding, however, I do also hope to favor my better, and probably least developed, self, the self of reason, by remaining faithful to my resolution and to the guardian spirit of *higher duty* who beckons to me from the distant goal and by being obedient to the demands fate proclaims through my circumstances. Yet, on occasion, I shall still sigh under the burden and turn to you saying: ora pro nobis ["pray for us," a liturgical formula addressed to the saints for their intercession].

(IV, 90, l. 21–91, l. 14)[10]

Social diversions and self-indulgence proved too much for him this time; but the same resolve gained steadiness in defeat, and during his next attempt it is fully realized. In his letter to Oppel, he refers to his misadventures in Leipzig and the resultant change in attitude with which he continued his studies at Wittenberg:

Mein Mißgeschick weckte meine Ambition und mein Glück führte mir vortreffliche Lehrer zu — so daß in fünf Vierteljahren das Versäumte nachgeholt und ich examinirt war. Diesem Zeitraume dank ich die Fähigkeit mich mit unangenehmen und mühsamen Gegenständen anhaltend beschäftigen zu können.

Failure aroused my ambition, and good fortune sent superb teachers my way — so that I was able to make up all requirements and pass my examinations within five Quarters. It was then that I gained the capability for perseverance in dealing with unpleasant and strenuous tasks.

(IV, 310, ll. 20–24)

From that time on, professional duty and intellectual inclinations no longer confront him in contrast; he has finally reached the position of balance from which he can do justice to both and enhance either realm with benefits derived from the other.

The juxtaposition of "duty" and "inclination" is hardly unintentional when it occurs in a letter addressed to Schiller, as it does in the one just cited at length. This obviously Kantian formulation is indicative of the philosophical context within which the deep emotional experiences at Jena assume their lasting significance. The imposing system Kant had just constructed in honor of moral certitude was the cardinal intellectual event of the time, and Jena became the place where it was most impressively proclaimed. Reinhold, with whom Novalis also entertained friendly relations, was the first in a series of professors dedicated to the new doctrine of critical philosophy and Schiller had by then become thoroughly acquainted with it. Their student undeniably received his share of indoctrination and his later evaluation ("however, I was much too superficial in order to gain more than a certain fluency in the language of philosophy" ["ich war aber viel zu flüchtig um es weiter als zu einer Geläufigkeit in der philosophischen Sprache zu bringen"] [IV, 310, ll. 4–6], seems rather too modest. His appreciation of Schiller shows more than a superficial familiarity with Kantian concepts since he appraises him as a moral individual and intellectual guide entirely in those terms.[11]

Schiller's influence did not merely extend to imparting principles of moral conduct to his disciple. His unique appeal lay in the fact that he insisted on a common ground for ethics and aesthetics, and Novalis was well aware of this. In April of 1791, "Klagen eines Jünglings" ("A Youth's Complaint"), his first publication, appeared in Wieland's journal *Neuer Teutscher Merkur*. The poem is a lyric rendition of the new self-evaluation Schiller had inspired in its author and it has been traditionally acknowledged as such; but beyond that it also clearly marks a break with all of Novalis's previous artistic exploration, which becomes strikingly evident in the current edition where it is included as one among a great number of early poems published there for the first time. Gone is the bantering tone, the air of noncommittal and aesthetic dalliance, the occasional sense of disproportion between too much poetry and too little to say; gone also is the general aimlessness of poetic purpose that characterizes this collection in its dependency on models. "Klagen eines Jünglings" has its own statement to make, has its own orientation that accomplishes the union of individual experience and general validity the other poems lack to a greater or lesser degree. Here, Novalis takes stock of his life, finds it dependent on favorable circumstances and consequently devoid of a strong central core; his self, he feels, has remained weak and untried in determining its own course. In the last two stanzas, he prays for adversity so that he might transform it into an asset by force of moral engagement. Since the ideological framework is Kantian, this hope is far from the shallow sentiments of moralizing didacticism; rather, it expresses the ambition both to establish self-identity by exercising the freedom of action, potential to all men, and also to attain, in this process, an ever-more-inclusive level of self-awareness. Kant's concept of the self as a free agent in its ability to act ethically arises from intricate philosophical reasoning with which the young student was not sufficiently conversant to reach independent intellectual conclusions that would permanently affect his life. It was Schiller's personality and his aesthetic creed that demonstrated these abstract reflections in their living, human actuality, and the immediacy of this experience forms the firm foundation that lends direction to Friedrich von Hardenberg's future and provides the essence for what may be regarded his final poem of those early years.

This remarkable change in poetic style and purpose is not an unconscious shift nor is it brought about by the accident of temporary emotions. It has its theoretical parallel in the history of Novalis's regard for Gottfried August Bürger, one of the foremost lyrical talents with an established reputation at the time. The second, enlarged edition of Bürger's poems had just appeared when he came to Langendorf in the spring of 1789 for an extended visit with his sister. The village is very close to Weißenfels and young Hardenberg immediately availed himself of the opportunity to meet the famous man whom he admired greatly. The letters he addresses to him in May of that year are impassioned hymns of adoration that have few equals in his correspondence. After he receives an affirmative reply to his plea for a personal interview, he bursts into verse, modestly adding that his poetic prowess may not entirely have been able to do full justice to his feelings.

Unquestionably, his own poetry cannot compete with the artistry of Horace, Wieland, and Bürger, whom Novalis mentions as ideal poets (IV, 73, ll. 12–18); however, his critical acumen is sharp enough to determine quality in others and to set very high standards. Above all, the passage shows to what degree he values Bürger's work, which, if somewhat exaggerated, could certainly be defended up to a point. It is quite startling, therefore, to find that a little more than a year later his opinion has undergone a complete reversal. Shortly before his matriculation at the University of Leipzig and still completely under the spell of his experiences at Jena, he writes his erstwhile professor from his home in Weißenfels, where he was spending his vacation. He tells of the productive mood that has been kindled in him by the season, mentions long walks through the autumnal countryside on which the *Odyssey* and *Don Carlos* keep him company, proceeds, in this connection, to reflect on the nature of poetic genius, and arrives at the specific topic of the public censure Schiller inflicted on Bürger's poetry.

Bey Gelegenheit der Lektüre des Don Karlos habe ich noch einmal die Rezension von Bürgers Gedichten gelesen und sie ist mir beynah in der Stimmung, worein Sie mich versezt hatten, noch zu gelind vorgekommen; Da wenigstens der Maaßstab, den Sie darinn nicht, wie viele gethan haben, von der Erfahrung mehrerer Jahrhunderte abstrahirten, sondern

ihn a priori aus einem den Gesetzen der Sittlichkeit correspondirenden
Gesetze aufstellten und dadurch der Wissenschaft zu einem einzigen
Gesichtspunkt verhalfen, der ihr bis dahin mangelte . . . da wenigstens
der Maaßstab, sag ich, sich zu den meisten von Bürgers Gedichten nicht
harmonisch verhält.

As I was reading *Don Carlos*, I took occasion to read your review of
Bürger's poems once again, and while I was under the impression of your
words it almost seemed to me that you had still dealt too gently with him.
Unlike many who abstract their criteria from the accumulated experience
of centuries, you have established a criterion of judgment in this review
that is a priori and derives from a law that corresponds to the moral law.
In establishing this criterion you have given us a standard perspective in
the science of aesthetics that had previously been lacking, and no matter
what else one might say about them, most of Bürger's poems fail to measure
up to it.

(IV, 100, ll. 17–26, 31–33)

The review in question makes emotional disengagement the prime condition
for the writing of poetry, an attitude Novalis still obviously lacked at the time
of his veneration for Bürger. The immediacy of emotional upheaval must never
control the pen, judges Schiller, because: "Selbst in Gedichten, von denen man
zu sagen pflegt, daß die Liebe, die Freundschaft u.s.w. selbst dem Dichter den
Pinsel dabei geführt habe, hatte er damit anfangen müssen, sich selbst fremd zu
werden, den Gegenstand seiner Begeisterung von seiner Individualität los zu
wickeln, seine Leidenschaft aus einer mildernden Ferne anzuschauen" ("Even
those poems of which it is generally said that love, friendship etc. did themselves
guide the poet's pen, even those poems could not have been written, unless the
poet had first estranged himself from his feelings, had disengaged the object of
his enthusiasm from his own individuality, and had viewed his passion from a
mitigating distance".)[12]
These pronouncements might seem astonishingly "modern" to readers of
Thomas Mann, for example, who are accustomed to take it for granted that art
belongs to a realm painfully separate from life. Schiller, however, is unacquainted
with the despondency of a Tonio Kröger and certainly would never suggest that
"the bliss of the commonplace" ("die Wonnen der Gewöhnlichkeit") could
ever be the legitimate goal of any man's aspirations. He does not have to long
for the "commonplace" in order to regain a sense of fellowship with other men
because art does not mean banishment from their midst. On the contrary, he is
convinced that the immediacy of feeling can only be experienced in the isolation
of individuated being, whereas the principles of art are akin to those which
endow each individual with the ability to proclaim his or her membership in
humanity. The general validity Schiller demands of the work of art cannot be
the product of the human condition encapsuled in subjective isolation but must

derive its power to be binding for everyone from the ideal of humanity itself. Freedom from being governed by the urgency of our affections, self-estrangement from the immediacy of experience, which Schiller makes the condition for true acts of poetic creativity, constitute the same freedom Kant requires for the possibility to act morally, that is, in a manner defensible in the name of all humankind. This moral or "categorical" imperative is the ideal of humanity, its "idea" if Kantian terminology were to be used; it is the regulative principle that inspires all human action insofar as it is characteristically human, which means free of those controls nature exerts over all other creatures as their sole motivating force. From the moment it begins to exist, the self is isolated in its individuality, and in its effort to gain objective authenticity it attempts by various means to overcome this limitation. Kant's solution recommends acting according to standards that potentially demand the self's readiness to will its own physical extinction, not in suicidal ecstasy but as the final consequence of a life freely defined in its totality. This ability to refuse the accident of existence any claim to self-sufficiency is shared by all people, as is the power to lend it human significance, and in realizing both, the actions of an individual assume genuine reality outside the confines of physically imposed self-interest. Schiller shares these Kantian views and discovers in them the basis for a new theory of aesthetics. In his answer to the outraged reaction directed at him for attacking Bürger, the ideological bonds that link moral philosophy and poetic practice in Schiller's thoughts become even more clearly apparent than in the initial review:

Leser, welche sich der gefühlvollen Lieder eines Denis, Goeckingk, Hölty, Kleist, Klopstock, v. Salis erinnern, welche einsehen, daß Empfindungen dadurch allein, daß sie sich zum allgemeinen Charakter der Menschheit erheben, einer allgemeinen Mitteilung fähig — und dadurch allein, daß sie jeden fremdartigen Zusatz ablegen, mit den Gesetzen der Sittlichkeit sich in Übereinstimmung setzen und gleichsam aus dem Schoße veredelter Menschheit hervorströmen, zu schönen Naturtönen werden (denn rührende Naturtöne entrinnen auch dem gequälten Verbrecher, ohne hoffentlich auf Schönheit Anspruch zu machen), solche Leser dürften nun schwerlich dahin zu bringen sein, idealisierte Empfindungen, wie Rezensent sie der Kürze halber meint, für nichtige Phantome oder gar mit erkünstelten naturwidrigen Abstrakten für einerlei zu halten.

Readers who recall the heartfelt lyrics of a Denis, Goeckingk, Hölty, Kleist, Klopstock, von Salis, readers who have come to understand that emotions can lay claim to general communicability only if they are raised to the level of general humanity — and only if they are made to shed all foreign admixture [of nature's compulsion] and are brought into harmony with [the specifically human law,] the laws of morality, emanating, as it were, from the womb of ennobled humanity, can they become beautiful sounds of nature (because affective sounds of nature can also escape the criminal's mouth without anyone's wishing to claim they are beautiful, I trust) — such readers would hardly be fooled into thinking that the concept of "idealized emotions," as I have called them for brevity's sake, refers to non-existing phantoms or, worse yet, constitutes no more than an artificial and unnatural abstraction.[13]

Novalis, who but a short time before had accepted Bürger without reservation as one of the great poets, fully agrees with Schiller's critical analysis and willingly subordinates the idol of his emotions to the superior force of rational principles. He openly acknowledges their Kantian heritage when he states his particular appreciation of the fact that they constitute an "*a priori* law" rather than *a posteriori* standards "abstracted from the experience of several centuries." He is also quite conscious of the intended relationship between ethics and aesthetics that furnishes the crucial basis for Schiller's argument and is its main point. "Morality" (*Sittlichkeit*), which his letter mentions in connection with the poet's art, is by no means understood in the traditional sense that the literary work impart moral advice or edification; on the contrary, no such intentionality can be allowed to mar the work of art: "O! ich lerne immer mehr einsehn, daß nur moralische Schönheit, je absichtsloser sie bewürkt zu seyn scheint, den einzig unabhängig, wahren Werth eines jedweden Werks des dichterischen Genies aus-macht . . . das Utile muß nicht Zweck werden, sonst sinken wir zu moralischen Predigern und Schlendrianisten herab" ("Oh! I am beginning to see ever more clearly that only moral beauty, unmarred by intention of moral effect, may constitute the independent and true worth of the poetic spirit's every work . . . there must be no utilitarian purpose, because then we would sink to the level of moral preachers and imitative dabblers") (IV, 100, ll. 33–36; 101, ll. 13–15).

As a result of his association with Schiller, Novalis has become convinced that goodness and beauty are intimately related, possibly even one, and the letter of 7 October 1791 contains the first detailed exposition of his newly gained assurance. He will never lose it, although its implications undergo considerable change as he develops his own point of view. Moral beauty, which he expressly recognizes as the stamp of true classicism (IV, 100, l. 33–101, l. 2), is more to him than a purely aesthetic qualification, of value only in the realm of art; the "moral" or rather characteristically "human" aspect leads right back into life itself and identifies artists and their works as an integral part of it with a definite function to fulfill. Just as Schiller does in his *Letters Concerning the Aesthetic Education of Man* (*Über die ästhetische Erziehung des Menschen in einer Reihe von Briefen*), which were not published until much later, in 1795, Novalis perceives this function to be "educational" in the sense that beauty points the way to goodness and truth: "Vielleicht daß auch die Linie, die hier sich um die Schönheit windet, dort auch an das Gute sich schmiegt und auf ihrem sanftge-schwungnen Pfade sich Schönheit und Wahrheit findet und Herz und Geist mit den zartesten Faden und im reichsten Bunde vereinigt. Jünglinge, die ihr mit mir einem gleichen Wege nachspürt, bey den Grazien, folget dieser Spur, die uns unser Lehrer, unser angebeteter Schiller zeigte'' (''Very possibly, the line that here traces the contours of beauty does there also nestle up close to the good and on its softly winding path beauty and truth may well coincide, uniting heart and spirit with the most tender of ties in a most bounteous union. Youths, you who are trying to discover the same path along with me, by the graces, follow this trail that our teacher, our revered Schiller, has shown us'') (IV, 102, ll. 9–15).

The certainty of his convictions still rests with the example Schiller's personality sets for him. As time goes on, the hopeful uncertainty, expressed by the *vielleicht* with which the passage opens, will no longer have to be outweighed by the reassuring presence of inspiring leaders; the insights that accompany his own attempts to traverse the indicated path will prove to be increasingly sufficient guides. In his biography of Novalis, Gerhard Schulz summarizes most effectively what Schiller meant to Friedrich von Hardenberg by pointing out the difference between the youth who adores Bürger and the more mature spirit who no longer can do so:

Die Begegnung zwischen Schiller und Novalis lag also nicht mehr nur in der Sphäre des ''Einflußnehmens'' eines älteren Dichters auf einen jüngeren, wie es bei Bürger der Fall war, sondern in der Auslösung eines Prozesses der Selbsterkenntnis. Schiller wurde ihm das Vorbild eines Menschen, der einem widrigen Schicksal eine innere Harmonie der Kräfte abzuringen vermochte, der Sittlichkeit mit Schönheit, Inneres und Äußeres zu *sittlicher Grazie* zu verbinden suchte und damit die Möglichkeit zur Bewältigung einer Lebensproblematik zeigt, die sich mehr und mehr vor dem begeisterungsfähigen, von Eindrücken und Empfindungen bedrängten jungen Manne auftat. Es war nicht mehr die dichterische Nachfolge, die Novalis in seinem Verhältnis zu Schiller anstrebte, sondern Selbstverständnis und die Festigung seiner Persönlichkeit auf ein Lebensziel hin.

Novalis's encounter with Schiller initiated a process of self-recognition that meant much more than merely an older poet's influencing a younger one, as had been the case with Bürger. He acknowledged Schiller as the exemplary individual who was able to wrest an inner harmony of his powers from an antagonistic fate, who sought to unite ethical imperative and beauty, the inner and the outer sphere, into *moral grace*; in doing so, he showed the possibility of overcoming a problematic aspect of life that had become of ever more concern to the young man, who was so easily roused to enthusiasm and far too dependent on impressions and emotions. In his relationship to Schiller, Novalis sought no longer to emulate a poet but rather to gain an understanding of self and a steadying of his personality that would allow him to give his life a purpose.[14]

The terms *Selbstverständnis* and *Festigung seiner Persönlichkeit auf ein Lebensziel hin* do not only specify the consequences for the young man of his encounter with Schiller but they also return our attention to appropriate points of orientation from which Friedrich von Hardenberg's early history, as it was outlined in these pages, may be surveyed. As I noted, from childhood on his positive affinity for all life had to offer led him to assimilate whatever was akin to his nature, even against some obstacles, such as those the limited resources at home must have presented to extensive literary ambitions. This tendency to expand the self had to be balanced by a sense of its identity, a necessity Novalis repeatedly considered most urgent. He did so with good reason. What he thought of as lack of steadiness in purpose, a certain indulgent aimlessness, was essentially the lack of a defined center to his intellectual and social pursuits, which was also clearly evident in his early poetry and in the way he subordinated himself to those he admired. The consciousness of self that henceforth imparts direction to his life and coherence to all he asembles within his expanding world was kindled by Schiller, the personification of the moral self-definition to which Kant's new philosophy gave voice. The self, so it proclaims, harbors the law that endows all deeds with general human validity and declares the individual free to fashion the circumstances of his life as a phenomenalized testimony to the idea of humanity; all other actions, although they may be designated as 'selfish," do not originate with the self and are determined by circumstance. These considerations gave Novalis his initial concept of self; it served to establish for him not only the necessary "stability of personality oriented toward a life goal" and, with the help of Schiller's interpretation, a source of aesthetic criteria for his own eventual poetic independence, but also a clear functional relationship connecting the two spheres between which "duty" and "inclination" had previously torn him.[15] At this point, however, this concept of self is still essentialy based on the unreflecting assurance of conviction, rather than on its true intellectual comprehension gained along the stages of philosophical insight that lead to it. The "Fichte-Studies," begun after he had successfully concluded his university career and entered professional training, constitute that next step toward theoretical independence and the correspondingly higher degree of self-awareness.

II. Sophie von Kühn and Philosophical Studies

Mein Lieblingsstudium heißt im Grunde, wie meine
Braut. Sofie heißt sie — Filosofie ist die Seele meines
Lebens und der Schlüssel zu meinem eigensten Selbst.

My favorite study actually bears the same name as my
future bride. Her name is Sophy — Philo-Sophy is the
soul of my life and the key to my innermost self.

Novalis

Das ächte Dividuum ist auch das ächte Individuum.

The true dividual is also the true individual.

Novalis

Mikrologische Tugend — warum denn keine Makrologische?

Micrological virtue — why not also a Macrological one?

Novalis

Chapter 3
The Encounter and Novalis's Twofold Love: Love of Sophie and Philosophy

The factual aspects of Novalis's encounter with Sophie von Kühn offer few reasons why it should have evolved over the almost two and a half years of its endurance into the most celebrated love affair of the epoch. True, Sophie apparently possessed a captivating personality that could charm all those who met her, more in a childlike way, however, than as a full partner in an adult relationship. Aside from this, she possessed little that could account for Hardenberg's instant realization, when he met the twelve-year-old girl on 17 November 1794 at her home in Grüningen, that his future had been decided and that he beheld in her person the love of his life. This fateful meeting occurred on one of his first official tours, nine days after he had started his practical training in state administration under Coelestin Just, the renowned director of the Regional Office at Tennstedt.

If the significance Novalis attached to his initial association with Sophie seems unusual, the fact that this relationship continued with unabated intensity is much more astounding since the passage of time brought little to support such fervor. There is no doubt that the social circle at Grüningen exercised a compelling attraction on many others, so that Novalis's sense of well-being in its midst is quite understandable; however, Sophie lacked the maturity and, it appears, the inclination to return her "Fritz's" ardour in kind. It would almost seem that he had fallen prey to the blind self-delusion with which "romanticism" is all too often, and all too wrongly, considered synonymous, were it not for his keen awareness of reality uncompromisingly tabulated in documents like "Klarisse" (IV, 24–25). There, after he had known her for almost two years and their

23

engagement had long since become public knowledge, Novalis takes stock of his beloved's traits, her endearing ones as well as those less flattering. The result is a description of a child with undeniably admirable qualities for whom adulthood is a definite threat, particularly the thought of marriage and the serious commitment her lover's affection demands, a fault conscientiously noted by him without embellishment: "Sie will sich nicht durch meine Liebe geniren lassen. Meine Liebe drückt sie oft. Sie ist *kalt* durchgehends" ("She does not want to be embarrassed by my love. My love often oppresses her. She is *cold* through and through") (IV, 25).

There is no reason to doubt Novalis's claim that he did, indeed, experience Sophie's very being as the revelation of his life's goal. It is equally true, though, that the compelling nature of this experience eludes general verifiability if the manifest attributes of Sophie's person or her conduct were to be its sole guarantors. The chance meeting in 1794 does have the impact of a "beginning"[1] for Novalis but, once initiated, this unforeseen and blissful turn of events stands in need of conscious interpretation that would allow it to be translated from a mere fortuitous coincidence into a way and a philosophy of life.

External conditions of this crucial period that was to reach its ultimate crisis with Sophie's death on 19 March 1797 are not as decisive as Novalis's tendency to endow them with meaning. The decree of circumstance does not determine him exclusively; instead, it serves as the material from which he fashions his life. This practice represents an unbroken continuation of his earlier actions and aspirations; now, however, his performance is no longer instinctive, nor does it follow the patterns of conscious discipleship. Just as the manner in which he relates to Sophie shows how he actively transforms the course of objective events into meaningful reality, his philosophical studies, which he conducts at approximately the same time, reflect a similar spontaneity in the speculative realm and can be regarded as the theoretical counterpart for his actions. More than that, his determined efforts to gain full sovereignty over the new systems of critical thought must quite naturally have been accompanied by a state of mind prepared to view life and engage in it according to the insights and discoveries he had made. The fragment cited as the motto for these chapters is the succinct formulation Novalis offers in order to characterize the mutually supportive aims of his twofold activity. He extends inward, systematically observant of the processes of consciousness and their ultimate implications, and outward, ordering all his endeavors with reference to his beloved; both realms are united within themselves since each contains the regulative principle of an ultimate aim, and they are one, because the respective principles bear the same name. This latter aspect is not just a play on words if one considers the Greek or, more specifically, Platonic heritage to which the name "Sofie"[2] refers.

Sophie von Kühn is equated with the ancient ideal of wisdom, and rightly so since love proclaims them as the common goal. With this characterization of his relationship to "Sophie," Novalis offers the most compelling testimony that the events comprising the history of those two lives during the brief span of their mutual involvement do not harbor their enduring validity in themselves. Both avenues of Novalis's Philo-Sophia must be considered if either or both are to be viewed in the right perspective, and we have yet to examine the philosophical bias from which Novalis derives the standards that transfix his experiences into configurations of meaning and value.

The name most prominently associated with Novalis's intellectual development at this stage is that of Johann Gottlieb Fichte. He may not have initiated the "Copernican Revolution" of which Kant speaks, but he certainly was its most consequential prophet. His doctrine demanded an ideological commitment that most Kantians were unable or unwilling to make, and even Kant himself felt it was incompatible with his own position. At Jena, however, where he first presented his "system," he gained a solid following, and by 1795, it had been fully proclaimed in word and print to an enthusiastic audience under the title of *Wissenschaftslehre*. Among the faculty, Reinhold and Schiller, Novalis's former teachers, belonged to those who publicly endorsed the new teachings; Reinhold became an outright convert and Schiller supported some key arguments in his *Aesthetic Letters* with reference to "the author of the *Wissenschaftslehre*." Even though his university days were over and he had little leisure, Novalis must have been one of the earliest adherents since his "Fichte-Studies," the voluminous notebooks he kept from the fall of 1795 to the summer of 1796, leave no doubt that he was thoroughly acquainted with everything the Jena professor had published. True to his claim (IV, 188, ll. 8–10), it appears that aside from professional requirements, Novalis was almost exclusively preoccupied with the study of Fichte's philosophy throughout the time of his courtship and, again, for some months after Sophie's death had threatened him with the chaos of despair.

The *Wissenschaftslehre* presents its readers with an assembly of very intricate and often abstruse arguments, but its basic tenets may be stated briefly in comparatively simple language. The notion that objects exist as self-defined entities by themselves "out there in the world" is a mistaken one, Fichte contends. They exist in the mind; more precisely, the mind constructs them as self-identical units related to one another. Yet, we insist that the mind is not freely engaged in this process of setting up objects for itself, or "positing" them, as Fichte would term it. The compulsion thus felt can only be another action on which the one construing objects is dependent. We think our dependency originates with the object's acting on the organs of perception, but this, again, is nothing but a necessary construction of the mind in order to account for the sense of compulsory necessity that accompanies all positing. In effect we claim that if the mind constructs, or rather posits, an object as real, then the "if" signifies that we consider the object to have its own existence outside the mind. Fichte states it this way: "Wenn A *im Ich* gesetzt its, so *ist es gesetzt;* oder — so *ist es*" ("If A is posited *in the ego,* then *it is posited* or then *it is"* (*SW*, I, 94).[3] The condition under which the mind sets up objects, posits or constructs them, is called being or existence, and we think of it as outside the mind because we attribute existence to an object only insofar as our own being, the being of the self, is affected by it.

Being is thus attributed to the self by the self and only indirectly, by projection, to anything that affects this being. Here the "if" no longer applies: "If the self is posited in the ego, then it is posited or then it is" makes no sense because we never doubt our own being and have, therefore, posited our self without condition. The self simply posits the self, which is an act unconditional and primary to all other acts, so that unconditional identity is the criterion of unity, the point of reference, for all other posited objects as well as their mediate source of being. Stated in terms of an experience easily verified by everyone, the self is always conscious of itself, it is its own permanent object, and this identity of subject and object is that which we call "I."

The action of positing is thus dependent on the action of self-positing, which establishes the ground of being and defines it as the objective self or I, the prime unit part that determines the manner of interrelation between all objects, which is equivalent to determing their respective unity. This primary self-definition by self-positing is not dependent on any further "if"; it is primary and "free," absolutely necessary rather than relatively by means of compulsion from another action, and in this sense it is also the only true identity, identity pure and simple. Fichte refers by the name of *Tathandlung* to the free act of self-positing that must precede all acts of consciousness as their necessary point of reference. The term is his own creation with which he means to imply a pure sense of enactment without the attendant stationary features of agent and completed act customarily associated with the concept of action. According to pre-Kantian thought, also labeled "dogmatism" (*Dogmatismus*), which essentially envisioned human consciousness as acted upon by an external, objective reality, absolute or pure action (*actus purus*) was attributable to God as fountainhead of everything real. After Kant recognized that the objectively binding laws of reality originate in the mind, Fichte arrived at the conclusion that all things are only for the mind that posits them, which necessarily transfers the original act of positing from the realm of things to the realm of consciousness. Effectively, the Absolute, or pure activity, was no longer conceived as the pure object, or God, but as the pure subject or, in Fichte's language, the absolute Ego (*das absolute Ich*). It must be remembered, however, that both are Absolutes, and just as God could not be identified with any aspect of his creation (such confusion would simply result in any of the many forms of idolatry), the Ego, as the source of all consciousness, is equally removed from all we are conscious of, including our empirical selves.

Insofar as subject and object are one, the Ego posits itself; insofar as they are separate, the Ego posits a nonego. Both are absolutely posited and therefore have a claim to independence or, within the relative context of their interaction, each has a claim to dominance over the other. The Ego can thus be said to posit itself as determined by the nonego, which corresponds to the basic premise of all traditional, dogmatic philosophies. The Ego posits itself as determined by the nonego is a statement relating in abstract terms what our experience conveys to us as the individual's utter dependence on the infinite cosmos that surrounds it; but, and this is the emphatic difference that assures the freedom necessary for moral responsibility previous systems were unable to guarantee, the Ego can also be said to posit itself as determining the nonego. In the absolute sense, the Ego never does anything else, so that freedom for the relative ego, for the empirical self, is equivalent to the obligation of returning to the absolute condition. Since that is an unrealizable demand, the exhortation to be absolute takes the form of a constant command, a "categorical imperative," an eternal "ought to," which constitutes the directive for ethical conduct. Accordingly, moral action is equivalent to true self-determination, free of dictates other than the one to make human freedom manifest within a state of apparent bondage.

The fascination Fichte's system held for Novalis stems from its appeal to the human individual as a being endowed with the awesome responsibility of freedom; it offers a framework for all of reality within which the self assumes the central function, equally removed from the placid security of prescribed patterns and from the vacillation of license. Novalis's "Fichte-Studies" are his persistent and serious attempt to explore the system's web of thought, to spin it out on his own, and to assume his place in it.

True to the example set by his mentor's method and in accordance with its fundamental premise that philosophical truth can only be enacted in the mind, not learned, his fragments are really experiments in thought. For this reason, no individual pronouncement may be regarded as conclusive; throughout these studies contradictions abound, self-corrective statements occur, variations on the same themes are frequent; in short, sequences of reasoning are laid out as an overt product of careful efforts to trace the implications of certain premises or ideas arising from positions taken in the *Wissenschaftslehre* and publications attendant to it. It would hardly be useful to reexamine every phase and direction of Novalis's experimentation. As far as such an endeavor contributes to a better understanding of the overall coherence that prevails in the "Fichte-Studies," Hans-Joachim Mähl's comprehensive introduction and detailed justification for his painstaking editorial work has already accomplished all that was needed.[4] The purpose at hand is limited to an exposition of the theme that is common to the diverse topics treated by these fragments. That theme, as would be appropriate for reflections inspired by Fichte's philosophy, is the concept of the self and the pattern of functional relationships that comprise it. In connection with a letter Novalis wrote to his brother on 27 February 1796, Mähl acknowledges:

Der Glaube an 'die Universalität des Uchs', zu der Novalis den Bruder

hier beschwörend aufruft, enthält vielmehr einen Schlüssel für das
Verständnis der gesamten *Fichte-Stundien*.

Faith in the "universality of the self," which Novalis entreats his brother
to cultivate in this letter, is actually the key to the entire *Fichte-Studies*.
(II, 66)

The universality of which he speaks is not only of central importance to the
fragments but, even more basic than that, it identifies the self and its powers
with the point of orientation for all the actualities of life, as the passage cited
from the letter in question indicates:

> Bleibe fest im Glauben an die Universalitaet Deines Ichs. . . . Mache
> Dir Deine Lage interessant, denke alles, was Dich umgibt, im Verhältnis
> zur unendlichen Dauer — Resultat einer Ewigkeit a parte ante und post.
> Setze Nullen an die Einer nach Willkühr — ich denke Deine Fantasie soll
> müde und der *Raum* Deiner Seele voll werden.

> Remain firm of faith in the universality of your self. . . . Make of your
> situation one that is of interest to you, think everything that surrounds you
> with reference to eternal duration — think of it as the result of an eternity
> that precedes and succeeds the particular moment on which your thought
> concentrates. Add as many zeros to the ones as you like — I should think
> your imagination will have to grow tired as the *space* of your soul will
> have to grow full.
(IV, 172, l. 17; 172, ll. 32–36)

These admonitions clearly establish a direct continuity between the fundamental
objective of the philosophical experiments conducted from 1795 to 1796 and
Novalis's earlier tendencies to foster, ever more consciously, his stability of
self. That same continuity will also guide the ensuing discussion of the "Fichte-
Studies" in which I intend to show the development Novalis undergoes as he
attempts to understand his own being from the perspective of the *Wissenschafts-
lehre*.

Chapter 4
The "Basic Schema" as It Evolves from the "Fichte-Studies"

Fichte begins his demonstration of the Ego's absolute powers with the sentence of identity, A = A; he chooses it as an example of commonly acknowledged truth that is not subject to change and, therefore, independent of the variables arising from the circumstances of its concrete, empirical application. Derived from this tautology is the implication that the identity of any objective reality is necessarily dependent on the primary identity of subject and object or, in Fichte's words, *"Das Ich setzt ursprünglich schlechthin sein eigenes Seyn"* (*"Originally the Ego freely posits its own being"*) (*SW*, I, 98).

What Fichte wishes to communicate in this awkward language is the simple fact that the term "I" — or for that matter the terms "ego" or "self" — cannot refer to any object to which I attribute being outside of my consciousness. For example, I do not believe that this piece of paper ceases to exist as soon as I turn my attention away from it. I hold that same conviction with regard to any object, that is to say, any and all, except one. That to which I refer as "I" is an object always accompanied by my consciousness and, conversely, my consciousness has only one permanent object. This inseparability of subject and object to which the term "I" refers, and it refers to nothing else,[5] leads Fichte to proclaim that the original act of positing, before anything else may be posited, must necessarily be an act of self-positing; furthermore, this primary act is free since no compulsion attaches to it, as would be the case with any other object that happens to affect us and must, therefore, be posited.

Novalis begins his reflections with a critical analysis of that same sentence of identity. What fascinates him is the simultaneity of sameness and otherness expressed by the formula A = A. This seemingly self-evident assertion, which is axiomatic for any theory of logic and, in this capacity, had remained an unquestioned expression of certainty for centuries, proves to be quite problematic since it cannot affirm identity except by means of duplicity. For this reason, Novalis calls the sentence of identity a "sentence that really is not a sentence," a *Scheinsatz*, when he says, "d[as] Wesen der Identität läßt sich nur in einem *Scheinsatz* aufstellen" ("The nature of identity can be demonstrated only by a *pseudo-sentence* of identity") (II, 104, ll. 5–6). Essentially, this means that identity itself, or actually pure oneness, is undemonstrable, unless it be in relation to what it is not, which the next remark states most succinctly as: "Wir verlassen das *Identische* um es darzustellen" ("We leave the *identical* in order to represent it") (II, 104, ll. 6–7). This sentence at the beginning of what Novalis describes as "[d]ringende Einleitungsstudien auf mein ganzes künftiges Leben" ("urgent introductory studies of determinative importance for my entire future life") (IV, 159) contains in its brevity the principle his future speculations will discover as basic to the interrelation and interaction between all aspects of reality. Most important, at this point he states in effect that unity is manifest only in multiplicity and multiplicity, in turn, constitutes a relationship only with respect to unity. This is the fundamental pattern within which Novalis envisions the necessary pertinence of absolute and empirical values to one another; the term *darstellen* quite appropriately expresses that the relationship entails sameness fully as much as otherness since anything representative of another can take its place but is different nonetheless. The dividing and reuniting of A in the formula A = A merely serves to indicate that identity is apparent only within the medium of nonidentity or, if agency be emphasized, A leaves A in the process of demonstrating its identity; but in doing so, it has already exchanged the realm of identity for its opposite, a state of dichotomous reciprocity.

The sentence of identity is thus dualistic and representative in a twofold manner: it stands opposed not only as a polar antagonism from A to A but also with respect to identity as such and, conversely, identity as such is represented insofar as each polar opposite represents the other. Translated into terms with more immediate significance, A may be any particular set of objects; since nothing can be stated concerning anything except as it appears in the mind, A = A really means that the identity with which the mind has endowed the object in having it appear is the same as the one in which it appears for the mind. That is to say, the object as object is equal to the object as it is for me. In even more prosaic language, if we may, for the moment, assume the object to be a tree, the formula A = A can be read to infer: tree, posited by the mind but believed to be "out there," = tree, in the mind, or: object = subject only as manifestation of the intellect's absolute spontaneity. If we return now to Novalis's theory of representation, A = A stands for the mutually representative relation between subject and object, which is, in turn, representative of an absolute activity preceding consciousness. That Novalis thinks in terms of this total "representation" is quite clear from his opinions on the nature of signs, which follow immediately after the sentence last cited, "Wir verlassen das *Identische* um es darzustellen — " ("We leave the *identical* in order to represent it — "):

> Entweder dis geschieht nur scheinbar — und wir werden v[on] d[er] Einbildungskraft dahin gebracht es zu glauben — es *geschieht*, was schon Ist — natürlich durch imaginaires Trennen und vereinigen — Oder wir stellen es durch sein Nichtseyn, durch ein Nichtidentisches vor — Zeichen — ein bestimmtes für ein gleichförmig bestimmendes — dieses gleichförmig bestimmende muß eigentlich durchaus unmittelbar das mitgetheilte Zeichen durch eben die Bewegungen bestimmen, wie ich — Frey und doch so wie ich. Geschmack und Genie. Ersteres — wenn es durch ein Mittelbares, eine Vorstellung meiner Productionshandlung des Zeichens oder nur meiner *Absicht*, meines *Sinns*, lezteres, wenn es ohne dis Mittelbare, die Vorstellung *meiner* Causalitaet, es unmittelbar producirt — wie ich. Jenes ist bloßer Geschmack, dis Genie Geschmack.

> Either this takes place only apparently — and our imagination leads us to believe it [i.e., to believe that there is something out there which is reflected or represented in our mind] — that which already is, is just now taking *place* [i.e., the self can only be conscious of the self, but that self is constantly undergoing change; accordingly, the conscious self projects an object outside the self to which the particular change is attributed. There is only the immediacy of self-consciousness and all registering, or rather "positing" of objects is secondary] — naturally by means of imaginary acts of separating and uniting [i.e., the imagination first "posits" the object outside the self in order to compensate for the particular state the self is in, and then it introduces this posited projection as an external and independent object into consciousness. On a naïve level, we are only aware of this second phase, and for this reason Novalis says in the first sentence that this kind of leaving the identical in order to represent it is only apparent, that is to say does not really take place this way] — Or we represent it by means of that which it is not, by means of that which is not identical with it — [a sign is] something defined for something defining in a uniform manner — [uniform means that] this something defining in a uniform manner must without any mediation whatever [i.e., entirely on its own] define the communicated sign in the same manner as I do — freely and nonetheless as I do. Taste and genius. The former designation applies if the other defining entity produces the sign as I do by referring to a mediating ground, to an imaginary re-creation of my activity in producing the sign, or just to my *intention*, my *meaning*; the latter designation applies if the other defining entity produces the sign in a wholly unmediated fashion, just as spontaneously as I do without this mediating factor of having to think of *my* causality. The former is mere taste, the latter the taste of genius.

(II, 104, 11. 7–19)[6]

In essence, these lines develop the rudiments for a theory of communication and art from Fichte's contention that the identity of any one thing cannot be asserted except for the absolutely founded unity of subject and object in the pure activity he calls *Tathandlung* or Ego. Accordingly, the intellect's absolute agency in formulating the world of objects is necessarily on a preconscious level since consciousness can only contain the products of that activity; effectively, it has the power to formulate something as other than the self that has its significance only with respect to the self. This preconscious productivity can be likened on a conscious level to the fabrication of signs because, in accordance with Novalis's definitions, both are representative actions. The difference is that the use of signs presupposes the mediating ground of consciously established objects in relation to which the individuated, empirical self defines its purposes. Other than that, signs are related to their objects only in and for the human beholder, just like the object itself.[7]

Novalis's brief examination of Fichte's initial sentence of identity leads him directly to considerations that, far from isolating the ego in solipsist splendor, point to its absolute heritage as the ground from which interpersonal bonds may be established. Signs are a conscious reperformance of the same function that underlies the fusion of subjective and objective validity in all acts of consciousness. They may, in this capacity, relate more or less directly to the ego's spontaneous productivity. If the sign is as immediately effective as the object itself, both being produced in and for the mind, Novalis considers it a product of "genius"; if the technique, the producing aspect within the realm of established purpose, is prevalent, "taste" gave rise to it.

To the modern reader, the "sign of genius" obviously suggests characteristics he associates with his concept of "symbol." No doubt there is justification for that, abridged, however, by distinct limitations. Novalis's "symbol" is as far removed from the pure aesthetics of symbolist theory and practice as are the systems and concerns of Fichte's philosophy. In time, Novalis will reassess the position art, or rather "poesy" (*Poesie*), holds with respect to the metaphysics of morals construed by idealist philosophy, but he will never deny the legitimacy of the most intimate ties that, in his view, maintain the interdependence of ethics and aesthetics. Here, at the outset of the "Fichte-Studies," this close coordination is immediately made evident by his introduction of concepts like "representation" (*darstellen*) and signification as essential to thoughts evolving from arguments that supply the foundation for the system of ethics that is the *Wissenschaftslehre*.

In his effort to have Fichte's words assume the reality of active thought, Novalis becomes critical of the sentence of identity because it does not convey the problematic nature of this concept with sufficient urgency. His excursion into topics apparently unrelated to the reasoning with which the *Wissenschaftslehre* begins constitutes a substitution of A = B for A = A. Novalis found Fichte's choice unconvincing, and I suggest he did so because A = A fails to emphasize the empirical aspect of identity that furnishes, after all, the basis for postulating the primary necessity of the Ego's absolute agency. At its immediate level, the empirical condition is experienced as an all-pervasive dualism, as self and world standing opposed. Upon further reflection it becomes apparent that this confrontation takes place with respect to the opposing parties' underlying unity, because without it, no relationship is possible, not even one of opposition. In other words, subject and object are entirely different realms, yet the subject is part of the object's domain and the object part of the subject's. The relationship between subject and object is one that entails otherness and sameness simultaneously, with the immediate and obvious accent on the former. Novalis's focus is on this immediate aspect when he introduces his ideas on signs and representation in contrast to the sentence of identity, $A = A$, in which the dualism of its components remain almost unnoticed because of their sameness.

Awareness of the empirical dualism is basic to all of human experience and overcoming it the aim of every action. Essentially, this dichotomy is a problem that requires a continuing resolution, or rather it poses an ever renewed question for each individual as to what his or her definition of unity between subject and object might be. Even the most basic activities with which we respond to challenges from the environment are answers to this question, and with increasingly conscious behavior, the answers become, correspondingly, more complex and inclusive. In the final analysis, theological and philosophical systems of thought are the utmost attempts to offer as comprehensive an answer as possible and, consequently, they can assign an equally definite functional role to the self in its confrontation with the world. Fichte envisions this contest in purely moralistic terms. He regards the "nonego" as the Ego's self-imposed limitation, which means that all objects are created for the relative, empirical self and, in this capacity, fulfill a twofold function: on the one hand, their very existence is a permanent barrier to the original state and, on the other, they constitute a challenge to regain it.

The dependency each individual experiences throughout life is a feeling of impotence that spans the difference between relative and absolute agency; it is the negative awareness of pure action, the awareness of freedom, unity, self-identity, by its absence. However, the self constrained by those empirical bonds does have the power to reassert its absolute heritage and suspend all claims originating from the realm of objects by declaring itself the source of its action. The self is a free agent when it acts morally, because moral purpose identifies the aims of the self with those of any and all possible selves, which amounts to self-enactment or rather a definition of self that is not a composition derived from the clamor of empirical circumstance. In this context, the object assumes its contours and eventual significance entirely from the self and with respect to it; it is constructed as the self's medium for self-realization and, as such, it is an actualized representation of that which it can potentially elicit. Fichte essentially maintains that the subject freely creates the object and the object is itself invested with general validity insofar as this creation makes moral action possible, which refers the individual from subjective isolation to absolute authenticity.

His determination in proving the individual a free agent and therefore capable of moral action compels Fichte to ascribe a compensatory lack of independence to the object. Novalis is quick to appreciate the implication that the dynamics of symbolic representation show an undeniable kinship with the manner in which the object must necessarily relate to the subject within the framework of the *Wissenschaftslehre*. It is equally undeniable, however, that we are primarily aware of the object's general validity and not of our freedom in creating it, whereas symbols are, without question, freely created but may also be far more open to individual interpretation. The difference arises from the fact that the establishment of the relationship between subject and object initiates all processes of consciousness, so that only its results are reflected, which are, nonetheless, indicative of their origin.

Fichte, as I have pointed out, identifies primacy with the apodictic act of self-positing. Novalis's reasoning brings him to the same conclusion, and he elaborates on the significance of the formula I = I, the formula implicitly contained in the sentence of identity, immediately after his digression concerning signs and symbols:

Anwendung des bereits gesagten auf den Satz:
Ich bin ich.
Grammaticalisch enthält er dreyfach idem. Gehalt kann in dem Satze: Ich bin Ich nicht mehr, als im bloßen Begriff des Ich liegen. Was ist Ich? /Absolutes thetisches Vermögen / D[ie] Sfäre des Ich muß für uns alles umschließen. Als Selbst Gehalt kann es Gehalt erkennen. Das Erkennen deutet auf sein *Ich*seyn. Als Grund alles Bestimmens für d[as] Ich, oder aller *Form* ist es mithin Grund seiner eignen Bestimmung, oder Form. Kürzer: es ist eine selbstständige Bestimmung des Gehalts — damit hat es *sich* selbst *alle* Bestimmung gegeben.
Spontaneitaet seiner Bestimmung — Es nimmt z. B. A an, weil es a annimmt.
Warum die erste Handlung eine freye Handlung seyn muß — weil sie keine andre voraussezt — Sie ist, weil sie ist, nicht, weil eine andre ist. Folglich ist die Bestimmung des Ich, als Ich, frey. / Eine nichtfreye Handlung, kann nur durch eine andre Handlung nichtfrey seyn und so fort. Identität /

Application of what I have already stated to the sentence:
I am I [or I = I].
Grammatically it contains the same threefold. There can be no more content in the sentence I am I than there is in the mere concept of I. What is I? / Absolute thetic power / The sphere of the I must comprehend all for us. As content of its own self it can become conscious of content [i.e., the

self, or I, has only itself as its object, that is to say, it is its own content, and any other object or content can enter consciousness only insofar as it is believed to have affected the self]. Being conscious points to its being *I*. As basis of all definition for the I, or of all *form*, the I is therefore the basis of its own definition, or form. Phrased more succinctly: I is an independent definition of content — this means that it has given *itself all* definition [i.e., All this simply refers to the fact that "I" means both simultaneously that which is conscious and the object of this consciousness. As this consciousness it is "the sphere that comprehends all"; as the unconditional object of this consciousness it is delimited and defined by that sphere, that is to say, all its possible changes and variations are also defined within that sphere from the very beginning, even though all limitation is posited as an external reality, which is believed to enter consciousness from there]. Spontaneity of its definition — For example, it accepts A as an object because it does. Why the first act has to be a free act — because it is not preceded by any other — It is because it is. Consequently the I's definition as I is free. / A non-free action can only be non-free because it depends on another action and so on. Identity / [i.e., Again, these sentences refer to the self-conscious nature of the "I." Consciousness sets its object in front of itself, it "posits" the object; since the self is the permanent object of the self's consciousness, the first and free act of positing entails the self's positing itself].

(II, 104, 1. 22–105, 1. 7)

In exploring the concept of the ego, Novalis ascertains it is the only concept that necessarily entails its own existence; this is equivalent to saying the ego is the self-definition of being and everything else constitutes a modification of it. More simply, objects are in terms of the self's being since only that being is immediately apparent to the conceptual process, and the unconditional nature of such an awareness characterizes it as free, as self-enactment and self-definition, as that to which the term identity most fittingly applies.

Just as identity, the prime factor for the operation of consciousness, is ultimately dependent on the absolute act of self-positing that defines the sphere of being in all its potential modifications, nonidentity or otherness must be attributed the same absolute origin. In defining itself, the self delimits itself, and its own powers of limitation are now felt to be "outside," comprising a realm of nonself or "nonego" within which the self is totally determined. Insofar as anything is known, it can only be known within the self, within the confines of the defined unity that is the self functioning, in this respect, as the whole does with reference to its parts. Insofar as that which is known is different from the self as knowing agent, it must be external to it; but there all knowing ceases and only belief based on feeling effectively projects the object of knowledge beyond the self. Only the self is both, subject and object, whole and part, encompassing unity relative to the inner realm and point of departure for a projection toward external infinity. In this binary capacity, the self allows for the basic experience of empirical reality and for its conceptual framework as well.

Obviously, the absolute action prerequisite to the establishment of empirical reality cannot also be part of it. The primary act of self-positing with its corollary of self-limiting is thus necessarily beyond cognition; however, self-observation in the act of cognition leads to the recognition that dichotomy is only possible with reference to unity, absolute dichotomy with reference to absolute unity, ego and nonego only with reference to the Absolute, which bears no name, or rather any name signifying pure enactment. Fichte chose to call it Ego (Ich), because for him the Absolute is the guarantor of the empirical ego's inherent freedom over circumstance and determination made evident in its ability to act ethically. Novalis questions this nomenclature because the term "Ego" is all too easily associated with the relative, empirical subject, a dangerous possibility that would result in the very solipsist nonsense romantics are so frequently accused of advocating; instead, he wishes to emphasize the difference that exists between the absolute and relative realms. In a brief but thorough examination of the meaning attached to the concept of self, he arrives at the conclusion that the word "I" used in Fichte's manner is essentially a sign, a hieroglyph.[8] Stated more explicitly, he implies the symbol must not be confused with the symbolized, yet a relationship between the two must, nonetheless, exist.

These considerations at the beginning of the "Fichte-Studies" bring Novalis to the point at which it becomes necessary to develop the rudimentary outlines of a systematic schema for the relative interdependence of self, world, and Absolute. His formulation is very brief and precise:

> Es muß ein Nichtich seyn, damit Ich sich, als Ich setzen kann. These, Antithese, Synthese. D [ie] Handlung, daß Ich sich als Ich sezt muß mit der Antithese eines unabhängigen Nichtich und der Beziehung auf eine sie umschließende Säre verknüpft seyn — diese Säre kann man Gott und Ich nennen.

> There must be a nonego in order for the Ego to posit itself as ego. Thesis, antithesis, synthesis. The action of the ego's being posited by the Ego must be accompanied by the antithesis of an independent nonego, which, in turn, requires a simultaneous relationship to a sphere that encompasses both — this sphere can be called God and Ego.
>
> (fragments 7 and 8; II, 107, l. 30–108, l. 2)

These lines furnish the imagery within which Novalis's fundamental system of interrelation begins to assume shape. For the present, he merely points out that all of empirical reality may be reduced to the basic dualism between ego and nonego, self and world, which cannot, however, be established without reference to something that transcends either and is held in common by both. The latter is envisioned as a sphere, and its absolute nature is indicated by the stipulation that it may be referred to as God, in the traditional sense, and Ego, in accordance with Fichte's position. Both terms are equally appropriate, that is to say neither demands the exclusion of the other, but, at the same time, both are entirely inappropriate since they attempt to signify that which lies beyond the range of any and all possible experience, restricted, as it is, to the dualistic sphere of reality. Ego and God are simply expressions for the idea of absolute unity with reference to which we establish links of relationship throughout the infinite multiplicity we know as being. Here, the problem is stated in its simplest terms: all diversity is reduced to the fundamental opposition we experience as the difference between self and world, between ego and nonego, whereas the unity that inheres in this relationship all the same is also recognized and quite aptly seen as the sphere or circumference that determines the content not from within but from without by transcending it.

With respect to the self, whose distinguishing feature is its capability for free moral agency, the Absolute relates as Ego, as pure activity that directs the self to resolve the basic dualism on its own terms as long as they are representative of all selves. Whenever an individual acts morally, it leaves the isolation of its subjectivity, because for that moment all external limitation, all dependency on nature and circumstance has been suspended; insofar as the self assumes full responsibility for its actions, and in doing so determines the course of events according to the ever-present criterion of the categorical "ought to" that recognizes no dictates derived from empirical expedience, it defines its own being freely in terms of an Ego who re-creates everything after its own image, for whom the nonego effectively does not exist. This concept of self-enactment has nothing to do with either selfish egocentricity or self-deification. The selfish person defines his being in terms of the world of which he is a part, and in order to maintain his individuality he regards those aspects of the world within immediate practical range solely as means for self-aggrandizement, a process that is brought to its ultimate extreme when the subjective personality lays claim to absolute authority and, effectively, declares itself to be divine. Ethical behavior, on the other hand, does not define the agent in terms of the world nor is it aimed toward self-aggrandizement. Instead, the moral act defines the world in terms of the self who acts as a free agent on behalf of all other selves or free agents; consequently, the person truly engaged in moral action does not commit the idolatrous error of substituting absolute for relative values because he knows that his empirical being is not identical with the principle that governs it, with the Ego, and that no moral act nor any sum thereof could constitute a standard for moral action itself. This aspect of our selves constitutes true individuality and true selfhood, which can be experienced only during moments when the given state of physical dependency is suspended and made subordinate to directives that have neither their origin nor their goal in that dependency. Source and aim of such directives can only be the self's absolute freedom, which is, within the context of human consciousness, an unrealizable ideal that constitutes a permanent obligation for our actions and a necessary prerequisite for consciousness itself.

This then is the Ego, the all-inclusive sphere, of which Novalis speaks in concurrence with Fichte, and his justification for doing so is the very existence of the reality we all experience. However, this reality is twofold and also consists of a cosmic extension within which the self is merely a part determined by all the factors external to it. From this point of view, the all-inclusive sphere functions as the beginning and end of the exterior infinity insofar as it constitutes a related multiplicity that comprises the realm of objects for us, within which we envision the self as one of many. God, in the Judeo-Christian sense of the word, signifies nothing else but Unity, absolute and transcendental: God is the "creator," the uniform source of all things, who guarantees their relationship to one another but is, for that very reason, also excluded from their midst. God is manifest in every aspect of being since each one is a constitutive part and capable, as such, of relating to others; but God is not identical with any one particular aspect of creation no matter how large or small. When Novalis says the all-inclusive sphere can be called God or Ego, he states in the simplest possible manner that these names derive from the two basic perspectives with respect to which each moment of consciousness must necessarily relate to unity in an absolute sense if there be any consciousness at all.

As I have already noted, this is Novalis's first draft of the fundamental schema that transfixes the confusing complexity of all reality into a defined pattern of systematic interrelation between ego, nonego, and Absolute. At this stage, it serves to show that the ego is only in terms of the nonego, the nonego in terms of the ego, and this relationship only in terms of absolute unity; it also furnishes the framework from which the key issues that must still be resolved emerge and within which they are examined. Accordingly, those very issues are briefly introduced in passages immediately following fragment 8. Novalis begins with the notation, "Erfordernisse einer allgemeingültigen Filosofie" ("Requirements for a generally valid philosophy"), which may be regarded as the heading; the subsequent phrase, "Begriff des Nichts und des Was" ("Concept of nothing and something"), refers to the basic dualism between nonego and ego as fundamental to all conscious experience and therefore equally fundamental in its implications for any theory of knowledge, which he subdivides into three fields of inquiry:

1. Theorie des Zeichens oder was kann durch das Medium der Sprache *wahr* seyn?
2. über Filosofie überhaupt — Möglichkeit eines Systems etc.
3. System selbst.

1. Theory of signs or what may be *true* by means of the medium of language?
2. about philosophy in general — possibility of a system etc.
3. the system itself.

(II, 108, ll. 3–8; fragments 9, 10, and part of 11)

Hans-Joachim Mähl considers these programmatic points, under the heading "Requirements for a generally valid philosophy," to be the "germinal cell" from which the entire first 210 fragments, the first of the five "Groups" comprising the "Fichte-Studies," receive their topical coherence (II, 43). This is quite true, but I would also view the "germinal cell" as the most succinct formulation for those topics of main interest that evolve within the context of the first eight fragments in which Novalis records his reflections arising from the basic premise of the *Wissenschaftslehre*, from the implications contained in the sentence of identity, $A = A$. Furthermore, the exploratory survey comprising the initial seven fragments culminates in the first exposition of the "basic schema" that spans all aspects of reality and also spawns the "germinal cell" of which Mähl speaks. The enumeration of topics conducted there may be determinative for the next two hundred fragments; however, the basic schema of interrelation between absolute and relative values remains Novalis's cardinal concern and frame of reference throughout the entire body of fragments and beyond, so that this cyclic pattern of two opposing trends within an absolute sphere is actually the single most important intellectual configuration reflected at various stages of refinement and applicability in all of his work. The "Fichte-Studies," in particular, develop the "basic schema" from its rather simplistic beginnings to a high degree of theoretical sophistication.

At this juncture of his reasoning, Novalis continues his trend of thought by returning to his original speculative excursion, to the explication of the philosophic premises underlying the function of signs. Now he deals with the matter far more extensively, however, and he concludes his analysis by expanding the basic schema of interrelation to accommodate the functional relationship between the various factors involved in the process of signifying. Since that which is to be signified resides within the subjective realm of an individual's mind and since the choice of sign, the decision to consider the unrelated related by arbitrary decree, is equally private, it is puzzling indeed that we may nonetheless break through our respective isolation and are able to communicate. The compelling validity of signs by means of which thoughts are conveyed rests neither with the thought nor the sign and must therefore, be sought in the functional relationship subjective and objective moments assume with respect to the self. Only the self as the active nexus for whom subject and object are necessarily linked can presuppose a receptive recognition of the same necessity on the part of every other self. As a matter of fact, the more arbitrarily the respective combination is designed, the purer will be the manifestation of the self's agency and the more direct the appeal to a potential audience of equals. In other words, the process of signifying can only be understood in terms of the functional complex that is the self, and this complex is equivalent to the "basic schema." Novalis describes the connection very precisely in these words, which also emphasize the importance he attaches to the systematic diagram they are designed to outline, because here, for the first time, he refers to his concept of representative interrelation as the "basic schema" (*ursprüngliches Schema*), which terminology I have anticipated throughout this discussion for the sake of clarity:

> Die Nothwendigkeit der Beziehung eines Zeichens auf ein Bezeichnetes soll in einem Bezeichnenden liegen. In *diesem* aber wird beydes frey gesezt. Es muß also eine freye Nothwendigkeit der Beziehung beyder im Bezeichnenden vorhanden seyn. Frey soll sie seyn in Rücksicht dieses Bezeichnenden — nothwendig kann sie also nur in Rücksicht *des Bezeichnenden überhaupt* oder d[er] andern Bezeichnenden seyn. Freye Nothwendigkeit könnte man Selbstbestimmung nennen — folglich wäre Selbstbestimmung Character des *Bezeichnenden überhaupt* oder d[er] andern Bezeichn[enden] — das Wesen der Selbstbestimmung wäre sonach Synthese — absolute Sfärensetzung — These — bestimmte Särensetzung — Antithese nicht bestimmte Sfärensetzung. Jedes dieser drey ist alles Dreyes und dis ist Beweis ihres Zusammengehörens. Die Synthese ist These und Antithese oder kann es seyn. So die These; so die Antithese. Ursprüngliches Schema. / Eins in allem / Alles in Einem / Jedes *verständliche* Zeichen also muß in einem *schematischen* Verhältniß zum Bezeichneten stehn.

The necessary nature of the relationship between a sign and the signified is to be derived from the signifying agent. However, the sign and the signified are both freely posited within the signifying agent. Accordingly, there must be a free necessity of the relationship between the two present within the signifying agent. It is to be free with respect to this particular signifying agent, and since that is so, it can be necessary only with respect to the *essential nature of signifying agents in general* or rather with respect to the other signifying agents. Free necessity could be called self-definition; consequently, self-definition would be the essential character of *signifying agents in general* or, rather, of the other signifying agents — in this context, self-definition would essentially be synthesis—absolute positing of the sphere — thesis — positing of the sphere as a defined realm — antithesis [—] positing of the sphere without defined limits. Each of these three is all three in one and that is proof of their belonging together. Synthesis is, or rather can be, thesis and antithesis; the same holds true for thesis and also for antithesis. Basic schema / One in all / All in One / Each *comprehensible* sign must thus be in a *schematic* relationship to that which is signified.

(II, 109, ll. 15–31)

In this passage Novalis effectively identifies the correspondence between the sign and that which it represents with the necessity the self imparts to the relationship between subject and object. Again, highly abstract thoughts are rendered in more visible contours with the introduction of spheral imagery, which now, just a few lines after its initial appearance, has grown considerably more inclusive in its application and more complex in its composition. The key issue, apparent almost immediately, is the requisite that the self combine in its being freedom and necessity simultaneously: with respect to itself, it is free; with respect to others, who are equally free, a bond of necessity must prevail.

Within the framework of critical philosophy, the concept of necessity refers to the ground all individuals hold in common and shifts it from shared dependency on the physical universe to shared freedom in the human capacity for moral agency. The moral law of the "categorical imperative," and not the "thing in itself" or the "nonego," establishes the bond that links humanity. This bond is categorical and thus has generally binding, objective validity, whereas the decree of circumstance affects each individual differently and no such claim to objectivity can therefore attach to it or to any aspect of the world from which it emanates. As moral agents, human beings are considered free because a morally valid decision disavows dependence on any source of motivation, other than the imperative that applies equally to all, regardless of individual differences. Since it pertains without exception to all human beings, morally valid motivation is not only free but also necessary. Therefore, when Novalis speaks of "free necessity," he indicates primarily that an arbitrarily chosen sign derives its significance not from the thing to which it refers but from the same source that lets us endow our actions with meaning we expect others to share.

As my brief previous references to Fichte's philosophy have already suggested, the moral imperative may be considered to have epistemological significance because the synthesis of ego and nonego it seeks to effect has its equivalent in the unity of their origin with reference to which their relationship to one another is determined and made possible. In other words, the preconscious act of self-positing also establishes the sphere within which the nonego is posited as the object of a potential synthesis; it is with reference to this synthesis, which suspends the ego's individuated state of dependency and isolation, that the nonego assumes its differentiated contours and gains significance in the form of concrete objects for human consciousness.

With his concept of "free necessity," Novalis essentially states that the objects of human consciousness are as freely posited as the signs with which we refer to them, and that we are able to share the former by means of the latter because all selves are necessarily linked by their shared capacity for free moral agency. In order to be characterized by "free necessity" rather than mere necessity, the self must be supposed to have set its own limits and defined itself, as Novalis says. He also goes on to recognize that synthesis is the self's very essence, and he equates the primary act of self-definition, from which the power to synthesize is derived, with the absolute positing of the sphere, that is to say, with the defining of a point from which the absolute sphere, the sphere that contains all of reality, may be potentially drawn.

Only the Absolute can posit absolutely, and since there is nothing besides the Absolute, it can only posit itself. Self-positing, however, and self-definition are one and the same: both imply nothing else but an absolute act of self-limitation which suggests an image of totality in reverse or the reduction of the absolute sphere to its minimum, to a point that is its center, to a point that is absolute reality transformed into absolute potential. The self, or rather any self, is that point because from the limited perspective the One that is the Absolute becomes infinity, and within infinity, any point may be designated as center. What Novalis calls "the absolute positing of the sphere" does not mean drawing an absolute circumference; that would be a contradiction in terms since circumference means limit and absolute means none. Instead, his imagery suggests a point called into being absolutely — it simply is because it is, exactly as we experience our own being — with reference to which anything that may lay claim to reality assumes reality.

The self is empowered by its absolute heritage to expand its realm into infinity; potentially it is the Absolute, but that difference between actual and potential, limited and unlimited, has already introduced a dualism into reality as it pertains to the self. On the one hand, the self is that for whom everything is real, and in this capacity it functions as the defined sphere of reality. Novalis refers to this aspect as "positing the sphere as a defined realm" (*bestimmte Sfärensetzung*) or "thesis." It could also be envisioned as the inner realm or the realm of consciousness. On the other hand, reality is an infinite potential beyond the limits of the self; that would be the antithetical aspect Novalis characterizes as "positing the sphere without defined limits," which corresponds in our experience to the infinite expanse of the cosmos around us that seems to harbor everything our consciousness projects as real.

These are the three spheres; each time it is the same sphere viewed from a different vantage point that is, in its turn, merely an aspect of the others, and those vantage points are nothing else but the self in the three functional modes it maintains simultaneously: the self as potential Whole ("synthesis") with the power to relate the self as relative whole ("thesis") to the self as relative part ("antithesis"). This functional complex constitutes the basic schema of interrelation that is the self, and any process including that of signifying, takes place only within its context; it also establishes the bond of validity with reference to all selves that Novalis had sought to determine in order to explain the possibility of a specifically human form of communication involving freedom of choice rather than involuntary reactions to nature's impulses on nature's terms.

Freedom, as the distinguishing feature of the properly human, is the concept that might well be regarded as the soul of Fichte's philosophic "system" in all its variations from the first version of the *Wissenschaftslehre* on. As is the case with any genuine doctrine proclaiming human freedom, its perpetrators and disciples must be careful to locate a ground common to all men unless they wish to become entwined in a cocoon of subjective license where no path extends from I to thou, a cocoon of self-idolatry that may seem ludicrous in theory but in actuality demands to be fed human sacrifice, which is the wont of idols, be they of stone or flesh. Fichte's and Novalis's insistence on the sharp distinction between absolute and relative values serves as a fundamental deterrent for such confusion. However, it is difficult to oversee at one glance the various applied implications of these abstractions. Those empirical aspects particularly illustrative of the coordination between individual and general requisites merit, therefore, separate and specific attention. Communication obviously presents one such instance, but so do cognition and the trend to render a systematic account of its entire range in a philosophy; all these are topics marked for investigation by the "germinal cell" and all are commonplace, basic operations that involve the individual as a free agent who is nonetheless bound by what Novalis termed necessity. His basic schema for relating these two functions compresses the interaction of absolute and relative values in their necessary interdependence into a simple pattern that holds true for every being capable of saying "I" and affords us a ready link between experiential immediacy and theoretical abstraction. Essentially, the schema is the diagrammatic summation of Fichte's three axiomatic formulas (*Grundsätze*) with which the *Wissenschaftslehre* begins and from which all further arguments follow. Novalis's intent becomes readily apparent in these remarks that bring the discussion concerning the efficacy of signs back to the underlying relationship comprising the dialectic moments of absolute Ego, ego, and nonego:

/ Gegensatz ist vom Nichtsatz zu unterscheiden. Antipoden und Antiveci.
/ Auch hier in der Anwendung zeigt sich der Caracter der Alleseinheit des Schemas. Frey kann nur bestimmt, also nothwendig, Nothwendig nur unbestimmt, also frey, seyn. Ohne Sfäre müssen These und Antithese verwechselt werden können, Eins seyn, oder nichts seyn — welches hier einerley ist. So Ich und Nichtich, ohne absolutes Ich! welches aber nur Sfäre ist, nur unter der Voraussetzung (*Mit* [setzung]) der These und Antithese ist /

/ Opposition is altogether different from not-positing at all [Opposition involves] antipodes antivectors. /
/ Here, too, in its application, the schema's character of being one in all its aspects and all aspects in each one becomes apparent. Free can only mean definite, and thus necessary; necessary can only mean non-defined, and thus free. Without the [absolute] sphere, thesis and antithesis would have to be indistinguishable from one another; they would be as one or

nothing, which, in this case, amounts to the same thing. The same holds true for ego and non-ego without the absolute Ego! However the absolute Ego is only sphere, it is only insofar as there is thesis and antithesis /

(II, 110, ll. 9–17)

Here, once again, the emphasis is on the absolute sphere, which is identical with the Ego. However, Novalis makes it quite clear that this "sphere" exists only with reference to ego, or thesis, and nonego, or antithesis. As a result, the image maintains no concrete outline and quite obviously has the symbolic function to convey that source and resolution of the empirical dualism are one. Opposition, so the introductory words state, is characterized by an antipodal tendency, which, by implication, is possible only from a point that serves as common origin for the extension in opposite directions. If this point is viewed as the center from which the absolute sphere is approached along opposing vectors, then thesis and antithesis, ego and nonego, would indeed exist only as long as there is a center with reference to a potentially all-inclusive sphere. The spheral aspect accents ultimate unity or synthetic function, whereas the center marks the point from which unity takes on a twofold direction. Both are, however, one and the same: each is nothing without the other and both are expressive of unity as well as multiplicity. The difference is one of direction; whereas the sphere can only move from unity to multiplicity, the center initiates a multiple approach to unity. It is this very dynamic reciprocity between sphere and center that is separately represented in each of the two vectors emanating from the center. One is the thesis, or ego, which traverses an infinity of objects on the way from the inclusive unity of consciousness to the center and final object that would be the ego beheld in all its possible states of being affected. The other is the antithesis or nonego, which is the same multiplicity but traversed in the opposite direction from the self as the prime reference point for all of being to the sphere that would include it all.

Viewed together, the ego is the center in an absolute sense, which requires it to function simultaneously as relative sphere for the subjective reality of consciousness and as relative center for the objective reality of being. In its extension as subject, the ego is defined as sphere, the sphere of consciousness, but not as center, which varies in accordance with the context of consciousness. In its extension as object, the ego is defined as center, as the point of orientation for objective reality, but not as sphere, which is, again, as variable as infinity. However, the ego is simultaneously both relative sphere and relative center and can, in this capacity, supply the definition for the missing constant in each respective sphere from the other. When the ego functions in this manner, it functions synthetically by the power invested in it as center of the absolute sphere, which enables it to unite the subjective and objective moments into a conscious whole. Effectively, the ego draws the absolute sphere every moment it is conscious of the world around it, but never conclusively because the Absolute has no circumscribable limits and remains thus forever potential, a limit asymptotically approached by way of simultaneous extension into subjective and objective infinity. Only in its synthesizing action does the ego function as the Absolute's center and only in this activity is the ego fully itself; it is neither subject nor object but both, and paradoxically, only in this context do the moments of subjective and objective reality assume definite contours. As Novalis says in the last fragment cited, the Ego is sphere only with reference to thesis and antithesis, only with reference to the relative, dualistic realms of ego and nonego, subject and object. It is that, one must add, only by means of its center from which it can be drawn, the point at which both members of the dualism merge and emerge, by means of the self for whom both its moments of ego and nonego, subject and object, are.

In other words, the absolute sphere does not exist at all in concrete outline but rather in the ongoing productivity through which the self radiates in two directions at once in order to unite them within the scope of an ever more inclusive sphere. The self is one only as the productive center in its unceasing activity; the relative effect of this activity, however, the conscious image of the world, is always marked by that very dualism: consciousness and world, subject and object. Accordingly, the self must identify with either realm separately, either as subject where the world is seen in terms of the self, or as object, where the self appears in terms of the world; therefore, its true nature remains unrecognized, unless it becomes aware of itself as the active principle from which this twofold reality derives its coherence. Because it is itself activity, such awareness occurs only through enactment and cannot properly be referred to as consciousness since the distinction between subject and object does not apply. The enactment in question is equivalent to self-enactment, which entails any activity that unites subjective and objective criteria in one function. At the most fundamental level, for example, any act of knowledge constitutes the intentional exercise of the ego's synthesizing power and qualifies, in this respect, essentially as self-awareness. In short, all aspects of human experience must be brought into correct focus with reference to the ego's function as productive center if they are to be seen correctly. Or, in different words, everything is essentially a product of the self's activity, and to comprehend any phenomenon correctly simply means being able to behold it in this context; the contextual pattern, however, and thus the universal key to all insight, is the "basic schema."

For the moment, though, Novalis's immediate concern had been directed at the question of signifying and representation. In response to it, the "basic schema" took more definite shape, because the act of appointing a sign from the realm of objects to convey a thought sets the self's distinctive synthesizing powers into operation with such pronounced intentionality that it likens, in effect, this particular activity to an experiment from which certain analytical conclusions may be drawn for less controlled situations. The degree of conscious intent in any action demonstrative of the ego's unifying function is, therefore, not only a measure of the degree of self-awareness that may be achieved. It can, in this connection, also lead to a proportionately clearer theoretical understanding of self, world, and Absolute within a philosophical context. This is the more precise meaning in which Novalis's fragments are philosophical experiments; and since they entail the self's active participation as synthetic agent in an effort to formulate thoughts that have general validity and thus apply equally to the subjective and objective spheres, this practice of speculative experimentation would also have to be accompanied by the unmitigated experience of the self's agency, by self-awareness. In this manner Novalis proceeds throughout the "Fichte-Studies" to test the various facets and implications of the *Wissenschaftslehre* within the framework of his "basic schema," but I shall not attempt to reenact his every experiment. For the sake of clarity, it must suffice if only the results are pointed out that contribute to the further evolution of the "basic schema."

The "Fichte-Studies" deal with a bewildering array of topics; however, there is a systematic approach that lends coherence to the apparent disorganization. These fragments make it quite evident that the fundamental concepts of Kantian and Fichtean philosophy are being examined in all manner of variations, but — and this would seem to be equally obvious — it is done within a framework evolved from the structural principle of the "basic schema." The interrelations of various topical concepts change at a confusing rate as Novalis tries out each new set or combination of sets; he never arrives at a fully integrated system, and I suspect that was not even his major concern. The "basic schema" of interrelation is the unvarying element in his speculations, and it is actually this structural and dynamic principle that is tested in these philosophical experiments rather than the individual concepts under consideration.

For example, form (*Form*) and matter (*Stoff*) constitute one of the many dichotomies examined repeatedly with varying results, but the attempt to determine the unifying factor on which this relationship depends remains constant. The structural pattern that becomes apparent in the course of Novalis's efforts to align form and matter as reciprocal correspondents bears an undeniable resemblance to the "basic schema," as is easily perceived in this concise formulation: "Ich mit den Gliedern Form und Stoff ist der Punct des empirischen Bewußtseyns, die Pyramide aufwärts ist das Transscendentale" ("The self with the constitutive members of form and matter is the point of empirical consciousness; from that point upward is the pyramid of the transcendental") (II, 135, ll. 29–31). For the sake of amplification, one could also add the pronouncement, made some pages thereafter, that "/ Bewußtseyn muß Einfach and unendlich seyn. /" ("consciousness must be singular," like a point, "and infinite," as the pyramid with an open base would imply) (II, 221, l. 13). The image these words suggest is the familiar one of a dualism that stands opposed only with reference to a point both spheres hold in common and, because they must hold it in common, that point also refers to the absolute sphere within which those same opposing trends would be one. In this sense, consciousness is the self as the functional point for which material and formal aspects are one. It is also the point at which those same aspects merge and from which they are projected as united in the object that has both subjective and objective validity.

However, the ego is not only active as a conscious, theoretical being but also as a moral, practical one and, again, Novalis presents his reflections on the matter within the context of the "basic schema." One of his first deliberations concerning the topic of morality leads from a reexamination of the Ego-ego relationship to the conclusion that morality comprises religion and ethics. The initial part (fragment 53: II, 139, l. 32–140, l. 33) restates that the term "absolute Ego" is expressive of absolute synthesis, which must be envisioned as a sphere without limit (*Sphäre ohne Grenze*); but both the term and the image have meaning only from the perspective of an equally absolute point of division. That is to say, synthesis derives its meaning from analysis, and analysis means dualism, which translates into the encompassing unity of synthesis reduced to tangency in opposition, also called limit. With reference to the infinite sphere, the only limit conceivable would be its infinite concentration to a point; Novalis merely refers to absolute limit (*Grenze überhaupt*), which means point of opposition, that is to say "analysis" or, in this context, "analytical ego" (*analytisches Ich*) and potentially infinite sphere, potentially absolute and synthetic Ego ("das analytische Ich überhaupt erfüllt das synthetische Ich"). So far, this dynamic interplay outlines in familiar terms the movement from Absolute to relative and from relative toward Absolute. Even the following addition merely elaborates on some details that are not entirely surprising:

> Das analytische Ich wird vom Ich begründet und besteht in einem Setzen seiner selbst durch ein Entgegensetzen. Es sezt sich für sich, indem es ein Bild von seinem Begründenden sezt und so die Handlung seines Begründens reproducirt.

> The analytical ego is founded by the Ego and consists of positing itself by means of an opposition. It posits itself for itself by positing a reproduction (*Bild*) of its founder and thus it reproduces the action of its founding.
>
> (II, 140, ll. 28–31)

The cycle described is a movement from the infinite sphere to the infinitely potential point from which the sphere is approached in opposing directions and may be redrawn infinitely by uniting the two relative antipodes at any given instant. This reproduced sphere is the *Bild*, the image or reproduction — in this context, possibly, even reflection — of the original sphere but never its equivalent: the absolute sphere has no circumference and constitutes a movement from infinity to the point of its absolute reduction, whereas the movement from there tends in the opposite direction along opposing vectors which results in an infinite expansion of the punctual limit, that is, in effect, the constant redrawing of a circumference in an infinite approach toward the original Absolute.

Once the "basic schema" has been restated in terms of the ego's functional dynamics, Novalis continues by reformulating his abstractions in language that makes the pertinence of his conclusions more accessible (fragment 54: II, 141, ll. 1–14). He equates the absolute or synthetic Ego with God and the analytical ego with the concept of person, so that God and person are envisioned in the same absolute reciprocity outlined with respect to the synthetic Ego and the analytical ego. Accordingly, the concept of person designates nothing else but the two moments of that absolute reciprocity in a separate but simultaneous approach to God, which Novalis sees as an inner and outer direction toward the Absolute he terms "adoring God spiritually and in truth, striving infinitely toward God theoretically and practically ("Gott im Geist und in der Wahrheit anbeten — theoretisches unendliches Streben zu Gott — practisches Streben zu Gott").

The inner, theoretical or conscious realm is characterized by the consecutive influx of sense impressions, which is experienced as the sequential rhythm we call time. Once we become aware of the fact that it is I who undergoes this experience, that it takes place within me and is enacted by me, we gain a sense of personal continuity. When this person acts from a sense of freedom in which he recognizes himself as the source of action and assumes responsibility for it, all other determining factors lose their power and the temporal flux of circumstance lies suspended by the timeless validity of the self's action, its practical, its ethical action; Novalis calls that condition in this context "unity in time" ("Einheit in der Zeit"). Practical agency effects the most complete synthesis between the embattled dualism of subject and object because it is accompanied by the highest degree of self-awareness, an awareness that is proportionately keener the closer a person comes to his absolute origin. The same awareness must also be introduced into the theoretical realm if it is to be truly a striving toward God. Only in this respect does the accumulation of knowledge assume proper significance and coherence, which, with a view to its projected totality, might then be called religion. Novalis's laconic observation that the ideal, the highest good, is morality and that "morality consists of religion and ethics" ("Moral zerfällt in Religion und Ethik") (II, 141, ll. 9–10) loses its initial mystery and constitutes not only a succinct summary of his complex deliberation but also a useful formula for future orientation.

The oft-cited pronouncement that God has made man in His image gains new meaning in this context and is most persuasive when Novalis uses it to circumscribe the source and aim of the activity that is the self ("Gott hat uns nach seinem Bilde geschaffen" [II, 141 l. 13]). In its theoretical function, the self strives to formulate totality in its mind by construing an image of nature, the realm of objects, along a progression from thing to thing that would reach completion only with the final drawing of the sphere, with the beholding of ultimate unity, the vision of the Absolute or divine. As a practical agent, on the other hand, the self creates its own image within nature each instant an action reflects the freedom that is the ego's absolute heritage and unchanging identity; here, too, the direction is toward the final drawing of the sphere, which would entail regaining the original state where the realm of objects has no meaning other than in terms of the Ego, of the Absolute that is identical with God.

As Novalis says, God made man in His image, which is an abbreviation for saying we only know the Absolute, be its name Ego or God, insofar as we know the self, and we only know the self insofar as the subject reflects the object and vice versa. The subjective and objective realms are the only immediate realities for us, but because they constitute reciprocal moments engendered by the self's agency, we can become aware of the self in this function and thus approach recognition of the self as pure activity, as Ego or God, in accordance with the degree of freedom the self manifests in its relative activity. If the Absolute is infinitely remote as a goal, it is, nonetheless, proximate in its function as origin of the generative principle that gives rise to the mutually representative dualism of subject and object. Novalis, who occasionally refers to the basic dichotomy of empirical reality as relative synthesis and analysis, points this out emphatically and summarily when he says:

/ Ich ist blos der höchstmöglichste Ausdruck für die Entstehung der Analyse und Synthese im Unbekannten.
/ Das Unbekannte ist das heilige Nichts für uns. /

Ego is merely the highest possible expression for the origin of analysis and synthesis within the unknown.
The unknown is the holy Nothing for us.

(II, 144, ll. 28–30)

The "holy Nothing" signifies the pregnant absolute sphere, the womb giving birth to the self as opposing trends that relate on the basis of a mirrorlike reciprocity and strive to fill out the very sphere into which they were born; but the ancient mystical term "holy Nothing" also conveys the complete otherness of the divine or absolute realm as compared with the "something" that comprises the entire range of our experience. The path to the Absolute is, therefore, a negative one, that is to say, it must necessarily confine itself to that which the Absolute is not, and it can thus circumscribe its goal negatively. This negative approach actually means the gradual elimination of nonabsolute reality in favor of absolute Reality. For us, reality is characterized by the dualism of self and world, subject and object; its progressive elimination through increasing awareness of its origin and through its suspension in the self's agency is the course Novalis attempts to outline for himself in greater detail.

The "basic schema" proved to be a cycle of mutually representative action where each aspect presents an image of the others. From the very beginning, Novalis emphasized the self's function as image maker and signifier, and now it has become evident that this activity is so fundamental to the entire complex of relationships that awareness of the self's agency could best be gained by observing it in the execution of this, its functional designation within the "basic schema." Accordingly, the "Fichte-Studies" return to that very topic repeatedly, in an effort to determine the various levels at which the self's agency becomes ever more apparent in the representative interplay between the dual realms of inner and outer reality. In general, the trend of Novalis's thoughts begins with analyses of the most basic operation, the production of the conscious image, and goes on to link this process with its counterpart in reverse, with the production of a sign, which leads him to locate the power of imagination as the functional center for the ego's activity. Simply put, he says: "[Conscious] images are sense perception in terms of thought perception. Signs are thought perception in terms of sense perception" ("Bild ist eine vorgestellte Anschauung. Zeichen eine angeschaute Vorstellung"); to which he adds that one is effected by the imagination as mere imagination, whereas the other is the product of the imagination functioning as the power to formulate symbols (II, 171, ll. 16–18).

Neither sense perception nor thought perception exist in a pure state; they modify each other reciprocally at various levels and effectively constitute a cycle with the power of the imagination as its dynamic center (II, 171, ll. 19–21.) This operation circumscribes the self's free agency as formative action, in which it suspends the antagonistic dualism between the realms of sense and thought by uniting them within the contours of either image or sign. Unity of those two realms with respect to form is founded on the principle that, in its purest manifestation, is known to us as beauty; or as Novalis says, "Princip der Schönheit — begründet die Vorstellung und Anschauung" ("the principle of beauty furnishes the foundation for both, thought perception and sense perception") (II, 177, ll, 21–22). The principle of the imagination is, therefore, beauty, and since it arises with the self's free agency that also effects the very same synthesis on a speculative basis between the realities of the objective and subjective realms, beauty can be equated with truth, or "Man kann so gewiß seine Filosofie wahr nennen — so gewiß man etwas schön nennt" ("one can call one's philosophy true with the same degree of certainty as one can call something beautiful") (II, 177, ll. 17–18).

Novalis states quite explicitly that "freedom" is the proper term to describe what he calls "the condition of the hovering imagination" ("Zustand der schwebenden Einbildungskraft"), by which he means to convey that the imagination is neither one nor the other of the opposites it unites, and yet, because it unites them, it is both (II, 188, ll. 20–21). The law of the imagination is only manifest in its product, or, rather, freedom enacted becomes concretized as relative unity and all transition from one realm to the other (*Transitus*) is thus effected by the imagination, even though this is not always obvious to us in the same degree. Relative to conscious images (*Bild*), for example, the conscious effort invested is overridden by the perceptive activity of the senses ("im Bild [praevaliert] die Anschauung"), whereas signs are the product of a definite conscious intent ("im Zeichen praevaliert der Begriff"), so that the most commonly used sign, language, is, for Novalis, a linguistic or, better yet, conceptual image (II, 188, ll. 18–19). More particularly with reference to language, he states further: "Sprache: Verknüpfung des besondern sinnlichen Gedankenstoffs mit sinnlichen Zeichen. Zeichen ist eine hypothetische Anschauung, bedingt durch eine Vorstellung" ("Language is the linking of specific thought-matter with sensual signs. Any sign is a hypothetical sense perception conditioned by a thought perception") (II, 189, ll. 1–3).

Since thought, and with it consciousness, play the determinative part in speech or any other form of signification, the process is accompanied by a relatively greater awareness of the self's agency in effecting the transition from the subjective sphere to the objective one. In his deliberations concerning the power of the imagination, Novalis ultimately identifies it explicitly with the dynamic center of the "basic schema," with the functional nexus that truly is the ego and not merely its manifestation in the final relative pattern where it must always stand opposed by the nonego. Just as this central self never becomes apparent, except for the results of its agency, which really hide it from view because they are always partial to either the subject's or the object's sphere, the imagination is also evident only in the product of its activity. The term imagination is essentially nothing else but another name for the self, which emphatically conveys its true nature as free activity.

Toward the end of the "Fichte-Studies," Novalis comes to identify the self ever more closely with the power of the imagination, with free agency, and consequently with the principle of freedom in its most distinct manifestation, with practical, that is to say moral, activity. "Practische Vernunft ist reine Einbildungskraft" ("Practical reason is pure power of the imagination") (II, 258, l. 3), he says, and acting (*handeln*) becomes a key concept in the fifth, next to last, group of fragments, which may be regarded as an approximate summary of his thoughts on the *Wissenschaftslehre*. Here, Novalis begins again with the sentence of identity, A = A, but moves on quickly to proclaim morality (*Moralität*) as the cardinal principle for the entire sphere of the ego's being, for its theoretical and practical endeavors, as he had already done earlier in his deliberations concerning religion and ethics. Now knowledge (*Erkenntnis*), or rather philosophy as the attempt to expose and systematize the operational framework for all potential knowledge, takes the place of religion, so that the self is the goal in both directions: active search for full comprehension of the free self in one, and active realization of the free self in the other, or "Die höchste Filosofie ist Ethik" ("philosophy in its highest sense is equivalent to ethics") (II, 267, ll. 3–4). However, neither philosophy nor ethical practice can attain that goal since it is absolute and only discernible in the respective activities themselves. The self is on an unending path to itself along which it can only recognize itself negatively, as that which it is not, or, one might add, only in representation; Novalis specifies this quite precisely in these words:

> Durch das freywillige Entsagen des Absoluten entsteht die unendliche freye Thätigkeit in uns — das Einzig mögliche Absolute, was uns gegeben werden kann und was wir nur durch unsre Unvermögenheit ein Absolutes zu erreichen und zu erkennen, finden. Dies uns gegebne Absolute läßt sich nur negativ erkennen, indem wir handeln und finden, daß durch kein Handeln das erreicht wird, was wir suchen.

> As a result of our voluntarily abstaining from the Absolute, infinite and free activity originates within us, which is the only possible Absolute that can be given us, that we can find only through our inability to attain and apprehend an Absolute. This Absolute that is given us can be known only negatively, only insofar as we act and in acting realize that we do not attain what we seek through any of our actions.

> (II, 269, l. 33–270, l. 6)

Here Novalis clearly outlines the path he envisions. It is a *via negativa,* which does not mean nihilistic resignation because the ultimate goal of the empirical dualism's total elimination in the absolute unity and freedom of its origin is never reached. On the contrary, this permanent denial of final attainment is an infinite affirmation of that very goal because in its pursuit the ego ceaselessly suspends the opposition between subject and object, ego and nonego, self and world, with ever new and progressively more inclusive variations of union and, by doing so, furnishes a constant demonstration of freedom in an unending attempt at its absolute realization. To recognize the ego as pure agency, that is as not locked into either its subjective or objective moments, is the first and final insight to which philosophy leads, and thus all theoretical effort points to practical endeavor, the free exercise of the self's power in a continual process of self-realization, or "[Das Universalsystem der Filosofie muß] Compass der Freyheit seyn" ("philosophy must be the compass of freedom") (II, 290, l. 3).

The emphasis is clearly on the active life, the *vita activa,* and the task that arises from these philosophical experiments demands that the self grow in its awareness of its true nature through the active representation of its absolute heritage, through the demonstration of its freedom. Within the context of the "basic schema," this means that the relationship between the self as absolute center and absolute sphere be demonstrated in two directions: inward, in the conscious or theoretical realm, the self is actively to take possession of the objects in an ever greater knowledge of the external material world ("Wir müssen suchen eine innre Welt zu schaffen, die eigentlicher Pendant der äußern Welt ist — die, indem sie ihr auf allen Puncten bestimmt entgegengesezt wird, unsre Freyheit immer mehr erweitert" ["we must seek to create an inner world that is the real pendant of the external one, which — insofar as it is defined by us — increases our freedom correspondingly"] [II, 287, ll. 32–35]); and outward, in the objective realm, the self is to demonstrate freedom by every one of its actions and thus endow all aspects of temporal existence with human significance, a significance that defies the dictates of time and circumstance since it is derived from the self's free agency and is, thus, valid for all other free agents. Within the context of the "Fichte-Studies," such external self-enactment entails, as we have seen, an ever clearer self-representation from the most basic level of signifying to the most demanding acts of ethical self-determination, which, in its most extreme consequence, requires that it be extended to include even dying as the ultimate act through which human freedom may be professed.

The ego is essentially practical, that is to say, active as a free agent, be that in the inward direction, where it fashions the multiplicity of sense perception into units, into the objects of consciousness, within the theoretical context of a coherent whole, or in the outward direction, where its actions subsume the objective realm's claim to independence within their determinative sphere. In both directions, the object, the nonego as the limiting force that confines the ego, is progressively overcome as the ego unfolds its activity. Each realm mirrors the other and each realm is representative of the ego's true nature, only in different ways, in different directions; but since the image each bears is also essentially the same, difference must give way to correspondence and this correspondence is overtly effected in the externally directed practical act. Novalis calls this aspect of human activity *Kunst* by which he means art in the widest sense of the word, ranging from expertise or craftsmanship to self-enactment and self-representation in the moral act. "Ich ist Handlung und Produkt zugleich. Wollen und Vorstellen sind Wechselbestimmungen — das Ich ist nichts anders, als Wollen und Vorstellen" ("Ego is activity and product of that activity simultaneously. Willing and conceptualizing are reciprocal — the ego is nothing else but willing and conceptualizing"), he says and continues, "Nur das practische Ich kann wahrgenommen werden — denn dies ist auch das eigentliche Grundich. . . . Vollständiges Ich zu seyn, ist eine *K u n s t* — " ("Only the practical ego can be apprehended, because it is the basic, fundamental ego . . . . To be ego completely is an *a r t* — ") (II, 294, ll. 20–26). This art consists of the effortless movement between the inner and outer spheres, which means bringing them into correspondence from their point of tangency, their mutual center, from the activity that is the ego and with reference to it. "Kunst," Novalis had specified a little earlier, "ist: Ausbildung unsrer Wirksamkeit — *Wollen auf eine bestimmte Art* — einer Idee gemäß — Wirken und Wollen ist hier Eins" ("Art is the active training of our effectiveness, it is *willing in a definite manner*, according to an idea. Being effective and willing is one and the same for art") (II, 284, ll. 7–8). This simply means that the ego in its externally directed practical activity is able to suspend the object's or nonego's opposition so completely that for that instance the dualism ceases, the inner and outer spheres correspond, become one, and the absolute sphere is reestablished — not permanently, to be sure, since that is impossible, but at any given moment anew.

The theoretical realm is only an indirect manifestation of the ego's practicality or agency, and for that reason the objects retain some independence, which they would only lose if viewed from the perspective of their totality, from the perspective of God or the absolutely active Ego. The unity of consciousness remains the same and active throughout, but it is constantly expanded by new experiential data, so that the limiting function of the nonego is never exhausted. In its theoretical activity, the ego expands its knowledge by unifying the empirical data in its consciousness and by testing in experience what it defines within this unity as constitutive parts. These two aspects of the ego's theoretical endeavor Novalis calls *Wissenschaft* (science), which signifies the aspect of unity, and *Kenntnis* (pragmatic knowledge), which signifies the partial, experiential application (II, 283, ll. 21–24). Art, however, as the direct administration of the ego's free agency onto the objective realm is the synthesizing complement through which the correspondence of science and pragmatic experience is established; it is essentially the active, practical projection of the sphere of consciousness into the external realm. With these deliberations the "Fichte-Studies" effectively draw to a close. The last fragment reads:

> Über die Menschheit. Ihre reine, vollständige Ausbildung muß erst zur Kunst des Individui werden — und von da erst in die großen Völkermassen und dann in die Gattung übergehn. Inwiefern ist sie ein Individuum?

> About humanity. Its pure and complete realization must first become the art of being an individual, a self, and only from there can the great masses of the nations be affected and then the species. In what respect is the species an individual?
> (II, 296, ll. 28–31)

Novalis's philosophical experiments have led him to a vantage point from which human existence, as it appears through his own being, can be viewed clearly, so that the basis for self-orientation he had longed to attain is firmly established. He came to recognize the self not as a fixed object but as a functional schema of interrelation that extends from the Absolute to the potentially Absolute from which the Absolute may be reapproached along two ways that run in opposite directions but reflect one another insofar as their relative point of origin and their absolute goal are the same. This complex relationship is best represented by the image of a circle or sphere in flux; that is to say, as absolute origin it constricts to a point that serves as center for a circumference that, as absolute goal, can never be drawn conclusively. With the absolute sphere as origin and goal eliminated in the form of a concrete outline, the image that emerges is one of a dynamic point that expands continually in opposite directions; yet, at the same time, this common point of tangency in opposition can, in its capacity as potentially absolute center, unite these opposing trends under its ever-expanding, potentially absolute sphere. Without such reference to absolute unity, subject and object, ego and nonego, are mutually limiting opposites. Not to remain embattled in this apparent dualism but to establish correspondence of the two realms is to realize the self's potential, because nothing else except the self in its true function within empirical reality was to be illustrated by the dynamic center. The self is potentially absolute, which means it is one, self-identical, pure agency, and free; to realize its potential is to exercise it as a free agent for whom the mutually limiting opposition between subject and object lies suspended in unity, not permanently but at any given instance anew. This feat, so Novalis recognizes, is accomplished by the imagination, which hovers over both realms and is engaged in projecting the object into the subject and the subject onto the objects. Truth and beauty have their common ground in the functional unity of the imagination because, insofar as it is one and free, not encumbered by the limits of opposition, it is equally responsible for form and content. In other words, what the imagination conveys from one realm to the other has, through its power, validity in both, which is what we call truth; how the conveyed is represented also reflects the imagination's unifying agency, which, as the principle of all form, is also the principle of beauty, the clearest reflection, in either realm, of the two realms in harmony. The products of the imagination are not real in themselves, even though they constitute our only reality. They are real only as functions of the self's free activity. That freedom is most pronounced in those actions the self directs outward, against a realm that stands opposed to it, not in an effort at pragmatic accommodation but as active proof of its sovereignty. Such acts are ethical, and since they are nothing but a manifestation of the self's basic freedom in action, Novalis proclaims "Die Moralität muß Kern unsers Daseyns seyn" ("morality must be [i.e., is] the core of our being") (II, 266, 1. 34). However, the self is active not only in an outward direction but also inward. "Inward morality" actually refers to the theoretical attempt to approach total knowledge of the material world, to form as complete and comprehensive an image of it as possible, whereas "outward morality" entails ever clearer self-representation from the most basic level of signifying to the more complex in craftsmanship, art, and personal conduct.

Life, as Novalis envisions it in the "Fichte-Studies," is exclusively characterized by activity. It is a *vita activa* that consists of the unqualified pursuit of knowledge and the steady "development of our effectiveness" (II, 284, 1. 7). It means constant practice in exercising the self's free agency with the aim of gaining that free state of "moral" preparedness in which willing and acting are one, in which the transition between the spheres of subject and object takes place with the effortless grace he defines in this context as art. This loose definition leaves the exact relationship between ethics and aesthetics quite vague. As the issue becomes more pertinent later on, he will redefine the state of moral preparedness, which actually constitutes the highest level of achievement in the empirical realm, as the precondition for artistic inspiration and expression, as an openness and a state of receptivity for contact with the Absolute. But even here, at the time of the "Fichte-Studies," the accumulation of knowledge and the practice in effectiveness are complemented by a more direct affinity with the Absolute. His love for Sophie is the entire sphere of his being and subordinates everything else. In his relationship to her the world around him has lost all vestiges of estrangement; through her he is really one with it in a manner that cannot be explained in terms of the strict moralism that permeates Fichtean thought. Our attention must therefore return briefly to this profound human encounter that accompanies Novalis's philosophical experiments and continues after their conclusion.

Chapter 5
Death and the "Decision to Live"

Novalis had not been wrong when, shortly after the chance encounter with Sophie in November of 1794, he informed Erasmus, the eldest and favorite of his younger brothers, that a quarter of an hour had decided him (IV, 361, l. 1).[9] There is no doubt that the effect of this meeting must have seemed disturbing to his correspondent, who found little in their shared past that could have served to explain or justify such a drastic turn of events experienced with such decisive finality. On the contrary, along with that selfsame Erasmus and a younger brother Carl, Novalis had proven himself quite ardent and experienced in the pursuit of female companionship before leaving for Tennstedt, so that everyone, himself included, had expected no more of a change in these matters of social diversion than one of locale. Instead of diversity, however, he found at Grüningen the one being through whom all of reality was to derive its meaning for him. Everything else fell into place with reference to her and she became the ubiquitous point of orientation for all his future plans and activities. Novalis's reaction to meeting Sophie von Kühn is by no means one of self-abandonment in passionate intoxication nor does it come about as the result of careful calculations measured on the scale of pragmatic reason and consideration. He simply knows, as he beholds the girl, that the stability, so ardently desired in the past, was now established, that the self's beacon had been sighted and a true course could be plotted for his life. There has never been an explanation in rational terms of cause and effect that would account for the compelling attraction any one person may have for an other; neither objective criteria of external beauty nor those according to which the more elusive inner beauty of character is judged offer reliable or even observable standards for the most intense and most binding of human relationships. That moment when the realization sets in that the other person is not so much "other" than "I," when the veil of estrangement drops and the self finds itself in the other, that moment is the philosopher's and lawmakers' moral idea of interhuman unity concentrated from the inclusive infinity of reflective abstraction to the point of pure, individual experience. Novalis understood his love for Sophie exactly in these terms, that is to say as the experiential revelation of the Absolute, of the completely objectified ego referred to in Fichtean terms as the absolute Ego, and in more commonplace parlance as the principle of humanity. He makes this quite clear in a poem composed very soon after that first meeting, for which reason it bears the caption "Beginning" ("*Anfang*").[10]

It cannot be intoxication or I
Would not have been born for this star as though I had,
    By chance, come drifting much too close to
      It, to the sphere of its magnetism.

How could full consciousness of moral grace
Be mere intoxication? Faith in humanity
    A game for but an hour's amusement?
      What's life if this be madness of drunkards?

Am I to be eternally separate?
Is the anticipation of our union
    With that which we knew here as ours but
      Could not quite fully possess — is that

Intoxication too? Were it so, truth and
Sobriety would then have mere matter left to them,
    Mere clay, mere emptiness, mere loss, merely
      The gaping void of renunciation.

What, after all, could possibly reward
A life unwilled, a self divided, and — as the heel
    Of fate grinds us into the dust — the
      Smile barely mustered to claim our freedom.

You are no craze, you voice of the spiritual
Realm, nor are you, immortality revealed
    To mortals' eyes, nor you, ideal
      Of meaning glimpsed through reality's fragments.

Mankind will be, in time, what Sophie is
Now for me: human perfection — moral grace —
    Life's higher meaning will no longer
      Then be mistaken for drunken dreams.[11]

These lines, along with other documents of that time, convey, above all, Novalis's amazement at what had befallen him; there is a keen sense of wonder, vacillating between happy disbelief in his good fortune and joyous acceptance of the gift bestowed on him, a gift that amounted essentially to a new state of being. True, "falling in love" is quite commonplace and so is much that has been said on the subject, to which even Novalis's own life and correspondence, before November 1794, will bear witness. On the other hand, in some instances, that same experience may also prove to be the gateway to a new life, to a life transformed from busied aimlessness into a coherent process of self-realization, as so many have attested, from Plato to thinkers of our own age.

The difference between the commonplace and the extraordinary would seem to entail, at least in this case, a specific predisposition or receptivity that allows the beholder to see the physical apparition of another individual and recognize it as the manifestation of an entirely spiritual reality, as a reflection of his idea of human perfection: in the beloved the lover encounters a glimpse of his highest aspiration; he encounters himself on his way to himself. In order to read the signs that prefigure the goal, one must be on the way that leads to it, and Novalis had started on his under Schiller's tutelage. He had endeavored to establish himself at the center from which the clash between subject and object can be muted by the self's free agency, and in the process he had gained an awareness of human reality as a distinctly different realm that supersedes the simple and exclusive acquiescence to the reality of things. The reality of human values has no concrete embodiment and names like "ethics," "categorical imperative," "humanity," or even "Ego" have nothing that would correspond to them as something one could point to saying "there it is." Yet these terms signify the real objectivity that inspires each subject's every thought and deed; they mean complete selfness without the ever present obstruction by otherness, which we tend to regard as animate and inanimate "things"; they stand for the subject's reality magnified to include all of being but — and that is the point at which the subject also becomes the perfect object — without annihilating it. As the subject recognizes itself in the other, the otherness remains, which guarantees objective validity to the standards of recognition, whereas the "thingness" drops in consequence of their kinship to the subject. This is the realm of moral conduct where neither subject nor object prevail and a new unity forged from both dominates.

When the emphasis in a person's relationship to other people lies on their otherness, on the objective validity of the conduct association with them elicits, the guidelines for action are essentially negative. They are that since the pure object, humanity or the Ego, is not discernible, except for the demand that the subject give up its singularity, its interests based on the individuated nature of its being, and become one with the interests of all through its action. This prevalence of the negative criterion for moral action accounts, in my opinion, for the strictures of Kantian moralism on personal inclination, which effectively cast suspicion on the moral legitimacy of any act committed in accordance with one's natural tendency to benefit others. If, on the other hand, sameness rather than otherness is the predominant factor in a relationship, the self indentifies with the other in a positive transfer of affection that makes the ascetic measures of self-denial stipulated by moral philosophy pale by comparison. Such sameness is, however, difficult to ascertain for the entire spectrum of humanity with which a person might come into contact. At best, it remains a rather diffuse effort to embrace a disembodied notion of humanity in spite of the antagonism one might feel against some offensive individuals. This very characteristic of sameness occasionally appears to a person concentrated from the vague infinity of mankind to the point of its realization in one individual; when this occurs, it inspires the kind of love Novalis felt as he set eyes on Sophie von Kühn. His joyous bewilderment at the experience he had been granted was accompanied by the certainty that his life had been changed forever since he would never again be able to identify exclusively with the isolated instance of individuated being most of us mistake for our respective selves.

For Novalis, moral law, the categorical exhortation to exercise his freedom, had become a labor of love and with it the antagonism between the self's subjective and objective claims, the classic moral conflict between inclination and duty, was not only harmoniously put to rest but had been transformed into a new dynamic unity of mutually supportive forces. That unity also happens to be the same one with which Schiller is concerned throughout his work, even before his major treatises on the subject appeared.[12] A schema evolves from his aesthetic reformulation of moral freedom in which the polar extremes of physical determinateness and reality on purely human terms must merge at a point of nonopposition since they are constituent aspects of one and the same individual. Every person exists in this twofold fashion, determined as well as determining, and, according to Schiller, freedom has its truly human face when the individual unfolds from the inherent point of unity, from the point of merger for these two trends, and encompasses both in that mutually supportive harmony between nature and spirit for which Shaftesbury furnished the name of "moral grace." Novalis employs this term in his poem (*sittliche Grazie*, I, 386–87) to characterize the representative phenomenalization of absolute unity in a person whose entire bearing betrays the effortless coincidence of natural inclination and moral obligation. This unity of self, which may well have been due to the childlike simplicity a thirteen year old is capable of bringing to adult concerns, was the source of her aesthetic appeal for Novalis; and as he was granted the vision of natural humanity in her person, for whom the moral disparity between the physically determined state and the self's claim to freedom did not exist, his own self dropped the last vestiges of isolation and gained the same state of effortless unity in the experience of love.

This kind of love, as Novalis begins to realize after he becomes conscious of his situation, is not the product of one's own effort; it must be kindled, instead, from the outside, by a revelation of absolute congruence between subject and object, a revelation of that perfect freedom toward which all efforts have become directed in a concentration that amounts to the negative realization of their goal. Its positive realization can be effected only when the self lives what the self is: perfectly integrated moments of subjective and objective reality. As there are two moments, each will have to be realized in the other, so that the moral act, in which the subject attains to objective validity, must be complemented by a transformation in which the objects shed their otherness and assume a reality identical with the subject's. In the moral act, or rather in the preparedness to act morally, the self identifies consciously with the center of its being through which its subjective moments gain legitimacy as objective ones. Essentially, the movement is one of concentration from the dichotomous dispersion into opposing moments to their common point of origin. At that juncture, where the self is at one with itself and free, it holds a position from which a direct relation to unity all-encompassing and absolute becomes possible. This relationship actually constitutes an inversion of perspective: in it the self has been transported to the all-inclusive circumference, to the vantage point of absolute unity, for which there is no otherness, no object estranged into an externalized reality, and the dichotomous realities of the self's subjective and objective extensions are revealed as one identical reality within their common sphere.

But all such talk of a common, absolute sphere, of divinity or humanity, remains suspiciously fictitious since common experience offers no basis for such pronouncements. On the contrary, the self remains locked in between the dualistic stress of its subjective and objective realities, between the potentially infinite multiplicity of its inner and its outer dimensions. Any degree of self-awareness, of identity, the self may experience in its theoretical or practical operations, in thought or deed, will always bear the mark of a temporary resolution to the conflict and will, consequently, be in terms of it. The self can only effect unity as a form of the subject's gaining general validity; yet, even in a person's most conscious effort to obtain genuine objectivity, in the moral act that allows no criteria short of those from which the law for all mankind could be construed, the realm "out there," the objects' realm, maintains its independence, so that the self is actually denied that perfect objective authenticity, that absolute inclusiveness, toward which it strives.

Indeed, it would be but blindness to reality, "intoxication," as Novalis refers to it in his poem, to exert one's efforts toward a goal that remains forever remote, without the slightest trace of its existence. Against those who are drunk with such aspirations, "realists," so called, may well contend that it is far better to submit and accept the object's seeming ultimate authority. Within the context of such "realistic" arguments, gaining general validity now means estranging the subject from itself, reducing it, and thus the self's entire range, to one realm only, to the realm that knows no "I" and holds only the limits imposed by otherness, which we experience as things. This is the realm of dead "matter," of "clay" and "dust," to which Novalis refers in the fourth, fifth, and sixth stanzas, refusing to accept it as his prison and grave. He, so the poem announces, has found an assurance of the ideal's reality not apparent to those realist skeptics.

In Sophie the forbidding, alien expanse of objectivity revealed its basic kinship to Novalis and, to his expressed amazement, he experienced the transformation of the world of things from an obstacle that hides the human goal into a medium for its revelation. This experience is the love he describes in the poem that marks the beginning of his relationship to Sophie; now he no longer merely hopes and believes but *knows* that the self's efforts to maintain its "moral grace," its unity as the common ground for its dualistic moments, is not in vain, that the self need not become a thing in order to gain objective currency for its subjectivity, that the forbidding otherness out there may smile back, that the object can shed its rigid independence and grant the subject its reality, that the circumference will come to meet the center, that the I must no longer be either conqueror or conquered because it is confronted by a relentless It, that the I can encounter the Thou[13] and be transformed from a subject complemented by the ever-present antagonism of the object into a self for whom there is but one reality. This mutation from It to Thou is a given complement to the self's striving. It is, as Novalis says, a revelation of that perfect unity for which subjective and objective values are one, a revelation of that toward which all those aspire whose faith seems like intoxication to the "realists." It may also be regarded as the coincidence of a circumference drawn by the self from the center, within which it unifies its dual extension into subjective and objective realities, and a circumference drawn independent of the self, but for it, in a manner amounting to a constriction of the infinite inclusiveness that is the Absolute, the One.

It is quite clear from Novalis's poem that his love for Sophie added an unexpected experiential dimension to the philosophical guidelines and precepts with which he had become acquainted at Jena. Evidently, the encounter with adversity, which he had longed for in order to test the vigor of his moral freedom,[14] is no longer deemed as necessary. Instead, the sharp clash between inclination and duty has been superseded by their harmony in the state of moral grace,[15] not by way of mere theorizing, nor on the more sensual level of aesthetics, but through the incontestability of experience, an experience in which that ideal harmony, the goal of all the self's ambitions, appears phenomenalized in an other person; and furthermore, through the process of this revelation, this self-recognition in the other, the self became what it beheld.

At the time, when Novalis wrote his poem, in the early part of 1795, he had not yet thought out the full implications of the astounding transformation he had undergone. As his terminology indicates, however, he felt quite reassured about the direction in which his philosophical mentors had pointed him, but he gained this conviction, paradoxically enough, by means of an occurrence for which their theories had made no allowance. Contrary to their general emphasis on personal effort in the pursuit of self-realization, in the pursuit of realizing rather than abrogating freedom as one's inherent and essential human heritage, Novalis had been made aware that a gratuitous stage completes and complements that process. He had been met by that toward which he had striven; he had set out to conquer the world, to be a free agent, and that infinite, inconquerable world had turned around, dropped its defense of insurmountable infinity, assumed the concrete limitations of one person, and welcomed him. Such guidance from outside is easily associated with traditional notions concerning divine revelation, and it would not seem at all surprising if Novalis now thought they might prove valuable toward a new understanding of philosophy in general and Kantian or critical philosophy in particular.

I think it reasonable to bear these considerations in mind with reference to Immanuel Niethammer's reported comments on Novalis's conversation with Fichte at their first recorded meeting in May of 1795. We are told that there had been "much talk about religion and about revelation and that there were a great many questions philosophy still had to answer" (IV, 588, ll. 16–20).[16] Soon thereafter, Novalis begins work on his "Fichte-Studies," which actually constitute a systematic survey and independent development of material with which he had previously become acquainted; it is quite possible to view them as a continuation of that conversation at Niethammer's home, only in the form of a monologue.[17] These fragments are, therefore, not so much abstract intellectual exercises aimed at mastering the complexities of thought that stirred the brightest minds at the high seats of learning but reflect, rather, Novalis's very real, existential concerns, which move him to reexamine his philosophical bias with respect to the new direction his life had taken.[18]

This direction had been given him by Sophie and he is far from certain how or why she is in a position to exert such influence; all he knows is that she does, because ever since he had met her, he has experienced a hitherto unknown sense of certainty about his place in the world, which is accompanied by an even more immediate awareness of a miraculous coordination governing his actions, in that the severe, objective "I ought to" has become more akin to the subjective "I like to." Accordingly, Novalis's poem "Anfang" does not mark so much the beginning of his love for Sophie as his intention of accounting for it — a purely subjective experience — in generally comprehensible terms. But, at this time, his powers of expression are, apparently, no match for the task; imagery, concepts, and terminology are not very original and leave the impression that they had been borrowed for an extraordinary occasion. Particularly, the conceptual context remains vague, and established rhetorical usage does little to enlighten the reader concerning the complex relationship between ethics and aesthetics implied in the formula "moral grace." Novalis must, obviously, fashion his own language, his own means of bridging the gap between subject and object in a free creative manner. He must fashion his own "poesy" in order to reflect adequately the new level of awareness he has reached, and the "Fichte-Studies" function as the ambitiously inclusive theoretical prerequisite that enables him to translate experiential awareness into conscious experience.

His love for Sophie remains the perspective and frame for his philosophical deliberations; even though their abstract and private nature makes it difficult to recognize this association, Novalis's more public statements in his correspondence leave little doubt that, for him, Sophie and philosophy are inextricably linked. The best-known quotation to this effect occurs in his letter of 8 July 1796, the first addressed to Friedrich Schlegel after more than nineteen months. In it, Novalis not only alludes to the term "philosophy" as the univocal expression for his love of both "Sophies," of "wisdom," to which the Greek original refers, and of the girl at Grüningen,[19] but he goes on to elaborate in more detail:

> Seit jener Bekanntschaft bin ich auch mit diesem Studio ganz amalgamirt. Du wirst mich prüfen. Etwas zu schreiben und zu heyrathen ist Ein Ziel fast meiner Wünsche. Fichten bin ich Aufmunterung schuldig — Er ists, der mich weckte und indirecte zuschürt. Glaub aber nicht, daß ich, wie sonst leid[enschaft]lich blos Eins verfolge und nicht vor meine Füße sehe — Mein Vater [ist] zufrieden mit meinem Fleis und ich kann nicht über Langeweile bey ande[rn] Beschäftigungen klagen. Ich fühle in Allem immer mehr die erhabnen Glieder ein[es] wunderbaren Ganzen — in das ich hineinwachse, das zur Hülle meines Ichs werden soll — und muß ich nicht alles gern leiden, da ich liebe und mehr liebe, als die 8 Spannenlange Gestalt im Raume, und länger liebe, als die Schwingung der Lebenssayte währt. Spinotza und Zinzendorf haben sie erforscht, die unendliche Idee der Liebe und geahndet die Methode — sich für sie und sie für sich zu realisiren auf diesem Staubfaden. Schade, daß ich in Fichte noch nichts von dieser Aussicht sehe, nichts von diesem Schöpfungsathem fühle. Aber er ist nahe dran — Er muß in ihren Zauberkreis treten — wenn ihm nicht sein früheres Leben den Staub von den Flügeln gewischt hat.

Since I have known her, I have also become completely absorbed in the study of philosophy. You shall have an opportunity to test me. To write something [worth publishing] and to marry is almost one and the same goal of all my wishes. I am indebted to Fichte for inciting me; he is the one who roused me and, indirectly, keeps my intellectual fires burning. You must not think, however, that I am singleminded in my passionate

preoccupation and, as would have been the case of old, blind to everything
else; my father is satisfied with my work[20] and I cannot complain about
boredom with any of my tasks and activities, even if they keep me from
my favorite pursuit. I sense ever more keenly the sublime member-parts
of a marvellous Whole in everything, a Whole that I am to fill and that is
to be the fullness of my self; and must I not suffer all I encounter with
pleasure since I love and in loving love more than the figure of some five
feet in space and longer than the pulsations of our life–string endure.
Spinoza and Zinzendorf[21] have grasped the infinite idea of love and have
divined the method of realizing themselves for it as well as realizing it for
themselves on this speck of dust. I am sorry that I have not yet been able
to see anything of this vision in Fichte, felt nothing of this breath of
creativity. But he is close to it; he must step in love's magic circle, unless
his earlier years have robbed him of the power to lift his wings.

(IV, 188, ll. 10–28)

This letter furnishes an impressive survey of the full range to which Novalis
had grown in his self-comprehension since he had first recorded amazement
and gratitude in response to the startling discovery that everything life could
possibly offer would fall into a pattern of meaningful coherence through Sophie's
mediating presence. In the meantime, the ''Fichte-Studies'' had progressed
considerably and Novalis was in a better position to give an account of his
experience in terms that rendered it intelligible to others, even to those who,
like Schlegel, had known him under very different circumstances, during a period
of development and amorous confusion he had definitely outgrown. His remarks
concerning marriage and publication may, at first, seem odd in their insistence
that both constitute nearly the same goal for his ambitions, but they are less so
if one considers them as indicators of Novalis's own sense of maturity; the stated
desire to publish and take responsibility for a family is a proclamation of his
preparedness to draw objectively valid conclusions from his subjective experience
in both a theoretical and practical sense.[22]

Fichte had been the silent partner in the ongoing deliberations through which
Novalis had worked his way to a clearer understanding of his situation and its
philosophical implications. These intellectual advances have been accompanied,
so he reports, by a sense of personal equilibrium, in contrast to the relative lack
of stability Novalis tends to ascribe to himself before his encounter with Sophie.
Now, however, he deems his frame of mind to be steadied by his love who,
unlike objects of passion, functions as focus rather than restriction for the entire
domain of human enterprise. Novalis effectively describes his condition as one
in which everything he does is done as a free agent since he experiences his
many assignments and obligations not at all as actually or potentially opposed
to his wishes. In other words, he acts as a total being, without having to assert

his freedom over the claims of his dependency, and this harmony of self in action is the practical counterpart to the coincidence of human and natural factors perceived in the phenomenon of moral grace.

Quite unmistakably, Novalis ascribes here a definite moral function to love, or rather he experiences love as pure affirmation of freedom. For Fichte, however — and this is the point that leads to the critical conclusion of the quoted passage — the self can only act freely as a moral entity, that is to say, only insofar as it is engaged in the constant task of overcoming whatever dependency arises from the state of its physical existence. The intensity of his love, so Novalis explains, has carried him beyond the confines of physical apparitions, so that his conscious awareness is no longer bound to the perspective of limitation or initial dependency from which, one might add, all consciousness, according to Fichte, takes its origin.[23] Fichte is right, of course, and anyone who takes a moment to observe himself in the process of theoretical acquisition would have to agree with him, that the self depicts itself as acted upon by the objects it depicts in its consciousness. But, as Fichte fails to recognize, this relationship need not necessarily be one of limitation only; it can also be one of attraction, in which case the limiter that had prevented access to the Whole could also become a conductor to It.

When Novalis writes about Sophie in his letter to Schlegel, he indicates that she has channeled a force of attraction to him through which he has been raised out of his individuated isolation into a state of affinity with all of being. He now experiences everything as "parts of a Whole," as conduits to It and Its reflections, which constitutes an advance from common theoretical acquisition, based on the primacy of self-limitation, to a higher level of intellectual receptivity based on the primacy of the self's freedom.

There is an aspect to freedom that is not agency — which is where Fichte's deliberations stop — but inactivity, not mere striving but in striving a readiness to accept each stage along the way as representative of the final goal. Fichte considers only the first movement, extending from ego to Ego, as the manifestation of freedom appropriate to the self since movement in the direction from Ego to ego precedes consciousness, even though it must necessarily be presupposed to explain it.[24] Novalis, on the other hand, takes both moments to be equally important in the human process of conscious self-realization, so that freedom is not only a matter of free moral agency aimed at suspending the nonego's encroachment but also an encounter with the Self, a recognition that the otherness "out there" is really sameness.[25] In the moral act, the self extends human significance to the constellation of circumstances as they relate to it at any given moment, and if the infinite expanse of nature were to assume a human face for the self, the circle could finally be closed. Then, the extension from the center would have been met and complemented by one from the circumference, and the moral rigor of overcoming nature through self-enactment would change to a loving correspondence with it through self-recognition.

Once the moral imperative has been augmented by love, the self's dual progression into internal and external infinity will have been established in total correspondence with respect to a common point of origin as well as to a common goal. Novalis says as much when he regrets that Fichte has not yet entered the "magic circle" in which the individual is linked to the Unity of all being by the bond of love. This circle can be entered from either direction as the references to Zinzendorf and Spinoza indicate: the one is a pietist who encounters God along the inward path and the other is a philosopher for whom the outside world speaks but the language of its creator. Religious preference or orthodoxies are obviously not at issue but rather religiosity itself, which may, in this context, be understood as the ability both men display in regarding the infinity of being as a Whole and not as open-ended, locked into permanent estrangement. Through Sophie, Novalis, too, feels himself to be firmly fixed in his position from the absolute perspective of the Whole; but, more than that, he also feels himself to be on the way toward that ultimate comprehension he defines within the context of his basic circular schema, with Fichtean rather than Spinozistic or pietist terms, as the "fullness of self."

This is the last letter Novalis can write to his friend with such self-assured optimism. As a summary documentation of the existential and philosophical harvest that had accrued over the months since November 1794, it stands at the very edge of time before the possibility of Sophie's death began to cast its shadow on Novalis's hopes for the future.[26] In this respect, it establishes quite clearly that the love Sophie inspired in Novalis had never been one that was confined to her physical existence, that her function in this relationship had always been one of mediation through which generally valid Reality was made personally real for him in an other, as real as his own being. Consequently, Novalis saw his future task in an active expansion of this Self-encounter or, as he would later call it, of this "being oneself outside the self" ("*außer sich . . . seyn*, mit Bewußtseyn jenseits der Sinne . . . seyn") (II, 420, 14), until it encompassed all of being and he would enter into the "fullness of self" that is the absolute Unity his wedded life with Sophie was to anticipate.

His expectations were not to be realized. Under the growing awareness of Sophie's possible death, Novalis hopes to thwart despair by withdrawing inward, to the intellectual realm, where meaningful coherence remains preserved. Thus he writes to Frau von Thümmel on 8 February 1797:

so wird es Sie nicht mehr befremden, wenn ich, zufrieden das Nöthigste gethan zu haben — mich so tief, als möglich in die Fluth des menschlichen Wissens versenke, um, so lange ich in diesen heiligen Wellen bin, die

Traumwelt des Schicksals zu vergessen. Dort blühn allein mir die
Hoffnungen auf, die ich hier verliere —

thus it will no longer seem strange to you if — after I am satisfied that the
most pressing demands of the day have been attended to — I plunge as
deeply as possible into the flood of human knowledge in order to forget
the dreamworld of fate as long as I bathe in those holy waves. Only there
do those hopes still bloom that are lost to me here —

(IV, 201, ll. 13–17)

However, he is far from certain of his sanctuary, because the letter concludes
with a fervent wish for Sophie's final recovery, so that he might no longer have
to live like a desperate gambler whose very fate is at stake. Similarly, some
days later he praises the healing power of intellectual endeavors to his brother
Erasmus, who had himself become seriously ill:

Dein Entschluß Algebra zu studiren, ist gewiß sehr heilsam. Die
Wissenschaften haben wunderbare Heilkräfte — wenigstens stillen Sie,
wie Opiate, die Schmerzen und erheben uns in Sfären, die ein ewiger
Sonnenschein umgiebt. Sie sind die schönste Freystätte, die uns gegönnt
ward. Ohne diesen Trost wollt ich und könnt ich nicht leben. Wie hätt
ich ohne sie seit 1½ Jahren so gelassen Sophiens Kranckheit zusehn, und
außerdem so manchen Verdrießlichkeiten ausgesezt seyn können. Es mag
mir begegnen, was will; die Wissenschaften bleiben mir — mit Ihnen hoff
ich alles Ungemach des Lebens zu bestehn.

Your decision to study algebra is certain to be of benefit to your health.
The sciences possess marvelous healing-powers — at least they kill the
pain, like opiates, and lift us into spheres that are radiant with eternal
sunlight. They are the best refuge we have been granted. Without this
consolation I should neither wish to go on living nor even be able to do
so. Without them, how could I have witnessed Sophie's illness with any
degree of calmness for these one and a half years and have suffered all
manner of other adversities. Come what may, the sciences remain as my
staff — with them I hope to overcome whatever misfortune life may hold
in store.

(IV, 202, l. 24–203, l. 2)

But by the middle of March, after he had left Sophie with the "apodictic certainty"
that she had but few days to live, he reports to Friedrich Schlegel:

Die Gewisheit ihres Besitzes ist mir zu unentbehrlich geworden — jezt erst
fühl ich, wie Sie, mir selbst unmercklich, der Grundstein meiner Ruhe,
meiner Thätigkeit, meines ganzen Lebens gewesen ist. Der Lebensüberdruß
ist entsezlich — und ich sehe kein Ende. Ich hoffte, die Wissenschaften

sollten mir einen Ersatz bieten — aber alles ist auch hier todt, wüste, taub,
unbeweglich. . . .
Leb wol — guter, lieber Schlegel — mit mir hats bald aufgehört — Sey
glücklicher, als ich — Nur ein Wunder kann mich selbst mir wiedergeben.

The assured certainty that she is mine has become far too indispensable
for me — only now do I feel, how she had been the foundation of my rest,
of my activity, of my entire life, without my being fully aware of it. My
weariness of life is terrible — and I see no end to this condition. I had
hoped that the sciences, the realm of the intellect, were to make up for
the loss — but, here too, everything is dead, barren, deaf, without
sparkle. . . .
Farewell — good, dear Schlegel — I shall not last much longer — Be happier
than I — Only a miracle can restore me to myself.
                    (IV, 204, ll. 19–25; 204, l. 31–205, l. 2)

Novalis's worlds have collapsed into a meaningless shamble; with Sophie gone,
the desolate cosmos that confronts him is matched by his spiritual emptiness. In
this state of total isolation he is reduced to the innermost core of his selfhood,
a self he can experience initially only in terms of loss, in terms of having lost
everything this same self had previously invested with the power to give its own
existence meaning. The process of reduction had already begun when he concen-
trated the power to give meaning to his life in the person of Sophie; now fate
had decreed that the last step be taken, that the self assert its value-giving potency
without mitigation in the comfortless void, which is the price of freedom, or
fall prey to the beckoning shelter of extinction.

Death was the all-pervasive reality surrounding Novalis after Sophie had
become its victim and, accordingly, he felt that his own being could now be
real only in terms of its being absorbed by the same gaping nothingness of
extinction. "Es ist Abend um mich geworden" ("The darkness of evening has
settled around me"), he says to Woltman the day after he had received the news,
"und es ist mir, als würde ich früh weggehen" ("and it seems to me as though
I am to leave very soon") (IV, 206, ll. 13–14; ll. 19–20). A few days later, he
confesses to Karoline Just that life holds nothing for him but all the terrors of
lonely darkness (IV, 206, ll. 29–30), and goes on to say: "Wollte Gott, den ich
flehentlich darum gebeten habe, daß [meine übrigen Tage] kurz wären" ("So
God wills, whom I have fervently beseeched for this, [my remaining days] will
be short") (IV, 209, ll. 10–11). But in the same letter, actually a continuation
of it after an interval of four days, the passivity of despair begins to be replaced
by a strikingly different attitude. Much to his surprise, Novalis must recognize
that his state of utter isolation entails not only total negation, which he had
experienced as an unconditional preparedness to die, but also total freedom, the

freedom to enact one's own life, to live and in living affirm life's final outcome rather than to *be* lived punctuated by the ultimate indignity of having to suffer death. This letter, which had started on a note of lament, makes reference to Novalis's reawakened intellectual activity, and although he considers it a poor substitute for his loss, he goes on to speculate in an ever more optimistic manner concerning Sophie and his own existence. She continues to occupy the same place she had held before, but now her physical absence refers him directly to the realm of absolute unity that he had seen reflected in her person, and he begins to realize the implications:

> Während ich dieses schrieb, ist es mir recht warm aufs Herz gefallen, ob meine Klagen nicht selbstsüchtig, kleinlich und beschränkt sind. Wenn ich ein wahrhaft hoher Mensch seyn wollte, sollte nicht jezt eine ewige Heiterkeit meine Augen und meine Stirn beseelen — und himmlischer Enthusiasmus meine Brust erfüllen. Wer bin ich, daß ich so irrdisch klage? Sollt ich nicht Gott danken, daß er mir so früh meinen Beruf zur Ewigkeit kund machte? Ist es nicht Beruf zur apostolischen Würde? Kann ich im Ernst Sofieens Schicksal beklagen — Ist es nicht ein Vorzug für Sie — Ist nicht Ihr Tod und mein Nachsterben eine Verlobung im höhern Sinn? Gott hat mich und Sie für die schleichende Ansteckung der Gemeinheit bewahren — er hat Sie in eine höhere Erziehungsanstalt bringen, diese zarte Blume unter einen bessern Himmel verpflanzen und mich den stärkern, den rohern Mann noch in der Erdenluft zeitigen wollen. Sollte Gott von mir jezt ächte Erhebung, männliche Vollendung, tiefes Zutraun zu seiner Liebe — unverwandten Blick auf den Himmel und meine höhere Bestimmung, ewiges Gelübde der Tugend und des Glaubens an die Samenideen der innersten Menschheit fodern? So eben treten diese Ideen mit einer ungewohnten Wärme in mein Bewußtseyn — ich fühle was ich seyn könnte — aber Gott sieht wie gebrechlich und schwach ich bin — Kann ich hoffen, daß in dieser kraftlosen Seele solche Ideen haften und nicht vorbeygehn werden. Jezt ist einmal Leben in mir — aber wird es gegen die Nervenstumpfheit, gegen die Gewöhnlichkeit und das Verwöhntseyn sich halten können? Sophie weiß, was mir gut ist — Sie bittet Gott gewiß mit für mich — und nur dann muß meine Klage perenniren, wenn selbst solche Ideen nicht mehr Bleibens haben.

As I was writing this, I began to wonder in my heart whether my plaintive lamentations are not selfish, paltry, and narrow-minded. If I am to be a human being in the truest and highest sense, ought not my eyes and my forehead radiate an eternal cheerfulness at this time — and ought not my breast be filled with heavenly enthusiasm. Who am I that I lament in such an earthbound manner? Should I not thank God for letting me know early that my calling is to dedicate myself to eternity? Is it not a calling to apostolic dignity? Can I seriously lament Sophie's fate — Is it not to her advantage — Is not her dying and my desire to follow her a betrothal in a higher sense? God wanted to save me and her from encroaching contagion by pragmatic and commonplace concerns — He wanted to bring her to a nursery of higher quality, wanted to transplant this tender flower where it can flourish under a summer sky, and He wanted to season me, the stronger, the coarser man, for a while longer in the earth's atmosphere. Is it that God demands from me now true elevation of spirit, manly perfection, deep trust in his love — eyes unswervingly directed at heaven and at my higher destiny, eternal faithfulness to virtue and to the ideological seeds of innermost humanity? Just now these ideas fill my consciousness with unusual intensity — I feel what I could be — but God sees how frail and weak I am — Can I hope that such ideas will stay in this soul bereft of strength and will not be a passing fancy. For the moment, there is life in me — but will it prevail against dullness of mind, against the humdrum world of the commonplace, and against the prison of habits? Sophie knows what is good for me — She will surely intervene with God on my behalf — and only then will my lamenting have to continue when such ideas no longer inspire me.

(IV, 211, 1. 26–212, 1. 19)

I have cited from this letter at such length because these passages permit an unusual insight into the writer's mind as he, quite unintentionally, becomes aware of the new direction his life will have to take. His death is no longer the immediate and only reality, and he recognizes that union with Sophie will be preceded by some years of living, which must not be spent in idle expectation but rather in constant activity devoted to proving himself worthy of her.

Subsequent letters written by Novalis continue to reflect a growing sense of inner strength, the "sciences" (*Wissenschaften*) assume a new and higher meaning (IV, 215, ll. 21–23), as does his life, and that same awakening to a new sense of affirmation can also be detected in those records he kept only for private use. Among many one could choose, the following pronouncement is of particular interest: "Abends in Youngs *Nachtgedanken* geblättert — viel über *Meister* nachgedacht — " ("In the evening, I read in Young's *Night Thoughts* — thought a lot about *Meister* — ") IV, 30, ll. 15–16). These words describe, in part, the day's activities as he records them in his diary on 23 April 1797, thirty-six days after Sophie's death. The first part of the entry has found ready acceptance in the canon of Novalis, the death-intoxicated romantic, that has been traditional for so long. Young's *Night Thoughts* have frequently been cited, along with *Romeo and Juliet*, as literary influences or antecedents of some, if indeterminate consequence to the poetic expression Hardenberg's love and bereavement found in his *Hymns to the Night*. The reference to *Wilhelm Meister*, however, represents as obvious a contrast to Young's *Nights Thoughts* as life does to death, yet it appears without the slightest hesitation or excuse, as though the relationship were complementary, which, of course, it is. Novalis's own inclination not to dwell on the night thoughts of death exclusively hardly fits the image his admirers as well as detractors have fashioned over the years; since they preferred to think of him as the youth whose reaction to the loss of his beloved is to follow her in death, his turning at the height of mourning to Goethe's novel, a work singularly devoted to the pursuit of life, seemed to make little sense and was, therefore, completely disregarded or misinterpreted to fit the established prejudice.[27]

Only recently has attention been called to Novalis's curious and intensive preoccupation with *Wilhelm Meister* at this apparently most inappropriate time when he was supposedly deaf to all voices that would draw him back into the world of the living.[28] The fact is that this novel, which had been published in four volumes over a period from January 1795 to October 1796, was Novalis's constant companion at the time. No other work by any other author appears as persistently in the pages to which Novalis entrusted the emotions, thoughts, and actions that comprise his struggle for meaning and direction after the one person whom he had chosen as focal point for his life was no more. Hardly a day passes in late April and early May of 1797 without comment on *Wilhelm Meister,* and there is good reason to believe that Goethe's craftsmanship, his ability to execute, to realize genius fully rather than imply its potential in fragmentary flashes proved to be a decisive impetus for Novalis's own emergence as an artist and, one might add, as a man. Goethe shows the path outward, the path into life, into finite realization, into form, which must complement the oft-quoted "inward path," if a person is to be whole rather than one-sided or isolated and ineffectual despite all the glory of the subject's spontaneity. Life as the art of accommodation to the finite, and art as the craft that harnesses the spirit's power within the bounds of form are unquestionably concepts that guide the entire course of Wilhelm Meister's apprenticeship, and — after his intensive study of the novel — Novalis might well have joined them into a composite ideal of man and artist, which he came to consider his future vocation.

In addition to their importance for Novalis's future and artistic development, the diary entries also function as indicators of the fundamental existential change their author had undergone in consequence of his beloved's prolonged suffering and death. The juxtaposition expressed by the laconic "Abends in Youngs *Nachtgedanken* geblättert — viel über *Meister* nachgedacht" refers not only to the chance occurrences of one particular day, nor even of some, but to the mood that pervades the entire period from April to July 1797. From the beginning, Novalis speaks of his *Entschluß,* his "decision," which is accompanied by so many concerns directed at the process of living that it would be impossible to suspect its real nature, were it not for occasional statements expressive of his definite expectation death would soon prove him worthy of Sophie and reunite them. But then again, Novalis had already previously shown a remarkable tendency toward regarding all aspects of life as diverse manifestations of an ultimate unity, a common ground that guarantees those bonds by which all multiplicity and opposition are joined in a cosmic web of interrelation.

The disposition to view empirical reality from an absolute perspective that transcends all limitation is commonly attributed to romantics in general, frequently accompanied by some critical remarks as to their supposed escapism. In Novalis's case, however, such generalizations implying a vague mystical longing for submersion and loss of self in the murky ocean of infinity are entirely misapplied; at most, he may be said to have been sufficiently disoriented under the initial impact of his loss that he no longer attached any value to his life and longed to rid himself of its burdensome and pointless continuance. However, he undergoes a drastic redirection of perspective during his period of mourning, until he thinks no longer of his own death as the tired avoidance of living born of despair but as an act of decision by which the self establishes free reign over its own existence. Actually, there is equal or even greater justification to regard Novalis's famous "decision" *(Entschluß)* , which is primary among the concerns that inspired the "Journal" he kept from April until July 1797, as a decision to live rather than die. True, death is his ultimate aim, but this death must be attained through a life that has earned it; it must be achieved as the final culmination and fulfillment of all endeavor. Sophie is still Novalis's guide along the path of life; now, however, only in the sense of a preapparition of what is to come at its conclusion, whereas previously she had been an integral part of it. Alive, she had lent direction to his actions with reference to realizable ends centered around a life spent together; with her dead, Novalis was confronted with the difficult task of striving toward a goal that bore no concrete outline in terms of empirical reality other than the implication that it was to be the full unfolding of his being.

Thus his own "apprenticeship" begins, and *Wilhelm Meister*, a work with which he had become acquainted some months before,[29] is his obvious choice for intellectual companionship and guidance. Wilhelm, too, must pursue a course of development without benefit of a preconceived goal; he, too, is free and not bound to a narrow sequence of positive accomplishments prerequisite to its attainment, and, as a consequence, he, too, will have to find his way without the comfort of external standards by means of which he could determine how far along he had come or whether he was even going in the right direction. Yet, Wilhelm is not lost; "mich selbst, ganz wie ich da bin, auszubilden, das war dunkel von Jugend auf mein Wunsch und meine Absicht" ("to realize my full potential, that has been my wish and my intent ever since the days of my early youth, even though I could not associate a clearly defined goal in my mind with this ambition"),[30] he says, and goes on to state that he has become more certain of the means for realizing his ambition. The stage offers him this opportunity, he believes, because, so his argument proceeds, there the end of one functional, subordinate role within society will not determine the exercise, and thus the one-sided development, of his faculties; instead, the theater makes demands on all his potentials in order that he might represent humanity as fully as his capabilities permit. Wilhelm's entire career, not merely his association with the theater, is summarized in these pronouncements. Whatever he does, he does freely and for its own sake because he is not committed to a predefined purpose with which he could permanently identify. All his experiences contribute to the process of self-realization in which he is engaged, where self-realization means the ability to dispose freely over circumstance according to one's proven talents and capabilities. At least, that is the direction Wilhelm receives when he first meets his mentor,[31] an emissary of a secret society devoted to guiding the formative development of certain chosen individuals by permitting them to learn through error; but, since he divulges neither his identity nor his designs, Wilhelm has no idea that he is the object of an educational experiment and the reader is more impressed by the discourse than is the supposed tutee. However, Wilhelm also receives a more concrete indication of his ultimate goal; as he lies wounded from a battle with brigands, a girl comes to his aid and in his feverish state she appears as a vision from another world. Her memory never leaves him and henceforth he tries to find a trace of her. The apparition had been Natalie, the "beautiful soul," or rather "moral grace" personified, who was to become his betrothed at the end of his apprenticeship.

This encounter is also the topic that occasions the first mention of *Wilhelm Meister* as part of the very first entry in Novalis's "Journal," as he refers to his diary. It is, furthermore, one of the two more specific references that make identification in the text possible. It reads: "Im Wilh[elm] Meister fiel mir eine passende Stelle aus dem 4 ten Buche — ein Selbstgespräch Meisters — auf" ("In *Wilhelm Meister* an appropriate passage in Book 4 caught my attention — a monologue by Meister") (IV, 29, ll. 10–12). This is the passage in question:

Unaufhörlich rief er sich jene Begebenheit zurück, welche einen unauslöschlichen Eindruck auf sein Gemüt gemacht hatte. Er sah die schöne Amazone reitend aus den Büschen hervorkommen, sie näherte sich ihm, stieg ab, ging hin und wider und bemühte sich um seinetwillen. Er sah das umhüllende Kleid von ihren Schultern fallen; ihr Gesicht, ihre Gestalt glänzend verschwinden. Alle seine Jugendträume knüpften sich an dieses Bild. Er glaubte nunmehr die edle, heldenmütige Chlorinde mit eignen Augen gesehen zu haben; ihm fiel der kranke Königssohn wieder ein, an dessen Lager die schöne, teilnehmende Prinzessin mit stiller Bescheidenheit herantritt.

"Sollten nicht," sagte er manchmal im stillen zu sich selbst, "uns in der Jugend wie im Schlafe die Bilder zukünftiger Schicksale umschweben und unserm unbefangenen Auge ahnungsvoll sichtbar werden? Sollten die Keime dessen, was uns begegnen wird, nicht schon von der Hand des Schicksals ausgestreut, sollte nicht ein Vorgenuß der Früchte, die wir einst zu brechen hoffen, möglich sein?"

He recalled that event which had left a lasting impression, over and over again. He saw the beautiful amazon as she emerged from the underbrush on horseback; she approached him, dismounted and began to go about various tasks in an effort to comfort him. He saw the garment that had protected her slip from her shoulders; he saw her face, her entire figure fade away in radiance. All the dreams of his youth were united in this image. He thought that he had beheld the noble, heroic Chlorinde with his own eyes; he remembered the ailing prince again who is approached by the beautiful, compassionate princess as he lies on his sickbed.

"Might it not be," he said to himself quietly every now and then, "that in our youth, as happens in our sleep, images of what the future may hold surround us and become intuitively visible to our naïve and undistracted eyes? Might it not be that the hand of fate has already dispersed the germs of events bound to affect us later on, might it not even be that it is possible to be afforded an anticipatory taste of the fruit we hope to pluck one day?"[32]

If we recall that Novalis considered Sophie already during her lifetime a prefiguration of the ideal and that this aspect of his relationship to her became exclusively emphasized after her death, it is quite likely that he was quick to apply Goethe's words to his own situation.[33] Wilhelm strove toward self-realization and thus became worthy of the woman who had appeared to him as the ideal of womanhood, who, indeed, united in her person the disparity between spirit and nature in harmonious reciprocity. Novalis had set out on the same venture, had beheld the same vision of "moral beauty" ("*Anfang*"), had seen her disappear beyond his reach and decided to follow her, fully confident of ultimate reunion when his life had ripened in ever greater realization of the self's freedom to the point of final and absolute independence.

The process of maturation Novalis undergoes in consequence of his experiences with Sophie is also reflected in his philosophical experiments. Existentially, it culminates in his gaining an attitude of firm resolve and direction for conducting his life; intellectually, it leads to his completion of the "basic schema" in the concept of an expanded version of Fichte's philosophy he calls "*höhere Wissenschaftslehre*." How he reaches this concept and what it entails comprises the topic of the next chapter.

Chapter 6
The "Basic Schema" Completed or
"höhere Wissenschaftslehre"

"Zufall und Empfänglichkeit waren bis jetzt Deine Führer, Bestimmung und Humanität sollen es ins Künftige sein." Und doch soll der Zufall die wichtigste Begebenheit Deines Lebens, die Wahl Deiner zukünftigen Frau, Deiner treuesten Freundin und Begleiterin, bestimmen? — Dann erst, wenn Bestimmung und Humanität Deiner Wahl den Ausschlag geben werden, dann und nicht eher werde ich Dir zurufen: "Fritz, Du hast klug, Du hast lebensweise gehandelt." —

[You said in your letter that] "chance and your susceptibility to outside influence had been directing your life in the past, whereas now self-determination and the idea of humanity have become your guides for the future!" And yet chance is supposed to determine the most important occasion of your life, the occasion of choosing your future wife, your most faithful friend and companion? — Only after self-determination and the idea of humanity have decided your choice, then and not before will I call out to you and say: "Fritz, you have acted wisely."

(IV, 370, ll. 29–36)

With these words, Erasmus lends forceful expression to serious doubts concerning the decisive conclusions his brother had reached in consequence of the encounter at Grüningen. It is his second letter, dated 6 December 1794, obviously written in response to an elaborate account in which "Fritz" had sought to justify his state of mind as more than an emotive affect of questionable duration and value. Since Erasmus quotes from this letter to refute the tenability of the argument it

76

contains, he actually points out the very core of the problematic context within which Sophie assumes reality and significance for her lover.

It is quite clear that even then, at the very beginning, Novalis ascribes a moral dimension to his experience. Not only has the encounter with Sophie curtailed his lack of stability, a constant source of concern here referred to as susceptibility to outside influences and dependence on chance, but it has also established self-determination and the idea of humanity as the uncontested source of directives for future action. Evidently, the concepts of "self-determination" and "human-ity" circumscribe the equivalent of free moral self-determination in the Kantian or Fichtean sense, that is to say, they refer to a state in which the self has found its way to itself and is not deterred by anything from being what is to be. However, this independence from circumstance and mood, to which Novalis had aspired all along with varying degrees of success, this sense of stability was now itself to be owed to the courtesy of chance, a contradiction duly noted by Erasmus.

Clearly, for Novalis the experience itself, with all its contradictory aspects, is real and remains unquestioned; the problem is philosophical and it is one for which his previous exposure to the new school of thought had not prepared him. On the one hand, he understands his love for Sophie very definitely to be a reliable compass that points in the same direction as do the theoretical precepts of Kantain moral philosophy; on the other hand, what he knew of that moral philosophy — and expressed, for example, in "Klagen eines Jünglings" — of-fered no means of justifying the gratuitous and unwilled element of his experience within the conceptual framework at his disposal.

The poem "Anfang" in particular, but also the other examples cited (the correspondence with Erasmus, the birthday poem of 1796, the letter to Schlegel of the same year, etc.), refer to Sophie as a revelation of the moral idea capable of mediating a continuum of identity that extends from the absolute "idea of humanity" ("Einst wird die Menschheit sein, was Sophie mir/ Jetzt ist — vollen-det — sittliche Grazie") over the beloved as the manifest expression of "moral grace" to the "self-estranged and isolated self" ("Soll ich getrennt sein ewig?"). From the very beginning, Sophie is mediatrix, revelation, grace bestowed on her lover, in short, a religious phenomenon without reference to any particular or established religion, and she maintains that status. Small wonder, then, that "there was much talk about religion and revelation" and about "the many questions" — obviously relative to these topics — "philosophy would still have to answer" when Novalis had occasion to converse with Fichte at some length in May of 1795. Not the social or traditional institution of religion was at issue but rather the question whether Fichte's system would allow for the possibility that truth may be revealed *to* the self and not merely *by* the self through the exercise of its free moral agency. Novalis's experience points beyond the moralism of transcendental philosophy because his moral certitude, inspired as it was by Sophie, entails the addition of a passive, or essentially theoretical, moment to the practical sphere of purely free activity. How to accommodate this passive moment was obviously the basic question still to be answered by philosophy and Novalis sets out to explore this task in his "Fichte-Studies."

Fichte maintains that the self in its capacity as moral agent is free to effect its release from confinement to subjective isolation that characterizes the state of determined, or rather physical, existence. Through the moral act, the self may attain objective validity because it is no longer determined by the object but, instead, determines it according to standards valid for all possible selves. In effect, the morally engaged self elevates itself for the duration of the engagement to the level of identity with its absolute heritage, which Fichte refers to as Self or Ego. But — and this is Novalis's experience — the same movement can also be executed passively, that is to say the self can also be transported out of its subjective isolation when it recognizes itself in an other being. Consequently, the nonego loses its forbidding "non" and assumes value and reality that is no longer confined to its limiting function relative to the ego. The relationship between ego and nonego is thus no longer exclusively reflective of the isolating opposition between limited and limiter and allows the common sphere that informs both moments of this opposition to be in evidence.

With these considerations in mind, it is not surprising that the "Fichte-Studies" have as their favored topic the reduction of polar extremes to their commonality. It is also easy to understand why Novalis deviates from Fichte and employs the concepts of Ego and God in an interchangeable manner. He does so because the common sphere of absolute unity may be regarded either as separated from the self by a gulf of infinite limitation or as related to it across a bridge of infinite revelation. In the former case, the ego has to overcome the infinity of nonego, of otherness, in order to attain self-identity, which it aspires to do in the moral act, and then "Ego" would be the appropriate designation for absolute unity; in the latter case, the ego encounters itself in the nonego, finds its identity in the other, and then "God" would be the more appropriate terminological choice. Since the common sphere of unity is an absolute concept, no name is actually proper to it; the terms Ego and God merely serve to indicate the difference of perspective from which the self may perceive its position in the universe. Ever since his encounter with Sophie, that universe has a twofold function for Novalis: it is limitation as well as revelation, and throughout the course of his "Studies" he feels ever more keenly that Fichte recognizes only its limiting impact.

In his letter to Schlegel of 8 July 1796, Novalis defines his own philosophical position, summarizing, in effect, the results of his "Fichte-Studies":

1. There is no basic disagreement with his intellectual mentor; rather, they both travel along the same path, only Fichte seems to have stopped too soon.

2. Novalis not only understands his actions to be a progressive course of self-enactment through free moral agency, which would also be Fichte's position,

but he sees this process as a self-unfolding that takes place within the sphere of a matching reciprocal momentum; that is to say, he not only strives from part to Whole, from self to Self, but the Whole also presents itself to him in the part.

3. Within this context of reciprocity, Novalis defines love as the ability to experience the object not only as limit that separates self from Self but also as revelation from Self — or rather God — to self; he refers to Zinzendorf and Spinoza as exemplary in this respect since they were able to recognize the trace of the divine, of God, at every step on the paths along which they had directed their lives.

At this time, Sophie represents the singular point of mediation for Novalis that guarantees the reciprocal relationship he envisions. Consequently, her loss initially has the effect of leaving him totally despondent, until he begins to regain his sense of direction from the only source left him, his inner sense of freedom. At first he wants to die, purely as a reaction to the adversity of his fate; but soon reaction is transformed into a "decision." Death as the result of a free decision can only mean that it is to be the culmination of a life lived as a free decision. As the one decision gains in firmness, so does the other, and both are accompanied by a loving disposition, which Novalis now directs not at a mediatrix, nor at the void she left, but at the very source of the reality that had been revealed through her. Once the mediating figure disappears, so Novalis learns, its message does not disappear with it. That which has been revealed does not perish with the medium of its revelation; once it has been revealed, it remains as a promise, independent of further mediation, just as in Goethe's novel Wilhelm's brief encounter with Natalie retains the guiding quality of a promise for him. It is with this understanding and in this spirit that Novalis sets out on his future path, fully confident that his own efforts will ultimately be met by the final goal toward which he aspires.

The growing confidence with which Novalis begins to reapproach life is nourished by a renewed interest in philosophical and literary studies. Among the authors cited in the "Journal," Fichte's name is once again represented, at approximately the same time during which references to *Wilhelm Meister* dominate the entries. It is difficult to ascertain the entire range of his reawakened interest in Fichte since the only available document attesting to it is a rather brief collection of excerpts from the "Theoretical Part" of the *Wissenschafts-lehre*.[34] However, it is enough to indicate that he surveys Fichte's epistemology with an eye to the interrelation between the self's freedom in defining its content as the potential knower and its dependence in receiving the objects of knowledge. That relationship is possible because either aspect of it constitutes the same sequence of reflection only in opposite directions. Both the sequence of knowing and the sequence of the known arise from the original act in which the self posits itself as limited and determined by the nonego; both also "reflect" on the original act, that is to say, they take place with reference to it. Limited, the self is the unlimited self in a potential state and thus advances from potential, which is the possibility of all thought, toward its original state, which would be the conscious integration of the limiting momentum. However, the total realization of such conscious integration can never be attained because the limiting momentum would then cease to be just that, namely limit. This is the idealist or intellective sequence, and it advances toward the self's "facticity" (*Factum* is the term employed in Novalis's excerpts, II, 354, 1. 40), whereas the realist sequence covers the same ground in reverse. In the idealist sequence, "facticity" stands for the original state of self-identity as the projected aim of fully realized consciousness; in the realist sequence, "facticity" stands for the same unmitigated state of self-identity, but this time as the collective point of reference for all that may affect the self and thus become an object of consciousness. Both sequences are, of course, reciprocal, and only because they are that do conscious images and thoughts pertain with equal validity to an idealist or purely conceptual context as well as to a realist context in which the objects of the self's consciousness have reality independent of their being known.

The actual text to which my explication of Fichte's epistemology refers is an excerpt prepared by Novalis from the original (*SW*, 221–23):

> Die th[eoretische] W[issenschafts] L[ehre] besteht aus einer doppelten, entgegengesezten und eben deshalb vereinigten Reflexionsreihe — Die Eine geht vom Satz aus und endigt mit dem Factum — die Andre geht vom Factum zum Satze. Jene ist ideal, frey, enthält Denkmöglichkeiten — diese ist real, *gesezt*, enthält *Denknothwendigkeiten*.

> In the "Theoretical Part," the *Wissenschaftslehre* exposes a dual sequence of reflection moving in opposite directions yet united because it is one and the same sequence — One begins with the posited [self as limited and determined by the nonego] and ends with the facticity [of the self's identity in self-consciousness that encompasses the full conscious integration of the nonego] — the other begins with the facticity [of the self's identity in self-consciousness as prerequisite to being conscious of objects that affect the self] and ends with the posited [self as limited and determined by the infinite range of objects comprising the nonego]. The former is ideal, free, it contains the possibilities [or the form] of thought — the latter is real, *posited*, it contains the *necessity* [that determines the content] *of thought*.
>
> (II, 354, l. 38–355, l. 2)

From these remarks, Novalis draws his own conclusion, which he expresses in this formula:

> Jene ist die Auflösung des Satzes, oder der Aufgabe — Diese der *Beweis*. Das Factum ist der *Schlüssel*.

> The former is the resolution of the posited [condition of the self as limited and determined] or [the resolution] of the task [of reintegrating the limiting

moment within the self] — The latter is the [resolution's] *proof*. Facticity is the *key* [to both].

(II, 355, ll. 3–4)

Stated in simpler terms, Novalis reduces Fichte's systematic and extremely complex analysis of cognitive processes to the fundamental insight that the act of knowing entails two moments: one is the knowing agent's free disposition to receive a potential object of knowledge and the other is the givenness of the object. In other words, knowledge requires that the self be freely active in disposing itself to be receptive and that it be simultaneously passive in receiving the object. The entire process could also be described as active passivity — a concept Novalis is to employ a few months later — and the "key" to it is the self's "facticity." Actually, the "key" is, once again, the "basic schema" within which the "idealist" progression in the realm of consciousness and the "realist" sequence in the realm of objects comprising the world are freely posited, the one as the self's free activity in knowing, the other as its dependence on being given the objects of knowledge.

The pattern of congruence between ego and nonego, self and other, that emerges for Novalis from the "Theoretical Part" of the *Wissenschaftslehre* corresponds to the one in which he viewed his encounter with Sophie. However, that experience had moral dimensions and cannot, therefore, be accounted for in the same manner as an act of simple cognition. If freedom lies in the form of thought for the self's theoretical agency, it lies in the form of action for the self's practical, or rather moral, agency; and, so the parellelism would continue, if the Self's free self-positing action in the original act (*Tathandlung*) prepares the self to be a receptive agent, moral agency, which constitutes the reenactment of that original free act in the relative context of the self's limited estate, might well be considered to have a similar effect. Both as a theoretical and as a practical entity, the self is limited by the nonego; however, in its capacity as cognitive or theoretical agent the self is determined by the nonego, whereas in its capacity as practical agent that relationship is reversed.[35] The nonego remains the given factor in either case; only in each one it will reflect the difference of perspective from which it is approached. As the object of cognition, it will be formed into a world that is self-sufficient in its own being but devoid of any indication relative to a purpose with which the self could identify its existence. As the object of moral action, the world loses this self-sufficiency and becomes a medium capable of conveying the self's Self-hood. Once the self relates to the world from this perspective, that is to say, as a moral agent, its perception of the world is no longer reducible to acts of simple cognition. The objects such acts present to the mind remain the same, but viewed from the perspective of freedom their value to the self is not exhausted by their self-sufficient otherness or limiting function. In other words, the self as moral agent not only acts upon the world from the perspective of Self-hood, which is as far as Fichte's claims in the *Wissenschaftslehre* go, but also stands ready to receive the world from that same perspective, and that is Novalis's ever growing conviction. He comes to believe that the "Practical Part" of the *Wissenschaftslehre* is incomplete; it merely accounts for an "idealist" sequence, which actually ought to have a "realist" complement, just as the "Theoretical Part" stipulates a reciprocity of "idealist" and "realist" moments. Over the next months he develops his ideas more fully and ultimately arrives at a position to which he assigns the name of *"höhere Wissenschaftslehre."*

By autumn of the same year, Novalis had become very interested in the Dutch philosopher Frans Hemsterhuis (1721–90) from whose works he excerpts passages, occasionally lacing them with his own commentary (II, 360–78). He is not unfamiliar with the world of this thinker's Neoplatonism; after first meeting Novalis in Leipzig, Friedrich Schlegel reports to his brother in January of 1792 that fate had brought him into contact with an extraordinary young man by the name of Hardenberg whose "favorite authors are Plato and Hemsterhuis" ("seine Lieblingsschriftsteller sind Plato und Hemsterhuys — ") (IV, 572, ll. 5–6). Both these thinkers assign a prominent place to the concept of love in their respective philosophies, which would make Novalis's return to their world at this point quite understandable. Furthermore, the correlation of Platonic love and practical reason is not so farfetched because practical reason pertains specifically to the desirous faculty, just as theoretical reason pertains to the faculty of cognition.[36] Both these thinkers also share the view that the concept of love is expressive of the very reciprocity between idealist and realist moments Novalis found lacking in Fichte's analysis of practical reason. Plato envisions love as the offspring of lack and plenty,[37] which is another way of saying that love entails the dual moments of fulfillment potentialized and realized, or rather it entails the same sort of progressive receptivity, or active passivity, Novalis recognizes in Fichte's reciprocal sequences of cognition. Hemsterhuis, more appreciative of the passive rather than active aspect, likens love's anticipation of its object to an organ's similarly predetermined receptivity and, in distinction to organs providing sense perceptions for acts of ordinary cognition, he introduces the concept of a "moral organ." Unlike Hemsterhuis, though, Novalis gives the attribute "moral" a post-Kantian meaning and consequently reformulates the entire concept of "moral organ" into an extension of Fichte's philosophical position.

The potential for moral agency does, indeed, constitute an extrasensory organ since it introduces a unique perspective from which the self may relate to the world, to the objects of theoretical reason. However, and here Novalis emphasizes the Fichtean component, that organ is not simply given but must be developed to its utmost capacity through the conscious exercise of the self's freedom. In effect, Novalis comes to view moral agency as a formative process *(Bildung)*[38] through which the self is conditioned to regard the objects of cognition ever less exclusively from the perspective of its limited and determined state and, conversely, ever more inclusively from the perspective of its freedom.

The perspective of freedom is the perspective of Self, which the self attains in the moral command and its execution. From this vantage point gained in the enactment of its Selfhood, the self does not only recognize itself as Self but it may also come to recognize the Self in objects of cognition, as well it might since the nonego, which comprises the entirety of potential objects, is just as much a product of the Ego's positing as the self is.

Novalis's position becomes clearer if the major tenets of the *Wissenschaftslehre* are kept in mind. Consciousness is, first of all, the immediacy of self-presence we call self-consciousness. Since the self is always present to itself, without that presence being dependent on any influence outside the self, only the comprehensive unity for which the self is an object could have put the self there. That "putting the self there as an object" is what Fichte calls *Tathandlung*, a term with which he refers to the unconditional, that is, free and preconscious, act of self-positing summarized in his first axiomatic sentence (*Grundsatz*). However, the self is never simply present by itself but always in an affected state, a state of constant flux over which it has no control; to account for this situation, Fichte proposes in his second axiom that the self as the preconscious positing agent, simply referred to as Ego or Self, counterposits a nonego to the posited ego, or self. From the third axiom of mutual limitation, the self's theoretical and practical activity may be derived, as Fichte proceeds to do in the rest of the *Wissenschaftslehre*.

Since ego and nonego have the same source, there is no reason, so Novalis would argue, why only the self should reflect this common source, as it does in its capacity of free agent. Insofar as the self is a free agent, it also suspends the limiting function of the nonego; that is to say, if the self can be free of its limitation, which it is as a potentially moral agent, then its limiter is also free to enter into a relationship that is not restricted to limiting the self. A relationship not based on opposition is one of sameness, and it is in this sense that the self's moral capability constitutes an extrasensory organ with which it can behold not only the other, as it does with its sensory organs, but also the self in the other.

Fichte rests his case in the *Wissenschaftslehre* by deriving the self's capability for free moral agency from the same freedom of action that makes the world presented to the consciousness of our respective selves possible. In other words, the "Practical Part" establishes the self as desirous of being Self and capable of being that insofar as its freedom of action reflects the same freedom characteristic of the Self. Novalis adds a new theoretical dimension to this purely practical one and expands it, in effect, to include the possibility that the Self-reflecting self may also perceive the reflected Self, which is what makes a self-encounter in the other, or love, an essential corollary to the moral process.[39]

A number of fragments written later that same year and early in the next substantiate in greater depth and detail the outline I have just furnished concerning Novalis's effort to adapt Fichte's moralism to a reciprocal framework within which the self's free agency is not sufficient unto itself but entails, rather, a corresponding degree of passivity, of openness to receive that toward which the self strives in the ever repeated struggle to assert its freedom.[40] The mere capacity for free agency inherent in every person is already a form of receptivity which makes the revelatory encounter Novalis experienced with Sophie possible. He refers to it in these terms:

> Das willkührlichste Vorurtheil ist, daß dem Menschen das Vermögen *außer sich* zu seyn, mit Bewußtseyn jenseits der Sinne zu seyn, versagt sey. Der Mensch vermag in jedem Augenblicke ein übersinnliches Wesen zu seyn. Ohne dies wär er nicht Weltbürger — er wäre ein Thier. Freylich ist die Besonnenheit in diesem Zustande, die Sich Selbst Findung — sehr schwer, da er so unaufhörlich, so nothwendig mit dem Wechsel unsrer übrigen Zustände verbunden ist. Je mehr wir uns aber dieses Zustands bewußt zu seyn vermögen, desto lebendiger, mächtiger, genügender ist die Überzeugung, die daraus entsteht — der Glaube an ächte Offenbarungen des Geistes. Es ist kein Schauen — Hören — Fühlen — es ist aus allen dreyen zusammengesezt — mehr, als alles Dreyes — eine Empfindung unmittelbarer Gewisheit — eine Ansicht meines wahrhaftesten, eigensten Lebens — die Gedanken verwandeln sich in Gesetze — die Wünsche in Erfüllungen. Für den Schwachen ist das *Factum dieses Moments ein Glaubensartickel*. Auffallend wird die Erscheinung besonders beym Anblick mancher menschlicher Gestalten und Gesichter — vorzüglich bey der Erblickung mancher Augen, mancher Minen, mancher Bewegungen — beym Hören gewisser Worte, beym Lesen gewisser Stellen — bey gewissen Hinsichten auf Leben, Welt und Schicksal. Sehr viele Zufälle, manche Naturereignisse, besondre Jahrs und Tageszeiten liefern uns solche Erfahrungen. Gewisse Stimmungen sind vorzüglich solchen Offenbarungen günstig. Die Meisten sind augenblicklich — Wenige verziehend — die Wenigsten Bleibend. Hier ist viel Unterschied zwischen den Menschen. Einer hat mehr Offenbarungsfähigkeit, als der Andre —

> The most unwarranted prejudice is the belief that human beings are supposedly denied the ability to be *outside themselves*, to be conscious in an extrasensory manner. A human being is capable of being a supra-sensual being at any given moment. Without that ability he would not be a world-citizen — he would be an animal. Of course, it is difficult to maintain the concentration, the finding oneself, of this condition since it is so continuously and necessarily related to the state of change to which our other conditions are subject. The keener our consciousness of this condition can become, the more vivid, powerful, and satisfying is the conviction that arises from it — the conviction that a true revelation of the spirit is possible. It is not a seeing — hearing — feeling — it is composed of all

three — more than all three — a view of my life at its truest, true to itself
without any self-estrangement — thoughts take on the meaning of laws —
wishes are transformed into fulfillment. For the weak person the *facticity
of this moment is an article of faith*. This phenomenon occurs and becomes
obvious to us particularly when we catch sight of certain human figures
and faces — especially certain eyes, expressions, movements — when we
hear certain words, when we read certain passages — when we are struck
by certain aspects of life, world, and fate. Very many coincidences, some
events in nature, especially seasons and times of day give us such
experiences. Certain moods are particularly favorable for such revelations.
Most are of but a moment's duration — Some fade more slowly — hardly
any are lasting. There is a great deal of difference between people in this
respect. Some have more of a capability for revelation than others —
(II, 420, ll. 13–35; 422, ll. 1–2; *Athenäum* copy: II, 421, l. 8–43; 423, l.
2. Unless otherwise indicated, my text is based on the original version in
"Vermischte Bemerkungen.")

This fragment is the most coherent and encompassing statement that demon-
strates the philosophically assured position from which Novalis is now able to
account for the effect the encounter with Sophie had had on him. On the surface
his contentions seem to be "typically romantic" effusions of glorified emotion
at the expense of common sense and reason, in which spirit these pronouncements
and many of his others have all too readily been received. However, such opinions
are belied by the searching philosophical deliberations with which he attempts
to locate the purely isolated subjectivity of his emotive life within an objectively
valid context, an intellectual context common to all human beings. With reference
to the philosophical background that inspires this fragment, several, by now
familiar points emerge. First, Novalis is quite emphatic in saying that everyone
is capable of extrasensory perception but only insofar as everyone is also capable
of assuming "world-citizenship," which means a universal citizenship or rather
citizenship in the realm governed by the idea of humanity, the realm of the
categorical imperative. Next, he clearly characterizes this sort of perception as
a "finding of oneself" in the other that is accompanied by the very stabilization
of self he had experienced after meeting Sophie and had recognized as a reinforce-
ment of his self-identity. At the time, he speaks of it only in moral terms; now,
he calls it *Besonnenheit*, signifying a state of concentration in which the ever-oc-
curring flow of change to which the self is subject is suspended. This suspension
takes place not only with respect to the self, as it does in the state of moral
freedom, but also with respect to the objects, which attain a significance that is
equally undisturbed by the variation of conditions in time and place. That signifi-
cance is as subjective and yet as objectively valid as is moral agency, the sort
of agency that arises from the free and entirely personal decision to act in a
manner by which all possible selves would have to be bound as though it were

by the force of a law. In this sense Novalis speaks of thoughts assuming the force of laws when objects are perceived within the perspective guaranteed by the individual's capacity for moral freedom, the capacity for concentrating the diversely affected self to the point of self-identity.

With these reflections we are being returned to the structural complex of the "basic schema," because *Besonnenheit* means nothing else but a move to the center, a conscious self-identification with the self's true nature as the point held in common by the dual extension into an inner and outer reality. That balance is difficult to maintain, and for this reason Novalis mentions the weak, who are least aware of their own freedom, as experiencing the chance moment of revelation in the belief that they are entirely passive recipients during such an event, for which reason they regard it as an "article of faith." There are, furthermore, differences in degrees to which various people may prove capable of such an experience, and here, too, the emphasis is on capability rather than on the givenness of coincidental factors. Evidently, an active component is essential to the receptivity described in this fragment, only the topic is not fully developed beyond the stipulation that the capacity for free agency also determines the capacity for extrasensory perception. The question arises, for example, what part, if any, the individual can play in improving the *Offenbarungsfähigkeit* of which Novalis speaks. Such an improvement is not only possible but even necessary, unless the weak and their faith prevail and chance alone be left to govern the selection of a medium for self-encounter, which imposes an unwarranted restriction on the self's range of perspective, a range determined by no limit other than the self's awareness of its own freedom.

A few fragments later in the same collection, Novalis traces the advance from chance encounter to comprehensive vision. It is a progression along three possible stages of mediation, which actually constitute three moments within one and the same process he had previously identified as *Offenbarungsfähigkeit* and here refers to as "religiosity" (*Religiosität*). The terminology ought not to be misunderstood; it refers to no established orthodoxy, nor to any institution, but is indicative of the perspective or direction from which the self approaches the realization of its potential. Ever since the "Fichte-Studies," the terms "God" and "Ego" were declared to be interchangeable, and in the present context the concept of the "deity" is preferable to the concept of "Self." Novalis says:

Nichts ist zur wahren Religiositaet unentbehrlicher, als ein Mittelglied — das uns mit der Gottheit verbindet. Unmittelbar kann der Mensch schlechterdings nicht mit derselben in Verhältniß stehn. In der Wahl dieses Mittelglieds muß der Mensch durchaus frey seyn. . . . Man sieht bald, wie relativ diese Wahlen sind und wird unvermerckt auf die Idee getrieben — daß das Wesen der Religion wohl nicht von der Beschaffenheit des Mittlers abhänge, sondern lediglich in der Ansicht desselben, in den Verhältnissen zu ihm bestehe.

Nothing is more indispensable to true religiosity than a mediator — that links us to the deity. An unmediated relationship to the deity is impossible for human beings. In choosing the mediator the individual must be entirely free. . . . It soon becomes obvious how relative such choices are, which leads to the evident conclusion — that the essence of religion is not dependent on the characteristics of the mediator but consists, rather, of the attitude with which we regard that mediator, of the manner in which we relate to it.

(II, 440, l. 28–442, l. 3; 442, ll. 15–18;
Athenäum copy: II, 441 and 443)

With these words, Novalis stresses two crucial points: first, religion is not a matter of positive theological doctrine since it cannot even be defined in terms of a specific mediator, let alone in terms of a deity of which we know nothing; second, religiosity, if there be any at all, entails the same reciprocity of freedom, in the free act of choosing, and receptivity, in the dependence on a mediator, that characterizes revelation in the loving encounter. The chosen object must never be mistaken for the revealed itself because that would be "idolatry in its more inclusive sense" ("Götzendienst, im weitern Sinn") (II, 442, 19). Nor, Novalis adds in the same spirit, is it permissible to remain fixed upon one isolated form of revelation since all mediation takes place within a ring of mutual inter-dependence that progresses from any one object to one distinct object to all objects:

Die wahre Religion scheint aber bey einer nähern Betrachtung abermals antinomisch getheilt — In Panthëismus und Entheismus. Ich bediene mich hier einer Licenz — indem ich Pantheism nicht im gewöhnlichen Sinn nehme — sondern darunter die Idee verstehe — daß alles Organ der Gottheit — Mittler seyn könne, indem ich es dazu erhebe — so wie Enthëism im Gegentheil den Glauben bezeichnet, daß es nur Ein solches Organ in der Welt für uns gebe . . . welches ich also zu wählen durch mich selbst genöthigt werde — denn ohnedem würde der Enthëism nicht wahre Religion seyn. So unverträglich auch beyde zu seyn scheinen, so läßt sich doch ihre Vereinigung bewerckstelligen — wenn man den enthëistischen Mittler zum Mittler der Mittelwelt des Panthëisten macht — und diese gleichsam durch ihn zentrirt — so daß beyde einander, jedoch auf verschiedene Weise, necessitriren.

Upon closer examination, however, true religion seems, in turn, to be divided antinomically — into pantheism and entheism. I take the liberty — of not using either term in the customary manner — but rather to convey the idea — that pantheism means everything can be the deity's organ — can be a mediator by my raising it to that function — just as, to the contrary, entheism stands for the belief that there is only One such organ in the world for us . . . which I am to choose freely — because without my freely choosing it entheism would not be true religion. As incompatible as the two seem to be, their conciliation can be effected — if the entheistic mediator is viewed as mediator of the pantheist's mediatory world — centralizing it so to speak — so that both necessitate one another, but in different ways.

(II, 442, ll. 32–36; 444, ll. 1–2; 444, ll. 4–11;
Athenäum copy: II, 443 and II, 445)

"Pantheism" necessitates "entheism" and "entheism" "pantheism," which means the recognition of any one object as mediatory mediates the recognition of one particular mediator that mediates the recognition of all objects as potential mediators, and only because all objects are potential mediators is the initial recognition possible. In other words, mediation comprises three moments in a progressive cycle leading from one freely chosen object to a singular object that mediates the summary mediatory function of all objects, which it can only do by pointing away from itself to all other objects as potential mediators. Evidently, the function ascribed to the distinctive and singular mediator is one that can only be fulfilled by a given object or form of being no longer identifiable with any one part of the realm it is to represent summarily. That is, of course, the case with Sophie, who assumes the very role for Novalis others would attribute to Christ; actually, the two stand for the identical concept, a conviction that was to mature fully in his *Hymns to the Night*, which have their beginnings in the same period.[41]

In his theory of mediation, which he developed as a complementary expansion of Fichte's moralism, Novalis has not only accounted for the effect Sophie had had on him while she was alive but he has also succeeded in establishing her loss as a necessary moment in a progression toward the highest degree of *Offenbarungsfähigkeit*. The progression he describes is the one he has undergone. Love steadies him on his course and carries him along, but it can do so only if it is met by his own effort. The demand made on him is a moral demand, a demand to exercise his capacity for free agency ever more fully, ever more easily and readily, and to grow ever steadier in maintaining his place at the center. It is a formative process (*Bildung*) that requires he learn to live up to this demand and, since it is accompanied by love, also brings about a corresponding widening of his perspective for revelation, until he is receptive to the potential mediating power of all his surroundings. This changed relationship to the world marks the poet's perspective that allows for a poetic vision, a vision in which incidental objects and events may attain a meaning that cannot be reduced to the self's pragmatic concerns, be it in the pursuit of self-enhancement or in the execution of moral duty.

Already in a document entitled "Fragmentblatt," written a few weeks earlier, Novalis establishes a progressive linkage between the free theoretical moment he refers to as "absolute feeling" ("absolute Empfindung"), religiosity, and art: "All absolute feeling is religious. / Religion of beauty. Religion of art. / / Conclusion to be drawn from that. /" ("Alle absolute Empfindung ist religiös. / Religion des Schönen. Künstlerreligion. / / Schluß hieraus. / " (II, 395, ll. 22–23). A little later, in his "Logologische Fragmente," the "conclusion" to be drawn becomes more apparent when he develops the definition of a "*höhere Wissenschaftslehre*." First, however, Novalis examines the function of mythology, that is to say, the equivalent of a positively stated theology, and the pattern that emerges is the familiar circle of the "basic schema":

> Die höchsten Aufgaben beschäftigen den Menschen am Frühsten. Äußerst lebhaft fühlt der Mensch beym ersten Nachdenken das Bedürfniß die höchsten Enden zu vereinigen. Mit steigender Kultur nehmen seine Versuche an Genialitaet ab — aber sie nehmen an Brauchbarkeit zu — wodurch er zu dem Irrthume verleitet wird — gänzlich von den Endgliedern zu abstrahiren, und sein Verdienst bloß in Vereinigung näherer Bedingter Glieder zu setzen. . . . Jezt fällt ihm endlich ein in sich selbst, als absoluten Mittelpunct dieser getrennten Welten das absolute Vereinigungsglied aufzusuchen — Er sieht auf einmal, daß das Problem realiter schon durch seine Existenz gelößt ist — und das Bewußtseyn der Gesetze seiner Existenz die Wissenschaft kat exoxin sey, die er so lange schon suche. Mit der Entdeckung dieses Bewußtseyns ist das große Räthsel im Grunde gelößt. So wie sein Leben reale Philosophie ist, so ist seine Philosophie ideales Leben — lebendige Theorie des Lebens.

The most sublime problems preoccupy mankind at its earliest stages. As he begins to reflect, the human individual feels an urgent need to unite the ultimate ends. With an increasing development of culture, his intellectual constructions show ever less genius — but increase proportionally in pragmatic applicability — which leads him into the error — of diverting all attention from ultimate ends and attaching merit only to the uniting of closer conditional ends instead . . . [until] it finally dawns on him that he ought to seek the absolute point of union within himself since he is the absolute center of those separate worlds — He sees all of a sudden that the problem has really already been solved by his mere existence — and that consciousness of the laws of his existence is the science of science he had sought so long. With the discovery of this consciousness the great riddle has essentially been solved. As his life is realized philosophy, his philosophy is idealized life — [he is a] living theory of life.

(II, 527, l. 32–528, l. 4; 528, ll. 8–15)

The "ultimate ends" of which Novalis speaks may at first seem puzzling, but when their point of union is later identified as their "center," which is found to be the self, the terminology becomes less mysterious. "Ultimate ends" mean exactly what the words connote, namely the final points along the dual extensions into an outer, or "real," and an inner, or "ideal," world. If that final point could ever be ascertained in either of those "separate worlds," it would mean the ultimate circumference could be drawn that comprehends, and in comprehending joins, both ends, in which case they would be "united." The next fragment, which is an extremely concentrated summary of the preceding one, makes it clear that the ancient cosmogonies and theogonies constitute those inspired early attempts to furnish a total view from either the material or spiritual perspective.[42] In other words, mythology is meant when Novalis speaks of "uniting the ultimate ends"; but the mythological age has passed and attempts at drawing the ultimate circumference have been replaced by less ambitious designs that seek to harmonize the constellations of thought and matter around the self's state of dependency, which also happens to be the state that gives rise to all utilitarian needs. The encompassing vista of old shrinks down to the self, and this reductive orientation finally results in the discovery of the self's true nature as the center of that dual extension, center and thus the point of unity with reference to which the "ultimate ends" are united.

The discovery in question is initiated by Kant and completed by Fichte. The former first questioned the self's absolute dependence as a sufficient premise for the world our intellect presents to us and comes to the conclusion that the mind is not only reactive to experience but contributes independently in certain acts of cognition he calls "synthetic judgments *a priori*." Fichte establishes self-consciousness, expressed in the synthetic sentence *a priori* "$I = I$," as an act of uncontestable validity not only entirely independent of experiential data but prerequisite to it. This is the self-discovery of which Novalis speaks because with it the self does, indeed, come to understand itself for what it is, for the point from which the inner realm of thought and the outer realm of experience take their origin. That Novalis does have Fichte in mind becomes apparent when he refers to the "science of science" (*Wissenschaft kat exoxin*) as consciousness of the laws of existence arising from self-discovery. The title *Wissenschaftslehre* means "doctrine of science" which actually is equivalent to saying "science of science," and that philosophy does precisely what Novalis claims: it makes conscious the laws of existence as they arise from the discovery that consciousness of self, or rather the thought "I am," which accompanies all other operations of consciousness, is *the* synthetic judgment *a priori* and therefore the primary axiomatic sentence for the entire *Wissenschaftslehre*. Furthermore, it is also true that this philosophy is rooted in "reality," the only reality we have, the reality the self has for itself in the constancy of self-consciousness, and it is in this sense equally valid to say, as Novalis does in the last sentence cited, that the intellectual ("*ideal*") and experiential ("*real*") tracks of reality constitute an uninterrupted equation if we assume the vantage point Fichte affords us.

That very vantage point at the center, as Novalis sees it within the framework of his "basic schema," is maintained by the self that understands itself as free, which it can only do by enacting its freedom. This is as far as the *Wissen-*

schlaftslehre goes, but Novalis has gone one step further: the center is comple-
mented by the circumference and unity enacted may, therefore, be complemented
by unity received, as was outlined in the theory of mediation, which ultimately
pointed to the possibility of poetic vision, the sort of vision outlined in the defini-
tion of the "*höhere Wissenschaftslehre*":

> Es giebt gewisse Dichtungen in uns, die einen ganz andern Karacter, als
> die Übrigen zu haben scheinen, denn sie sind vom Gefühle der
> Nothwendigkeit begleitet, und doch ist schlechterdings kein äußrer Grund
> zu ihnen vorhanden. Es dünckt dem Menschen, als sey er in einem Gespräch
> begriffen, und irgend ein unbekanntes, geistiges Wesen veranlasse ihn auf
> eine wunderbare Weise zur Entwickelung der evidentesten Gedancken.
> Dieses Wesen muß ein Höheres Wesen seyn, weil es sich mit ihm auf eine
> Art in Beziehung sezt, die keinem an Erscheinungen gebundenen Wesen
> möglich ist — Es muß ein homogenes Wesen seyn, weil es ihn, wie ein
> geistiges Wesen behandelt und ihn nur zur seltensten Selbstthätigkeit
> auffordert. Dieses Ich höherer Art verhält sich zum Menschen, wie der
> Mensch zur Natur, oder wie der Weise zum Kinde. Der Mensch sehnt sich
> ihm gleich zu werden, wie er das N[icht] I[ch] sich gleich zu machen
> sucht. Darthun läßt sich dieses Factum nicht. Jeder muß es selbst erfahren.
> Es ist ein Factum höherer Art, das nur der höhere Mensch antreffen
> wird. Die Menschen sollen aber streben es in sich zu veranlassen. Die
> Wissenschaft, die hierdurch entsteht ist die höhere W[issenschafts] L[ehre]
> . . . Der practische Theil enthält die Selbsterziehung des Ich um jener
> Mittheilung fähig zu werden — der theoretische Theil — die Merckmale der
> ächten Mittheilung. Bey Fichte enthält der theoretische Theil die Merckmale
> einer ächten Vorstellung — der practische die Erziehung und Bildung des
> N[icht]-I[ch] um eines wahren Einflusses, einer wahren Gemeinschaft mit
> dem Ich fähig zu werden — mithin auch die parallele Selbstbildung des
> Ich. Moralität gehört also in beyde Welten; hier, als Zweck — dort als
> Mittel — und ist das Band, was beyde verknüpft.

There are certain fictions that occur to us, quite different in character from
all others because they are accompanied by a feeling of necessity, even
though there is no external cause for them [on which we could base this
feeling, as we do in all other theoretical processes of cognition]. In this
state, it seems to a person as though he were engaged in a conversation
and, in a miraculous manner, some unknown spiritual being caused him
to evolve thoughts of the most evident truth. This being must be a Higher
Being because it relates to the human individual in a manner that is not
possible for any being subject to the laws of the phenomenal realm
comprising our world — It must be a being akin to human being because
it treats the individual as a spiritual entity and summons him to exercise
his freedom of agency at the highest level. This self of a higher kind is to
the human being what the human being is to nature or what the wise person
is to the child. The human individual longs to be like that higher self just

as he seeks to make the nonego like himself. This facticity [of the higher self's revealing itself to the self] cannot be demonstrated. Everyone must experience it himself. It is a facticity of a higher sort [than the object's "facticity" in simple acts of cognition] that is encountered only at the level of superior humanity. Everyone, however, is to strive to induce this experience [by reaching the level of preparedness at which it can occur]. The science that comes into being in this context is the *"höhere Wissenschaftslehre."* . . . The practical part contains the self's self-education in order to become capable of receiving this impartation [from the higher self] — the theoretical part — [describes] the characteristics of a true communication. . . . With Fichte, the theoretical part contains the characteristics of a true conception [of objects] — the practical [part contains] the education and formation of the nonego so that it is fit to be truly affected by the self, fit to allow for true intercourse with the self — and that entails also the parallel formative process of the self's self-education. Morality, then, belongs into both worlds [that of the *"höhere Wissenschaftslehre"* and that of the *Wissenschaftslehre*]; in the latter as purpose — in the former as means — and it is the tie that links both together.

(II, 528, ll. 25–34; 529, ll. 1–9, 11–13, 15–20)

There is little that need be added to Novalis's words since they effectively summarize his deliberations to which this entire chapter has been dedicated. Some essentials do have to be pointed out, however. It may not be immediately evident, but the topic of discussion concerns the poetic vision. He speaks of *Dichtung*, which I have rendered as "fiction" rather than "poem" or "poetry" because the term does refer quite generally to constructions of the mind produced without the license of necessity that accompanies all presentations of external reality the imagination brings before consciousness. There are fictions, though, accompanied by their own kind of necessity, Novalis claims, and then, only after that distinction has been made, does the term *Dichtung* also assume poetic merit for him. The "feeling of necessity" that characterizes poetic vision has already been mentioned in the "Fragmentblatt" as "absolute feeling" and is equivalent to the feeling of "certainty" associated with revelation and mediation. The source of such unshakable assurance and "truth" is the "higher self," or rather the Self, which the self may encounter on its way to the Self; that is to say, the self expresses its "longing to be like the Self" in exercising free moral agency, which does not only "seek to liken the nonego to the self" but also — and most important — relates to the nonego as a potential medium that spans the abyss between self and Self. Again, the term *Factum* is used to express theoretical certainty, only this time it is "of a higher sort" since we are dealing with a "higher sort of *Wissenschaftslehre*" possessed by a "higher sort of person" (*höherer Mensch*). Each time the term "higher" (*höher*) is used, it means an advance beyond the moralism Fichte perceives as the final purpose of humankind;

however, it also means that Fichte's moralism, and with it the entire philosophical position supporting it, remains the firm platform from which alone this advance may proceed. Novalis acknowledges his transmutation of the *Wissenschaftslehre* and his continued reliance on it in the formula with which he concludes his remarks. Morality, or rather free agency, is Fichte's end station and Novalis's beginning; it is also their lasting bond because it is essential to both.[43]

If nothing else, the affirmation of Fichte's moralism makes it obvious that Novalis's poetics do not then, nor at any other time, proclaim art as an absolute or nonreferential endeavor; art originates with reference to the characteristically human capacity for free moral agency and it addresses itself to it. The poet has to undergo a formative process, a moral process referred to as the "self's self-education" through which he attains the "level of superior humanity" where he can encounter the poetic vision.[44] It is the very process Novalis had undergone in the course that presented him with the gift of Sophie and with her loss, a course he outlines in his theory of mediation. It is a *Bildungsweg* along the path of freedom, along the path of an educative formative process he calls "*Selbstbildung des Ich*," or as he tells August Wilhelm Schlegel:

Ohne Gegenstand kein Geist — ohne Bildung keine Liebe, Bildung ist gleichsam der feste Punct, durch welchen diese geistige Anziehungskraft sich offenbart — das nothwendige Organ derselben. . . . Wo ein fester Punct, ist, da sammelt sich Aether und Licht von selbst und beginnt seine himmlischen Reigen — Wo Pflicht und Tugend — Analoga jener festen Puncte — sind, da wird jenes flüchtige Wesen von selbst ein und ausströmen und jene kalten Regionen mit belebender Atmosphäre umgeben. Wer also nicht jene zu *fixiren* sucht, der wird dieser umsonst durch alle Räume nachfolgen, ohne Sie je erreichen, ohne Sie je sammeln und festhalten zu können.

Without any object there is no spirit — without the educative formative process there is no love. The educative formative process is, so to speak, the fixed point [i.e., focus] in which this spiritual power of attraction reveals itself — the necessary organ of it [, the organ through which the attracting power of love can reach the human spirit]. . . . Where there is a fixed point, there aether and light gather of their own accord and begin their heavenly round dance — Where duty and virtue [i.e., the imperative to act freely and its enactment] — which are analogous to those fixed points — are, there this aethereal essence [i.e., love] will flow in and out of its own accord and envelope those cold regions [of moral rigor] with an animating atmosphere. He who does not seek to *fix* those points [i.e., does not travel the *Bildungsweg* of the self's self-education in moral practice] will pursue his aethereal quarry in vain throughout the universe, without ever being able to reach it, to gather it and hold it fast.

(IV, 245, ll. 20–22; 245, ll. 30–36)

Not many travel the length of the difficult and demanding path Novalis has chosen; a few are prepared to receive a poetic vision of the world. Nonetheless, all people are "to strive to induce this experience," and their striving is complemented and aided by the mediated poetic vision, the poet's communicated vision, just as the poet's own efforts are complemented by the vision afforded him. However, the poet's function is not discussed in the context of the "*höhere Wissenschaftslehre*"; I have merely added an implication of it in anticipation of its demonstration, which Novalis supplies on the most comprehensive scale in his *Heinrich von Ofterdingen*.

III. *Heinrich von Ofterdingen*

Der Traum ist oft bedeutend und prophetisch, weil er eine Naturseelenwirckung ist — und *also* auf Associationsordnung beruht — Er ist, wie Poësie bedeutend — aber auch darum unregelmäßig bedeutend — *durchaus frey*.

Dreams are often meaningful and prophetic because they are effects of the natural functioning of the soul — and are *thus* based on rules of association — They are, like poesy, meaningful — but also for this reason irregularly meaningful — *entirely free*.

Novalis

Eine überraschende Selbstheit ist zwischen einem wahrhaften Liede und einer edeln Handlung.

There is a startling similarity between a genuine song and a noble deed.

Novalis

Chapter 7
Poetic Statement and
"höhere Wissenschaftslehre"

Almost two years separate the codification of a *"höhere Wissenschaftslehre"* from Novalis's work on *Heinrich von Ofterdingen*, the most ambitious and last of his literary projects. Much of that time was spent on scientific studies, but as always they, along with manifold other interests, occasioned extensive philosophical speculations that fill various notebooks and collections composed in the idiom of fragmentary notations peculiar to him. Also, his own evolution as a poet becomes more pronounced during that interim. Some of his religious poetry (*Geistliche Lieder*) falls into this period and, above all, his first attempted novel, *The Disciples at Sais (Die Lehrlinge zu Sais)*, which remained uncompleted because the more inclusive plan for *Heinrich von Ofterdingen* had taken precedence over it by November 1799.

The wealth of studies, experiences, projects, and reflections that fill those intervening months certainly serves to broaden the range of Novalis's vision but does not alter his ideological framework. The *"höhere Wissenschaftslehre"* retains its validity for him, and, more than that, furnishes the outline for a theory of poetry that determines both form and content of his artistic practice. Within this context, the poetic statement refers its audience to the same world the self's acts of cognition have construed to be its environment. There is no other world. There is only a difference of perspective from which it can be beheld and this shift in perspective is the poetic statement's singular topic, formal determinant, and potential effect. The poet can describe nothing else but the process through which he attained the level of self-consciousness that permits the world to appear as the poetically transformed phenomenon he presents it to be. In other words, the poetic statement must be justified through its own genesis since it originates from a perspective of self-consciousness that is different from the one for which the imagination produces the familiar world of simple cognition. However, this sort of poetic practice is not a matter of language becoming its own subject in isolated nonreferential splendor, with which the proper domain of the poet's art has come to be identified so frequently since the waning decades of the past century. For Novalis, the poet's genesis is at issue and not the poem's; that is to say, he derives the poem's authenticity from the primacy of moral rather than linguistic autonomy. Not that he would deny linguistic autonomy, which he had, after all, confirmed already in the "Fichte-Studies"; rather, he would deny that linguistic autonomy could be considered anything but a function of the self's capacity for free moral agency, and that is the crucial difference between Novalis and all those for whom art constitutes a self-sufficient enterprise, be they symbolists or their contemporary heirs. Consequently, his central topic is always the poetic work's own origin depicted as the developmental path by which the self gains consciousness of its inherent freedom. As this consciousness grows, the antagonism between self and world, or spirit and nature, diminishes and their fundamental identity begins to become apparent, which constitutes a poetic vision.

Novalis's poetry is consistently characterized by such visions of identity, be that in the *Disciples*, where nature drops her veil of estrangement before those who follow the true path, or in the *Hymns*, where the ultimate "non" of the nonego, the certainty of death, loses its power over those who are guided by love, or in *Ofterdingen*, where Heinrich's entire career constitutes a progression in world-encounter that is also a progression in self-encounter. It is not difficult to discern that these thematic variations are constructed according to the "basic schema." In each case, the fundamental dichotomy between the subjective and objective moments of reality is reduced to its point of unity in the self from where it can be, and is, complemented by an unfolding of its comprehensive unity. Not only the general theme but also the more detailed and formal aspects of its presentation reflect the same structure. The text of the *Disciples*, for example, advances along a steadily repeated pattern of dialectical triads carefully molded into a systematic sequence that also determines the arrangement of chapters and even paragraphs.[1] Moreover, the circular constellation of the "basic schema" finds its appropriate expression in imagery designed to symbolize the entirety of the task confronting the community at Sais: when one of the disciples, who had been particularly inept and thus barred from gaining entry into the secrets of nature, suddenly finds this barrier removed, he is depicted as having found a stone that supplies the missing center for a collection of nature's objects arranged in rows of opposing radii (I, 81, ll. 2–19).[2] The "basic schema" may even be revealed at the most fundamental levels of textual composition. A case in point would be the choice of personal pronouns in the first of the *Hymns* where the "it"-ness of light's cosmic expanse stands in contrast to "I"-ness, transfixed by death's limiting shadow, and all antagonism disappears in the limitless night of "thou"-ness that descends upon a loving heart (I, 131, ll. 1–31; 133, ll. 1–16).

These examples demonstrate sufficiently that the concept of the *"höhere Wissenschaftslehre"* affects not only Novalis's choice of topic for his poetic statements but also the formal aspects of their composition. The topic is the inner change the individual must undergo in order to perceive self and world in a relationship that is not frozen into a state of permanent opposition, which it is for all those people who attribute primacy to the nonego and believe the self to be as determined by an external causality in its actions as it is dependent on the givenness of sense perception in its theoretical function. Since the plot is one of inner development that has neither efficient nor final cause in the world of external circumstances, Novalis does not depict the environs in which his characters appear with "realistic" detail. Both his characters and their surroundings are strangely disembodied, which is hardly surprising, given the shift in perspective his works are to demonstrate. They reflect a changed world viewed from a changed relationship to it, and this change occurs when the theoretical premise of the *Wissenschaftslehre*, with reference to which the world of our accustomed reality emerges, is supplemented by the theoretical premise of the *"höhere Wissenschaftslehre."* The path that leads from one to the other, the move toward the center within the context of the "basic schema," is also the path that leads the reader through Novalis's work. In other words, the reader will have to reach the same perspective the protagonist attains, which is also the perspective the author aready holds. In this respect, the shift in perspective required by the *"höhere Wissenschaftslehre"* is not only the poetic statement's singular topic and formal determinant but also its intended, yet indirect, potential effect on the audience; furthermore, the corollary conclusion must be added that the poetic statement does have a referential dimension in the moral ground Fichte's *Wissenschaftslehre* and Novalis's "higher" version of it maintain in common.

These considerations have been offered in order to demonstrate the general criteria that may be derived for the poetic arts from the *"höhere Wissenschaftslehre."* To what effect Novalis actually comes to employ them is best exemplified in *Heinrich von Ofterdingen*, the novel that summarizes his poetic ambitions, even though its protagonist is prevented by the author's untimely death from traveling the entire length of the designated journey.[3]

Chapter 8
Dreams and Fairy Tales

Heinrich von Ofterdingen was to acquaint its readers with the full extent of the developmental path that must be traversed by a young man destined to be a poet. As it happened, Novalis did not advance much beyond completing the initial nine chapters that comprise the first of the novel's two parts, which bear the respective titles of "Expectation" ("Die Erwartung") and "Fulfillment" ("Die Erfüllung"). Unambiguous as those captions may seem by themselves, their relationship to the text is more difficult to determine. One might even be tempted to reverse their order. At least, it is quite possible to view the cycle of the first nine chapters under the heading of "Fulfillment" because it contains the successful completion of three highly important phases in the protagonist's life: his first exposure to the world outside the provincial seclusion of his native Eisenach, his encounter with the love of his life, and his admission to the poet's craft under the tutelage of one of its most renowned masters. Curiously enough, none of these events are even definitely envisaged goals and their occurrence to Heinrich appears to be far more unexpected than consciously anticipated. There simply is no ordinary sense of "expectation" in "Die Erwartung"; instead, there is a sense of preparation, a sense of development that entails a gradual opening of "the doors of perception,"[4] and only as a synonym for this sort of growth in receptivity does "Erwartung" or "expectancy" apply to the process Novalis describes. The ultimate stage of receptivity would be the one at which the last restriction, the limiting momentum of death's finality, is overcome. Novalis had reached that stage after Sophie's death and Heinrich, too, is not spared the fate of suffering the same loss before he is allowed to start on his way to "fulfillment."

The entire progression leading through the various phases of "expectancy," and beyond, is initiated by a sudden break in the accustomed normalcy of Heinrich's life. Of course, all constellations produced by the infinite flow of circumstances affect a person, and some do so more drastically than others, but this state of dependence is precisely the normalcy that has been unsettled. Essentially, Heinrich's situation at the beginning of the novel is as paradoxical as Novalis's had been after the encounter with Sophie. In Heinrich's case, it is not yet the full self-encounter of love — that will occur later — but it is the first tremor in the foundation on which the "it"-"I" relationship between world and self is based.

The novel opens with a brief descriptive statement, deceptively simple in its wording and imagery. The mere mention of sleeping parents and a ticking clock suffice to stake out a realm of placidity to which a sense of protective security is added by the wind's rattling at the windows and by the moonlight's only occasionally more successful penetration of the same barrier. The setting seems unproblematic enough in its common appeal, but actually the author employs it to intimate subtly that the poet's origins also furnish the background against which his development takes place. The vague outline of a dwelling, an enclosure circumscribed by human need, stands as a frail island amid the antagonistic forces of nature and night. Only the fantastic light of lunar illumination is testimony to the mysterious expanse outside, and the threat of invasion from that beyond goes unheeded in the unawareness of sleep marked by the monotonous rhythm of a clock ticking off seconds. With its dichotomous interplay between inner and outer spheres, the imagery obviously conveys the pattern of the "basic schema"; more specifically, it conveys the pragmatist variant to which Novalis had referred in the "Logologische Fragmente" (II, 527, 1. 32–528, 1. 4; 528, ll. 8–15, cited previously). The "ultimate ends" remain unresolved: outside, the threat of night prevails and inside, the lack of awareness; only the limited ends of need and use proscribe the uniform sphere within which the dichotomy of the self's inner and outer reality lies suspended, until — so one is led to conjecture — the clock completes its pointless round and the ultimate night sets in.

There is nothing inherently "wrong" with a pragmatic attitude toward life; later on in the chapter, Heinrich's father reveals his basically pragmatic inclinations but he cannot be summarily censured on that account. On the contrary, he is a craftsman whose work is evidently valued by his society. Pragmatic concerns are fundamental and necessary to human existence; however, they are insufficient as a validation of that existence since they only support it. The pragmatic circle is one within which the self defines itself solely on terms of those of its needs and desires that arise from its state of dependence on the world around it. In other words, the "I" defines itself as "it," and the enactment of this self-definition takes the form of self-expansion powered by the possessive rather than moral imperative. Accordingly, the limited sphere of the pragmatic world has no center, no "I," except as a potential core or offspring that emerges as the walls of the little home in the night are breached and the protective, yet also restrictive, confines of pragmatism open up toward the absolute sphere that completes the "basic schema."

Novalis has the self emerge in exactly this manner. The first descriptive passage is written in the third person; the second, still in the third person, introduces a youth, as yet unnamed but quite obviously the previously mentioned parents' offspring, who is unable to sleep because he is preoccupied with thoughts of a stranger's recent visit. Thereafter, the narrative shifts to the first person and assumes the form of a monologue in which the speaker registers a new self-aware-ness, actually tracing the unfolding of a consciousness of self that occurs as a reciprocal movement initiated by the stranger's tale of a blue flower. It is a vision from afar, from the beyond the mysterious stranger has introduced into the cottage. In response to this mediated vision, "I" is first pronounced, and with it the missing center moves into focus as a point of self-contemplative identity, which is what "I" really means. The newly gained theoretical ground of self-identity also has its practical counterpart in a longing for the blue flower that is devoid of any possessive interests. The monologue does, in fact, begin with the observation that an imperative other than the one to possess has become the singular motivation complementary to the stranger's conveyed message con-cerning the blue flower:

"Nicht die Schätze sind es, die ein so unaussprechliches Verlangen in mir geweckt haben", sagte er zu sich selbst; "fern ab liegt mir alle Habsucht: aber die blaue Blume sehn' ich mich zu erblicken. Sie liegt mir unaufhörlich im Sinn, und ich kann nichts anders dichten und denken".

"It is not the treasures that have awakened such an inexpressible longing in me," he said to himself; "nothing is further from me than greed [actually, 'the consuming passion to have, or possess']: but I do long to behold the blue flower. It is perpetually in my mind, and nothing else occupies my thought and imagination."

(I, 195, ll. 9–13)

As he continues, it becomes evident that no one else witness to the same event had been affected in a like manner. Their world remained undisturbed, whereas he, no longer confined by its walls, has left that very world in which flowers do not matter for an other one, and yet it is the same world, only more familiar, more of a "thou" than an "it."

The world has not changed, but his relationship to it has, and in the process the divisive limit between inside and outside, between ego and nonego, has become transparent. No matter how much nature is tamed in the service of human need, it always retains its forbidding otherness that ultimately claims the existence it temporarily supports. Once the self gains an inkling of its freedom, even that final barrier erected in testimony to the self's dependence loses it threatening power and nature assumes the features of another self. Accordingly, it now seems to the youth as though rocks, trees, and animals were about to speak to him, a state of mind that would have to be judged insane by previous standards were it not for the reassurance he derives from a greater clarity of vision and a heightened sense of understanding. At this point, he is still confused about this sudden change of perspective and far from conscious of what it entails. To grow into full self-consciousness as he receives an ever more comprehensive vision of the world from the perspective of his freedom, from the center for which the inner and outer realms merge, that will be his task.

The fullness of this consciousness will have been reached when he is able to communicate it, which is definitely not the case in his present state ("Daß ich auch nicht einmal von meinem wunderlichen Zustande reden kann!" ["And to think I cannot even talk about my singular condition!"], I, 195, ll. 21–22; Hilty, 15[5]). Since the degree of freedom realized by the self is attended by a proportionate range of receptivity to the world as a medium rather than a limit that constitutes a pragmatic challenge, communication of the self's true, that is to say free, condition can only be rendered in the manner of a poetic statement, as outlined by the "höhere Wissenschaftslehre." In other words, Heinrich will be able to "talk about his singular condition" when he has become a poet. That this is, indeed, to be the case becomes apparent in the ninth and last chapter of part I where Klingsohr's fairy tale not only exemplifies the poet's craft but also tells how a household, allegorically representative of the self's faculties, arrives at its deliverance from bondage into freedom. The "singular condition" is also the singular poetic topic, which can, of course, be told in innumerable ways but only by a free self addressing other selves as free in a language that reveals its own heritage of freedom from limitation to a pragmatically determined referential context.

Equally free of pragmatically determined referential contexts are dreams, and the youth's soliloquy that still refers its concepts to the "old world" ("[die] Welt, in der ich sonst lebte") (I, 195, 1. 15), if only by contrast, soon gives way to the more profound symbolism of a dream vision. In order to appreciate Novalis's special regard for the type of consciousness that occurs in dreaming states, it is necessary to recall that he considers all acts of cognition constitutive of our waking, or daytime, reality to be variables of self-consciousness and not the direct "knowledge" of objects as we believe. Those objects are products of the imagination with which it accounts for the varying conditions of the self's limited estate. The objects thus presented to consciousness have really no validity of their own, except as elements of a symbolic circumscription representative of the self. Objects constitute a language that does not speak exclusively in terms of an infinite range of limitation experienced as sentience. That restricted a medium conveys nothing but dictates to which a self, addressed as an entirely dependent entity, can offer no more than a pragmatic response. Far more important, the language of objects also speaks in terms of the self's formative power, which is best understood when that power is allowed to demonstrate its freedom by functioning without reference to the immediate impact of sense data indicative of the self's limited, or dependent, state. The freer the imagination is in forming its images, the more clearly do they display their function of serving to reveal the self's true nature.

Objects may assume such symbolic transparency in dreams, when the self lies suspended in sleep and for this very reason achieves a keener state of awareness than the distortions of waking reality would permit; actually, the dreaming self is awake and the waking self asleep to the truth of its reality, just as the parents are asleep to it and the youth awake in his dreamlike state[6] that effortlessly merges into a real dream. Dreams are, however, a purely subjective, or internal, experience that must be communicable if it is to have validity. Poetic statements are such dreams shared in common and fairy tales, as least referential to a pragmatic context, come closest to being objective, or external, counterparts to dreams. Consequently, part I of *Heinrich von Ofterdingen* begins with a dream and ends with a fairy tale, which completes the complementary arch of mutual validation that extends from internal to external vision. Also, this arrangement makes it evident that the structural pattern of the "basic schema" does not only underlie individual passages or some segments of the novel but informs the entire cycle of its completed chapters.

The dream that follows Heinrich's solitary musings is told in the third person and has three separate phases, which the narrator interrupts after the first one in order to relate the concluding section to the time of night at which it occurs. This brief interjection accomplishes a shift in narrative perspective by means of which the author succeeds in uniting the "it" and "I" dichotomies that have characterized the narration up to this point. The nondream reality and the dream reality have simultaneous validity from a viewpoint that transcends them both, which — for the moment — only the narrator and his audience hold. However, there is no doubt that the dreaming "I" is to attain the same perspective within its own domain; as a sign indicative of the direction where this attainment lies, the dreamer emerges upon waking as "Heinrich," so named for the first time, and enters the familial world where he is addressed as "thou" (*Du*).

The time of night to which Novalis refers his readers is also highly significant in its own right since it is the transitional period of dawn, the point where night meets day and their separate spheres of reality merge. As in the *Hymns to the Night*, daytime stands for the realm of life and its attendant pragmatic concerns, whereas night has a twofold meaning. It implies either the cessation of day, in a temporary as well as permanent sense, or a heightened awareness that comprehends both realms. Evidently, the latter instance applies in the case of dreamers who come to understand the language of their dreams as the language of reality. Furthermore, the confluence of night and day is also an important reference point for Novalis's concept of colors. He attaches definite symbolic value to their employment throughout the text, particularly in the two parts of the dream sequence that occur at the specified time of dawn. Briefly stated, Novalis's use of colors reflects the theoretical premises Goethe had outlined in his *Contributions to Optics (Beiträge zur Optik*, 1791–92).[7] In that publication, which Novalis held in high esteem, Goethe contends that colors originate at the points of tangency between the polar opposites of light and dark. As his experiments show, the edge of a light surface juxtaposed against a dark one will radiate the colors red in the direction of the dark area and yellow in its own direction, whereas the dark surface takes on a violet tint near the edge and projects a clear blue into its light counterpart. Most important for Novalis's scheme is the fact that light modified by darkness is yellow or golden in its own realm of light, and darkness projected into that same realm of light is manifest as blue.

Yellow and blue, the only true colors according to Goethe,[8] take their place within a framework of polar opposition Novalis would have had to regard as an obvious confirmation of the interactive complex typified by his "basic schema." Light and dark occupy the same positions with respect to one another as do ego and nonego, and both sets of opposites can maintain their relationship only within a sphere of mutual interaction. The circumference of the sphere is not apparent because there are no opposites from its vantage point; just as that sphere could be called "God" or "I" (II, 108, ll. 1–2), it could also be called "Dark" or "Light" since either nomenclature would be equally appropriate or inappropriate. Even though the periphery may be indeterminable, its center is very definitely determined by the point of tangency that allows for the interaction of opposites. As long as the self advances no further than the recognition of its determined state, it remains locked in opposition since it can only identify with the limited sphere of its selfhood and must grant full sufficiency to the limiting sphere beyond. Once the self comes to recognize ego and nonego as relative moments of interaction that originate with its selfhood and are potentially comprehended by it, the frozen state of deadly opposition begins to melt. In its stead, a field of living interaction appears that is nourished from the center, or rather from the tangential point, by the self's freedom of agency. As a restricted entity, the self is ego, identifiable with light or the daytime world, which is opposed by the otherness of nonego, the dark of night and death. As a free agent, the self is capable of integrating the nonego within its own sphere in two ways, just as light is capable of integrating darkness. With regard to the restrictive aspect of tangency, the self reflects the nonego's limiting effect on the ego and fashions it into images for consciousness to comprehend as the ego's world; this action would be the equivalent of light reflecting against darkness at the point of tangency and thus suspending the dualism of light and dark in the color yellow. With regard to the mediating aspect of tangency, the self attains the capacity to encounter the nonego freely without reference to its limiting agency; this "active passivity" would be the equivalent of light receiving darkness across the point of tangency and thus suspending even the last vestiges of dualism in the color blue.

The first of Henrich's dream sequences, which precedes the narrator's interjection, is remarkably eventful yet equally remarkable for its lack of descriptive detail and color. Uninhibited by the confines of time and space, the self appearing in the dream takes full measure of every experience the world has to offer and is carried along by the stream of being as it weaves its way back and forth between opposites that fall into a pattern of infinite repeatability. This dance of life moves according to the measures of war and peace, joy and suffering, life and death, only to end on a note of love and "eternal separation" ("auf ewig . . . getrennt") (I, 196, ll. 10–11).

Separation persists because the self is conceived solely as the entire range of experiences to which it may be exposed and not as the summary condition for the possibility of any and all experience. The self is not only the indirect object of consciousness viewed in the context of external circumstances that affect its feelings, thoughts, and actions, but also the direct object that is always self regardless of circumstantial affect. Self-consciousness is an act of consciousness that establishes self-identity as the necessary prior condition for all other conditions to which the self may be subject and to which its feelings, thoughts, and actions respond. If self-conciousness were not free of all other conditions but merely a secondary phenomenon that is dependent on them, there could be no consciousness of self since the self's identity could not be determined from the constant flow of changing conditions to which it is exposed. The ability to say "I," or rather "I am" feeling, thinking, doing, and so on, derives from the unqualified certainty of self-consciousness and not from a composite of experiences that span the interim between birth and death, even if that cycle were to be repeated indefinitely as the dream intimates. In other words, "I" does not mean an ego dependent on the primacy of the nonego, not world through which there is a self, but rather self-identity; and self-identity, in turn, means freedom of agency through which there is a self that entails the summary possibility of its determinability and therefore also the summary possibility of its determinant, the world outside. As long as "I" is not understood in its freedom as the potential sum and closure of its determinability and of its determinant, the self is not truly conscious of itself and persists in misunderstanding its relationship to the world. This misunderstanding occurs because the self is subject to limitation felt as sensory impact, which causes it to attribute the primacy of independent reality to the realm of the nonego and to the objects projected therein. Yet the self also insists on its own independence insofar as it recognizes itself as quite different from everything else. Consequently, ego and nonego, self and world, stand opposed, with the ego intent on claiming its independence on the nonego's ground, where it cannot be won because it has already been forfeit. This forfeiture makes separation permanent. It does not alter the range of possibilities for interaction, which takes place even on a reciprocal basis, but the nonego prevails and any union or sense of identity the ego attains with its opposite is always under the dictate of limitation and subject to dissolution.

The only mention of color in this segment of the dream is "colorful" (*bunt*), used to describe the manifold of life's adventures and to imply a sense of bewildering inconstancy as well. Soon therafter, the author announces the impending dawn and introduces the next phase as one characterized not only by more calm but also by greater clarity and constancy of image. That is, indeed, the case and the contrast is all the more striking because the preceding survey of life, which was conducted from a "realistic" perspective, contains not one single image but only abstract generalizations. The concrete "reality" of the outside world to which the self supposedly owes its experiences is actually depicted in thoroughly unsubstantial terms that belie any such assumption. In effect, Novalis has his dreamer reexecute Kant's "Copernican Revolution" by showing that there are no concrete objects as "things in themselves" to which experiential reality may refer. Things are not "in themselves"; rather, they are "phenomena," which means that the immediacy of their images refers to the self's creativity in forming them and not to the external origin of their givenness. After the dreaming self has dreamed the dream of pre-Kantian dogmatism to its unsatisfactory conclusion, it progresses toward an appreciation of the phenomenal quality that attaches to the objects of consciousness. This readjustment in perspective is indicated by the precision and detail of the imagery that now begins to appear, not with reference to the independent reality of a world determining the self's fate but expressive of the self's free agency in shaping that world.

First, Heinrich is shown to be moving away from tumultuous engagement, climbing through the isolating darkness of a forest to higher, brighter, and more distant spheres. After the upward movement of withdrawal, the journey proceeds inward, where it ends in a cave from which a bright light beckons. It is a sphere of light bathed in golden radiance by a fountainlike emanation, which rebounds off the ceiling's enclosing wall in countless sparklets that are gathered into a great pool at the base. The symbolism of the entire display, accented and reinforced by the Goethean color scheme, shows a spontaneous force reflecting against limiting confines in order to have those reflections comprehended into a whole, which is exactly the pattern of operation Novalis would ascribe to the imagination. But the pool is not yet world; to be that, it has to surround a self, an ego, with whom it can interact.

Confronted with colors to be seen and activity whose "holy silence" (*heilige Stille*) is registered by ear, the self Heinrich projects as the constant object of his dream approaches the basin, tastes its contents, and immerses himself in them. The flood, appearing as a manifold of colors, ("[das Becken wogte] mit unendlichen Farben'') (I, 196, l. 29) surrounds him and becomes his environment as sensation perceives it to be. All of the senses, except one, are carefully mentioned in order to establish them as areas of tangency, for which reason, it would seem, touch is the one most emphasized. In other words, the imagination transforms the otherness of pure limit into an inner reality for the self and that action is itself depicted within and for the self as a relationship of kinship between the self and the limiting realm. This kinship is experienced as sensibility and the various modes enumerated so far represent inner qualifications of the world outside.

Sight, hearing, taste, and touch modify the outer reality that is perceived and are therefore best suited to characterize the interaction between ego and nonego as one comprising the dual moments of external limit and inner creativity. The sense of smell requires a different sort of interaction, one that is based on reciprocity across the limit, just as the inhaling and exhaling of air in the life-giving act of breathing demonstrates. Consequently, olfaction only occurs in the third phase of the dream, which deals with the self's capability to enter into a free relationship with the nonego that allows for mediation instead of limitation.

In the second phase, there is no mediation; there is only limit. The dream's stage is restricted to a cave and the reality of an outer world can be recognized only as the limiting effect of the cave's confines on the fountain's activity. This relationship exhibits the same structural pattern as does light modified by darkness or self immersed in a continuum of sensual affect. In each case, the mutual ground for relationship can only be gained at the cost of the fountain's, the light's, and the self's respective identities. The fountain disperses into sparklets that are regathered in a common pool, light appears as the entire cave's golden illumination that is refracted in the pool's seething mixture of colors, and the self is lost in the erotic bliss of sensual communality.

All impressions to which the self is subject would remain as indistinct by themselves as the multicolored liquid that surrounds the bather in the dream. They do take on distinct shapes, however, with reference to the self's capability to think and order the universe of its environment. That very process is visualized by the dreamer as he sees the thoughts and feelings stimulated by the immersion actually materalize around him in the pool. With this last installment, the vision is complete and the conscious perception of a world containing the self has been shown to originate with a process that entails spontaneous action from within reflected against a limit imposed from without. The dreamer has seen himself, not just as the primary and only constant object of consciousness but as the creative force constructing the world within which that objectified self takes its place as one object among others. Expressed in the symbolic imagery of dreams — symbolic because it functions outside the framework of mimetic equivalence — Heinrich has just beheld the self as it is defined in the theoretical part of the *Wissenschaftslehre*.

The cave contains the fountain and its products, as consciousness comprehends the products of the imagination we refer to as objects. Objects, however, hide their origin because they seem to be conveyed to consciousness by the senses from an external reality or, to employ the language of the dream, the sparklets in the pool seem to emanate from the wall. The cave image traces the whole cycle, of which consciousness remains unaware while it is engaged in acts of common cognition. This lack of awareness results in the major tenets of pre-Kantian dogmatism that subscribe to the primacy of external reality, which would leave the self wholly determined in its cognitive and practical functions. The dream vision has the advantage of showing that the walls of limitation most certainly are a necessary and determinative requisite for the pool of perceptions from which we construct our world, but not its only requisite and definitely not its source.

Cognition, so the dream demonstrates, requires that the self be determined; however, it also demonstrates that the self be determined as a self whose identity is not the equivalent of any of its determined states. If action is not determined, then it is free, which means that the nondetermined state of self-identity is a condition of free activity that precedes its modification, just as the fountain's spontaneity precedes the wall's limiting effect on it. Objects of consciousness are modifications of the self's spontaneity and the golden aura of the cave's interior would be the proper lighting in which that truth could find recognition.

Light modified by darkness is yellow, with the accent on the power of light and not on the force of the modifier. This accentuation is amplified by the substitution of "gold" for "yellow," and it is gold whose radiance dominates the entire scene, allowing it to come into view. To the extent that the cavern is brightened by the jet's golden rays, the focus remains on the fountain's spontaneity, even though it may suffer the wall's impact, and on the self's identity, even though it may merge with the contents of the pool. Yellow is the visible manifestation of light's primacy in contact with darkness. This primacy is preserved in a state that necessarily entails its modification, just as the self's own freedom is preserved in its state of dependence on the givenness of sense perceptions that make the conscious apprehension of world and self in the world possible. Whatever the effect of darkness may be, gold prevails because it represents an absolute color in the Goethean scheme Novalis has adopted, the absolute color native to the sphere of light. It may be hidden from view in the multicolored mix of life but it is never lost. The task is to search it out behind the petrified walls of limitation that enclose it, be that task pursued as a dreamer who gains access to the self's innermost reaches or as a miner of the type to whom the fifth chapter, the central chapter of the nine, is dedicated, or as a poet who knows, as Klingsohr does, that Fable, the spirit of poesy, works her wonders with gold and spins her golden thread into eternity. Of the miner and Fable more will be said later on; they are mentioned now in order to furnish some indication how central the symbol of gold is to the entire novel and how consistent it is with the significance it acquires in the dream's context.

The fountain's light illuminates the cave but its golden yellow is not the only color mentioned. There is also a faint bluish tint along the walls. Blue comes into being as darkness crosses over into the sphere of light, and in this case, darkness is the impenetrable otherness of an opaque mass of rocks that may only gain entry to the fountain's domain as its limitation. The blue tint along the walls indicates that their limiting effect on the golden beam characterizes the relationship between the outer sphere of darkness and the inner sphere of light. It is a relationship where limit, or rather otherness, remains the prevalent feature, not because blue appears in the sphere of light — that underscores the sameness without which relationship would not be possible at all — but because blue must be identified with walls.

This reminder that there is an extraneous opposing force shifts the accent from the primacy of spontaneous action to the modifying influence it must undergo. Yellow is now hidden among the infinite variation of colors in the glittering pool, which reunites the fountain's dispersed energy just as consciousness gathers the variables of limitation the self's freedom of agency encounters and registers as sense impressions. All colors are derived from yellow and blue, according to Goethe's theory, and the colorful manifold at the base of the cave has no other ingredients. Here, too, the color symbolism parallels an aspect of consciousness, in particular the composition of its contents, which are products of freedom and limitation or, in terms of the dream's imagery, products of the golden fountain and its encounter with the bluish wall. The sense impressions, which result from this process and from which the self constructs the world of objects, are contained within the confines of consciousness insofar as they are the self's creation, but insofar as they are representative of the self's limitation, they also assume an external reality.

The dual reality of objects of consciousness is made obvious in the bathing scene where the inner and outer aspects of sensibility are treated as though they were indistinguishable in their uniform rapport. As a sign that the self's freedom of creativity is not left out from this image, the author employs color once again. When Heinrich is about to enter the pool after having established initial sensual contact, it seems to him as though he were enveloped in a reddish glow similar to that of the setting sun (I, 196, l. 36). This image not only conveys a transition from day to night but also, by way of parallel emphasis, a transition from light to dark that produces a red hue, which is the color the sphere of light projects into its dark counterpart. In the exact same manner, the objects of consciousness are projected outward as the formed reality that surrounds the self. Indeed, the entire inner world of the cavern stays behind as the dreamer leaves it and floats into the rocks, still immersed and carried by the pool's tide but overcome by sleep at the moment of transition.

He falls asleep to the world of his consciousness because its externalized version does not include the vision of the fountain as its origin and effectively denies the spontaneity of its source within the self's freedom. In the waking state, to which he would be released after the world has been constructed as shown in the dream, only the final product and not its genesis is apparent to consciousness. The world simply is there and is the environment on which the self depends. Viewed from its outcome, the process that brings world and self before consciousness appears in reverse order. Limitation is now the most immediate, and therefore primary, factor, whereas the self is once removed and its actions merely serve to provide for accommodation within the imposed limits. This is the daytime world of wakeful, pragmatic concerns, a world as unyielding in its otherness as the rock outside the cave, only the self has now become part of it and the magic cavern is lost from view. The gold is well hidden but it remains at the core, guarded by walls of stone and some, like the miner in the central chapter, prove capable of braving the barrier.

Heinrich is not yet ready to reenter this daytime world. He has glimpsed the secret of its beginnings, has observed it take shape, has caught sight of its golden essence, but that vision is incomplete and does not overcome the power of the walls. The self's inner spontaneity in constructing the world must be matched by an outer spontaneity, unless the walls are to retain authority over the self in the external realm from which they have blocked the golden fountain. Its rediscovery can only be effected by those who have the secret to penetrate the world of stone, who have the power to make it yield and cause it to be transformed from frozen rigidity into living organicity. That fluidity of interactive response between self and world has already been demonstrated in the cavern's pool. The relationship is one of sensual intercourse and occurs most definitely under Eros's spell. Externalized, the fluidity of that relationship does freeze, however, into determinative rigor where the limiting impact of physical dependence rules supreme, unless the self can prove itself to be as free of it here, in the practical realm, as it did in the theoretical realm.

In the third phase of the dream, Heinrich sees himself in surroundings quite different from the ones he had just left behind. Inanimate rock formations have been replaced by organic plant life and the oppressive closeness of walls has been supplanted by the dark blue expanse of the sky. The change is so dramatic that it is difficult, at first, to recognize any resemblance between this setting and the last. However, fountain, light, and self do make their reappearance and are as central to the present scene as they had been to the previous one. Here, as there, the complex of this triad stands for the differing functional contexts of triune selfhood: the fountain's spontaneity for the self's freedom of agency, the light's various hues for the self's interaction with the nonego, and Heinrich's own presence in the dream for the self's appearance before consciousness as its constant object that is endowed with sentience. These functional contexts remain the same but there is a marked difference in the circumstances under which they are envisioned. There are no more walls to obstruct the jet stream, which now extends upward without limits, in heaven's direction but not reaching it; gleaming gold has given way to a field of light, unusually bright and somehow superior to daylight, in which "light blue" (*lichtblau*) (I, 197, 1. 17) appears as the dominant color; and Heinrich has emerged from the pool, which has been replaced by flowers in whose midst there is a light blue one of such charm, it captivates all his attention, so that it comes to represent the central focus and sum total of his environment.

In contrast to the cave, a marked absence of limitation is the most pronounced feature in this phase of the dream. Nothing could better embody the elusive concept of self-enactment than the image of a fountain shaping itself by the unmitigated power of its own spontaneous energy. This fountain gives itself its own rule and it progresses unimpeded by any limitation that would curtail the domain of its authority. The rocks are there but they are at some distance and in no position to offer resistance to the fountain's activity, which freely extends outward, enacting its own being just as the self would in its capacity of moral agent.

The fountain ascends skyward, complemented by the absolute, inclusive sphere that its own efforts approximate. The heavens are "midnight blue," actually "black-blue" (*schwarzblau*) (I, 197, 1. 16), which signifies that they are infinitely removed yet turned toward the world since "black" is pure darkness and "blue" is the color darkness radiates into the sphere of light; moreover, they are also "clear" (*völlig rein*) (I, 197, ll. 16–17) so there is nothing to interrupt the continuity between the fountain and the absolute sphere, as there is nothing to obstruct the same relationship in reverse.

The moral idea, in accordance with which the self acts as a free agent, admits of no limit that might separate the self from it. It is as clear and as absolute in its inclusiveness as the sky at which the fountain is aimed; it is also as unattainable because it constitutes an imperative that may be realized in any one or any number of acts, but it is not a goal to be realized by them. The fountain striving ever upward in free self-assertion under the absolute sky's all-inclusive yet infinitely remote arch is the central image and it would have been sufficient if the self Heinrich has revealed to him in his dream were to be the one Fichte envisioned as a free practical agent. Novalis has, however, expanded Fichte's vision into a "*höhere Wissenschaftslehre*," and the imagery of the dream accommodates its added dimension of mediation and receptivity.

The fountain is central but right beside it are both Heinrich and the blue flower. Next to the fountain's pure activity, Heinrich's utter inactivity is all the more striking. He is completely passive, purely receptive and "sees nothing but the blue flower" ("Er sah nichts als die blaue Blume") (I, 197, 1. 21). It is the sort of receptivity that is only possible from the perspective of freedom, and that perspective is certainly the one under which this world appears, a world that holds no obstacles for the fountain's freedom of agency. Pure activity and pure passivity are here conjoined into the active passivity that is at the heart of the *"höhere Wissenschaftslehre."* Also at its heart is Novalis's theory of mediation, which finds its most compelling expression in the symbol of the blue flower.

A great many flowers surround Heinrich and this, his immediate environment, is as alive with colors as had been the one in the cave. Nonetheless, there is a slight but telling difference to which Novalis alerts the reader by a subtle variation in the terminology. He employs attributes indicative of colorful profusion to amplify the variability of circumstances comprising the world, or environment, within which we conduct our lives. In the first phase of the dream he uses the phrase "ein unendlich buntes Leben" (I, 196, l. 9), where "bunt" implies a collective of variegation without any detectable coherence or order. As the principles governing the interaction between self and world become more apparent and colors begin to assume their definite place within that framework, the panorama of life is still depicted as a colorful mix but one with more distinctive features. The phrase is now no longer "unendlich bunt" but rather "unendliche Farben" ("colors in infinite array") (I, 196, l. 29), and finally, in the third phase, the open-ended "unendlich" is dropped altogether in order to be replaced by the inclusive concept of "alle" ("all") (I, 197, l. 20), which converts the indistinct multiplicity of colors into a coherent totality.

Light and dark are not considered opposing spheres in this last context but rather the extreme ends of an expanded point of tangency that spans the entire range of color. Here the polarity of opposition reveals its true nature and proves to be a field of living interaction where the movement from light to dark is complemented by a movement from dark to light. As is the case with magnetism, the polar extremes of light and dark form an energy field. The two phenomena of color and magnetism are definitely associated in Novalis's mind, only magnetism stands for the principle of polarity in general — for which reason "Iron" plays such an important role in Klingsohr's tale — whereas color is less abstract and more specific in its immediate appeal to the eye. Organicity entails the same principle of polar resolution and identifies it as the principle of life for which the mechanistic dualism of cause and effect constitutes a sphere of reciprocal interaction where cause is as much effect as effect is cause. The organic complex is from the very beginning what it is going to be, and the causal chain of its development does not stretch aimlessly into infinity but is met at every moment by the comprehensive unity of its final form.

Heinrich finds himself in a world that is carefully depicted as one in which polar opposition has no place, except within the context of its resolution. It is a world of flowers where each particular object is an organic whole, an entity free in its own identity yet also representative of all others. There, the law of the individual is the law of all, just as it is for the morally free agent, and otherness does not constitute an exclusive or limiting moment but rather an inclusive continuum that extends from one to all because it also extends from all to one. The wall of separation between polar extremes has been transformed into a field of mediation that is an avenue from one to the other in either direction; or, more specifically, just as the self strives toward the full realization of the moral law under whose unifying authority the antagonism between self and world is suspended, the world may reveal its kinship and manifest that same law by presenting a human face to the self.

As Heinrich lies next to the fountain of freedom, the heavenly sphere and all the flowers under it converge on him in the one flower whose light blue color — the only color he sees — identifies it as a messenger to the field of light from the dark expanse the fountain approaches. Where the fountain of freedom emanates, there is the center where the dualism of the self's subjective and objective moments is suspended; there also is the center of the universe where the blue flower grows through which the infinitely removed sphere that comprehends the world may descend upon Heinrich and confirm this suspension in a reciprocal movement.[9] "World is to be self," longs the free agent, and "I am you," comes the response as the flower bends down toward Heinrich and opens its blue corolla to his view in order to display a human face at the center.

Spheral imagery is quite pronounced in this last phase of the dream. There are three distinctive variants and each represents a different aspect of the "basic schema" in its completed form as an absolute sphere that is the synthesis of two spheres tending in opposite directions. The absolute sphere is unlimited or infinite, that is to say, it is an expansive momentum, away from any potential center, and the sky in its black remoteness certainly depicts this relationship. No matter how expansive the momentum, the absolute sphere is also always identical with itself and forms a totality, an inclusive sphere that points back toward its center. The flowers of all colors are such a totality and the absolute sphere reflects back upon itself through them, which is indicated by their being grouped around one particular flower whose color is blue. The center itself must be a point of emanation into infinity and a point of return from there, a point of free agency and a point of passivity that stands ready to receive the countermovement from the outside as its own. As a free agent, the self moves into the center, which is where the fountain is and where Heinrich finds himself when he awakes next to it. However, the point of emanation is just the potential center of an absolute sphere, unless it is established in this position from the all-inclusive periphery whose center it is supposed to be. As a periphery, the infinite expanse of the absolute sphere assumes an identity only with reference to its center, and this relationship is symbolized by the final image, with which the dream concludes. The flower's petals form a sphere comprising a complex of radii, blue in color, that radiate inward merging into a "delicate face" ("zartes Gesicht") (I, 197, l. 26), the face Heinrich will later recognize as his love.

Fountain and remote *black*-blue sky, sky again — black-*blue* — bounding a field of vision filled with flowers centered around a blue one, and the round blue corolla from whose middle the world proclaims its identity with Heinrich, these are the three variants of the spheral image that dominate the dream's last phase. Collectively, they represent the "basic schema's" extensive and intensive spheres in perfect congruence not only with reference to a common point of tangency but also with reference to a common sphere, an absolute sphere that is called neither "I" nor "God" (II, 108, ll. 1–2) because it is both and its proper name would be "Thou" ("Statt N[icht] I[ch] — Du") (III, 430, l. 5).

Once again, Novalis has Eros forge the bond that links self to world and world to self. To be sure, that union has not yet been consummated and is still only a promise, but the power capable of bringing this event about has been identified. The story of the dream's fulfillment, which is also the story of Eros, is told in Klingsohr's tale. It is really more of an allegorical myth than a fairy tale, a product of his youth, as Klingsohr claims, a product of our culture's youth, as the variation on a Platonic theme makes evident. However, it is a variation quite new and youthful in its own right because, aside from the figure of Eros, it creates its own mythology against an entirely different philosophical background.

The dreamer in the first chapter dreams about himself and discovers the world; the narrator in the last chapter conveys that discovery in a dream of his own, in that peculiar kind of dream all can share. It is a spoken dream, spoken by someone who would actually have to experience the world as it had appeared to Heinrich. Unless that shift in perspective has occurred, dreams must retain the status of private illusions because they simply are not "true" if told in a language limited in its applicability to the waking state. Heinrich learns very quickly that dream reality is not easily translated into waking reality when his efforts to do so meet with his father's good-natured skepticism regarding the value of dreams in general (I, 198, ll. 11ff). The father knows himself only as a determined being, an individual whose link to others must be the determinant he has in common with them. Images, be they dreamed, thought, or expressed in words, can have validity for him only because they reflect this common ground of reference, which is the concrete givenness of the objective world as a causal nexus of necessity. He, too, had had a dream as a young man, quite similar to Heinrich's; he, too, had seen a flower, but he had also been quick to associate this vision with the world from where he had come, a world to which he returned after his dream with thoughts of marriage and eager to establish himself in his craft.

In his language a flower is a flower and a human face a human face. He is right, of course, because in the order of causal relationships, according to which our rational faculty understands the information received by sense perception, flowers cannot have a human face. He never dreamed his dream to an end since the waking world intruded too soon, and when he thinks or says "flower," it means something else than it does for Heinrich. The reason for this discrepancy is not that their words refer to different objects but that those words refer the same object to different levels of self-consciousness; Heinrich's refer to a self that is free in determining its activity but not awake, the father's to a self that is awake but not free. If both are to understand one another, it can only be with reference to a self that is conscious of its freedom in a waking state, and the self attains this sort of consciousness as a moral being.

The law according to which the self forms its images while dreaming is its own, and if that law is to have more than purely subjective applicability, it must be one all selves hold in common. The moral law is such a law, and how the world appears from its vantage point is a dream whose many versions all individuals may share. The act of dreaming is itself equivalent to the activity depicted in the cave-phase of Heinrich's dream; before he shares it, he will have to realize its last phase, which he does in the chapters that follow. Klingsohr's tale concludes this process with a demonstration of the poet's craft that enables those who have mastered it to speak the language of waking dreams and reclaim the imagination's sovereignty over the world. The poet speaks with moral authority, not as a moralizing pedant but as a free individual who invites everyone else to share his perspective of the world. His statements are those of a free agent and they proclaim the sovereignty of the imagination because they address an audience of peers capable of following his invitation and of acknowledging that sovereignty in themselves. Klingsohr's tale is a commentary on the liberating power of the spirit of poesy, a commentary vouched for by his own practice as he tells the story to a receptive circle of listeners. They, however, remain out of sight because those listeners are we ourselves, and it is actually we who are asked to realize the truth of Novalis's poetics as he has Klingsohr present them to us.

The loving union between self and world anticipated in the dream is the very theme with which the tale begins. Although they are separated initially, the two realms confront one another in mutual attraction, and, as the narrative unfolds, Eros bridges the gap, aided by Fable, the spirit of poesy. Their task will be to dispel the ice age that has settled over a world where everything seems entirely foreign, except for the familiar images of fountain and flowers. There is no sky that arches over this setting; instead, heaven with its stars now appears in the form of a palace whose king is lord over a city of ice and a garden of crystalline flowers that harbor the fountain's frozen jet in their midst. There are indications, though, that the great thaw is about to set in and that the palace grounds will come alive once the "beautiful stranger" (*der schöne Fremde*) (I, 292, l. 13) arrives and has completed his mission. When that time comes, as it does in the concluding scene, the ice will melt and the fountain will flow, the sparkling crystals will turn into living blossoms that burst forth everywhere, the king's daughter will be Eros's, the "beautiful stranger's" bride, and Fable will initiate the new era of their royal union with a final song in which she proclaims their rule to have been established forever. As Fable sings, she spins forth a golden thread emanating from within her, and this last image completes the cycle from dream to fairy tale because, in symbol as in deed, in Klingsohr's story as in his telling it, the golden stream of the imagination is obviously no longer confined to the cavern of internal freedom.

King Arctur's frozen world is the realm of nature viewed as the external counterpart of the dream's cave. It, too, is bounded by a "wall of rock formations" (*Berggürtel*) (I, 291, l. 6), and its law of dynamic flux remains hidden within those confines. Only after Iron hurls his sword against the wall of stone where it breaks up into pieces creating a shower of sparklets do the iron fragments and their magnetic properties point the way to nature's secret, which awaits its discovery by the self in an act of self-recognition; "ego = nonego — ultimate sentence of all *science* and *art*" ("*Ich* = N[icht] I[ch] — höchster Satz aller *Wissenschaft* und *Kunst*") (II, 542, l. 25), Novalis had already said more than a year earlier, and that formula applies here as well. Its fundamental truth is known to Fable because she is able to practice it, for which reason she is also the only one who moves effortlessly between Arctur's realm and the self's household. Her task is to remove the "non," represented by a third realm of total darkness where the Fates reside, and thus reveal the nonego's hidden identity with the ego.

Heinrich's dream is an entirely personal experience, and yet it is potentially everyone's. Klingsohr realizes this potential, and in order to do so his tale contains no persons at all but only a group of allegorical figures that represent the self's various faculties and features. This group forms a household with all the familial ties, economic implications, and isolating aspects the term suggests. The prevailing relationships and their allegorical significance are not difficult to discern. There are a father who goes in and out of the house and may be identified with the senses, a mother busy with housework who represents the heart as seat of the self's caring and nurturing inclinations, a nursemaid named Ginnistan, recognizable as the imagination, and the two infants Eros and Fable, the mother's and Ginnistan's offspring from the same father. Collectively, the first three circumscribe the self's theoretical (Ginnistan) and practical (mother) functions in its sense-determined state; the children are a generation removed, therefore freer of the senses and purer embodiments of their respective mothers' characteristics. Two further members complete the household. One is a scribe who composes a written record of information he receives from the father, the other a priestess, Sophie by name, who tests the scribe's pages and determines whether his words are to endure. The context in which they are presented identifies the scribe as "discursive reason" (*Verstand*) and the priestess as a form of reason superior to it. Such rational supremacy may be thought of in Jacob Böhme's sense as eternal wisdom descended to the human realm (I, 638, note to p. 291), but

Sophie's critical authority has a more appropriate parallel in the regulatory function Kantians assign to the "ideas" of "intuitive reason" (*Vernunft*).

Since it is externally determined, the scribe's activity is in itself an acknowledgment of a state of dependence that reduces the world to a bleak temple in which there can be no gospel other than the arbitrary decree of fate and no commandment other than pragmatic purpose. Sophie introduces an entirely different perspective. She is Arctur's wife, which means that the law of nature and the one she represents in the intellectual realm potentially coincide. The nether world of blackness and negation where the three sisters spin, measure, and cut the thread of life (I, 301, l. 16–302, l. 2) has no power over her because it is not her world. Her color is not black; it is blue[10] because she inspires not a sense of opposition but a spirit of continuity between the self's household and the whole of nature. Continuity means suspension of opposition, and this freedom has its priestess in Sophie, who is not only Fable's godmother (I, 310, ll. 8–9) but also a source of sustenance for Eros as he sets out on his journey into the world (I, 295, ll. 14–15). Both children can thus practice their inherited powers in freedom, which enables Eros to aim beyond the restrictions of sensual confinement and endows Fable with the capacity to reclaim the territory discursive reason usurped in the name of mechanistic causality and materialistic fatalism.

The spirit of poesy is not restricted to the literary arts, nor even to art itself. It pertains to all areas of human endeavor since it redefines the relationship between self and world from the perspective of freedom. Accordingly, Fable pursues her mission by redefining the self as free from the decrees of fate, which entails the corollary act of redefining nature as free from the petrifying decree that reduces it to a lifeless mechanism. "The great enigma," Novalis had said, "is basically solved" once the self discovers the outer world to be as much its own as the inner world because it is the "absolute center" for both (II, 528, ll. 8–15). That enigmatic aspect is depicted in Klingsohr's tale by the nether world of death and fate guarded by a sphinx who, true to her mythological function, poses a barrier of questions and riddles. In answering her, Fable shows that the poetic perspective leads to the very discovery Novalis had mentioned, that is, to the new philosophy by means of which the "great enigma" may be declared unreal. To the question, "What do you want?" ("was suchst du?") she answers "what belongs to me" ("mein Eigenthum") (I, 301, l. 27), and during her second interview, when asked "who knows the world?" ("wer kennt die Welt?") she presses the point by replying "he who knows himself" ("wer sich selbst kennt") (I, 308, ll. 9–10). She concludes each session with a reference to Sophie, which adds final authority to her statements and succeeds in confounding the inquisitive guardian. Once the Sphinx is defeated, the realm she protects no longer holds any threat and all of it is banished to the nihilistic void that the Fates had reserved for those who did not have the answer to the "great enigma" of existence. As the power of fate declines, so does the estrangement from nature and the rigidity of a materalistic universe gives way to an all-pervasive organicity. Again, it is Fable, this time as the spirit of poesy applied to the natural sciences, who possesses the clarity of vision to assemble the ingredients for a galvanic chain[11] and fashion them into a key with which she can release nature from the prison walls of matter (I, 310, l. 9–313, l. 30). The walls in question imprison nature as much as they do the self and the release of one means the release of the other. For this reason, Fable's key is also instrumental in effecting Ginnistan's permanent union with the father, which signifies the merger of outer and inner reality in perfect mirrorlike (I, 311, ll. 30–36) correspondence. Finally, the magic chain must work its wonder for Eros as well and help him in waking Arctur's daughter, Freya, to the new reality that is to be the era of their joint rule.

Fable's key could not have been put to such good use, unless Eros had been prepared to employ it. The story of his travels since he had left home in search of his beloved is one that follows a traditional pattern.[12] The peace that ends all longing, which is the "peace" Freya's name implies (I, 293; l. 24; 638, note to p. 291), is Eros's goal, but it cannot be found in a dreamworld that is mistaken for reality. Ginnistan, whom Sophie had assigned as his guide, leads Eros to her father's kingdom, which is the moon's kingdom of dreams, where she stages an elaborate performance for her companion's benefit. In it she shows him the final union with his beloved and, still under the impression of this dream display (I, 300, ll. 31–33), he believes Ginnistan to be the object of his love. She seduces him and the result is that, from then on, he continues to pursue his goal in the same disoriented manner, mistaking fictive substitutes for the true reality he actually seeks. As had been the case with Heinrich, dream reality is to become waking reality. Only this time the entire process of living is to become an uninterrupted waking dream told in a world where wakefulness does not mean the endorsement of an external criterion of objectivity, nor its replacement by an internal one, but rather the full and permanent realization that both are the same. That realization would also be the final realization of Heinrich's dream and the event leading to one would be of equal importance to the other.

Eros regains his original sense of mission only after his mother, the heart, suffers total devastation at the hands of discursive reason. However, her death also means the end of that usurper's rule, and thereafter the new era may be ushered in. It is an era in which she comes to be identified with all, as Sophie's last words proclaim: "The mother is among us, her presence will bless us in eternity" ("Die Mutter ist unter uns, ihre Gegenwart wird uns ewig beglücken") (I, 315, ll. 15–16). She describes a permanent state of self-identification with the other, one that is not bound to any one object because it applies to all. The heart, bound as it is to particular objects, will have to be "orphaned," as Novalis says ("verwaisen") (I, 319, l. 86), will have to lose the one object it treasures most before Eros can reach his goal. Giving up that object means giving up that one blue flower so that all may be blue. Renewal through bereavement had been Novalis's own experience. Dreamlike in its personal nature, his experience is the dream he has us share in Klingsohr's Tale. In Heinrich's tale, he tells us first of the preparatory path that must be traveled before the freedom of vision may be attained from which Klingsohr speaks.

Chapter 9
The Journey

Dreams, Heinrich tells his father, might well be a "significant rending apart of the mysterious curtain that extends with myriad folds into our interior" ("'ein bedeutsamer Riß in den geheimnisvollen Vorhang . . . der mit tausend Falten in unser Inneres hereinfällt'') (I, 198, l. 35–199, l. 1). He means to imply that the opaque otherness behind which the world we know remains hidden may not be as impenetrable as we are accustomed to believe. At least, that is Heinrich's suspicion kindled by the vivid impression with which the dream releases him into waking reality. Verification of this suspicion would mean that the curtain of estrangement is gradually lifted, giving way to an ever greater degree of transparence where self and world had stood embattled in mutual opposition. A journey into the world would then simultaneously be a journey to the self, or rather a progression in world-consciousness would also be a progression in self-consciousness, until both reveal themselves to be one. Fichte's entire philosophy derives from the fundamental insight that they are indeed one, and Novalis's *"höhere Wissenschaftslehre"* rests on the same foundation. Consequently, Heinrich follows an outward path that has its exact inward counterpart and each advance in one direction registers as progress in the other.

The first phase along this twofold path describes a movement that is best characterized in the author's own words at its conclusion: "Everything [Heinrich] saw and heard only seemed to push aside another crossbar in him and to open new windows" ("Alles was [Heinrich] sah und hörte schien nur neue Riegel in ihm wegzuschieben und neue Fenster ihm zu öffen") (I, 268, ll. 2–4). Heinrich's experiences essentially serve to remove the barrier of exclusion that separates

121

the inner and outer spheres of reality from one another. Each step reveals another facet of their possible coincidence and brings him closer to the center of their mutual identity. Initially, he ventures forth from his familar surroundings keenly aware of separation and of encounter with a world at once beckoning with promise yet also alien and overcast with the foreboding shadow of death's final authority. From this position of contrast at which self and world stand opposed, Heinrich advances toward the midpoint where the conflicting spheres merge. Each chapter highlights the goal of this journey from a different perspective but the concept of synthesis and the symbolic configuration of centrality remain constant, up to the fifth and central chapter of the nine from which Heinrich emerges ready to experience the world as Thou.

The narrative structure bears the unmistakable imprint of the "basic schema." At one extreme is the purely subjective reality of Heinrich's dream, at the other the objectified dream-reality of Klingsohr's tale, and their common ground appears at the center where the curtain of myriad folds swings open to afford a view of nature that uncovers the hidden gold beneath its stony surface and the self's identity amid the changing currents of time. The dream occurs in a timeless state suspended between the revolutions of night and day. Suspended, also, are the claims of an external world to products of the free imagination. Once the dreamer is awake, these claims, along with those of temporal succession, exert their right, and consciousness no longer is felt to be identical with its object but separated from it. As the dream showed, the cavern's pool, which constitutes the self's environment, does not have its origin from beyond the walls; they make it seem as though this were the case by redirecting the fountain's energy, but in doing so they also hide the true source of the world to which the self is consciously awake. That world appears to be alien and may seem unyielding in its otherness, yet at the core of its hardened layers there is the fountain's petrified trace, its golden essence that waits to be freed by those who, like the miner, approach nature in the spirit of selflessness. It is this spirit Heinrich is led to recognize throughout his sojourn to Augsburg, and as he recognizes it, he realizes its efficacy for himself.

Selflessness is the key that unlocks the crossbars of which Heinrich speaks and removes the barrier of dependence behind which the world would hold the self captive in a state of permanent separation. When it maintains an attitude of selflessness, the self relates freely to the objects comprising the world in which it lives; it is one of them and yet it has an identity entirely its own. As long as the self regards itself as dependent, it has no such identity and its sphere of interest in relating to the world remains confined to one of pragmatic accommodation within that world. Dependence imposes a servant's point of view, a servant who can exact a livelihood from his master by obeying orders without being able to account for the decision that gave rise to them. Incapable of determining the ultimate purpose for which he is used, the servant's own interest in the proceedings is necessarily reduced to the self-centered pragmatism of insuring his livelihood. Taken in this sense, selfishness is the practical attitude that lacks independence of purpose because the self fails to recognize its own identity. Such failure is founded on the belief that consciousness is entirely passive in its dependence on being given the objects it regards as real. However, not all objects are given to consciousness. The self is always present within it and that presence has no external cause, whereas any particular variant of the self's appearance does. Presenting itself to consciousness as affected by something else, the self seems to have no identity of its own, and the ever differing flow of its appearances tends to obscure the constancy of its presence. As the constant object of consciousness, though, the self is not susceptible to change and cannot be dependent on something else; rather, anything else introduced to consciousness is dependent on the unconditional identity of self-consciousness, which means that the self's freedom, and not its dependence, is the actual basis of the relationship between self and world. This truth is difficult to discern under the strictures the world imposes on the self's freedom in consequence of that relationship, but the difficulty is not insurmountable. The veil of objects that hides the self from itself may be lifted when selflessness replaces selfishness and the self knows itself to be free by being free. Once pragmatic interests are suspended, the world unfolds in its true relationship to the self and world-consciousness arises through self-consciousness, just as it does in the experience of dreaming. "World becomes dream" ("Die Welt wird Traum") (I, 319, l. 11), Novalis says in the introductory poem to part II of *Heinrich von Ofterdingen*, and his words can be read as a retrospective summary of the first five chapters where Heinrich's dream experience is complemented by his waking experience, until he sees "the world spread out before him in its vast and changing proportions" ("Er sah die Welt in ihren großen und abwechselnden Verhältnissen vor sich liegen") (I, 268, ll. 4–5).

"World becomes dream"; this transformation completes the first phase of the movement toward the center of the "absolute sphere" at which the "thesis" of self and the "antithesis" of world coincide. It is a movement marked by a shift in self-consciousness that establishes the immediacy of pure self-presence as the prerequisite rather than merely the subjective opposite of an objective reality. Once the self knows itself in a manner not based on opposition to the world, the world also ceases to oppose the self. It begins to speak the self's language and offers itself in confirmation of a reality that had previously been restricted to the freedom of association only granted in dreams. The dichotomy of self and world collapses as the self consciously assumes the perspective of freedom it inherently occupies in all processes of consciousness. That is its move toward the center, and while it occurs throughout the first five chapters, the world disappears from view as an opposing factor and "becomes dream." However, at the center the world reappears, now as the medium of the absolute sphere at whose center the self has taken its position. That is the reciprocal movement, the one anticipated outside the cave in Heinrich's dream and realized by him from the central chapter onward to the ninth, with which part I of the novel concludes. With this, the movement's second phase, the poem's line stands completed and "world becomes dream" is complemented by "dream becomes world" ("der Traum wird Welt") (I, 319, l. 11).

The pivitol remark has been cited in which Novalis describes Heinrich's condition at the beginning of chapter 6 as one resulting from a process of internal liberation that lets him see the world in its true proportions (I, 268, ll. 2–5). It refers only to the preceding chapters, to the movement's first phase, but already the next sentence points out the movement's complementary variant, which the protagonist has yet to experience. Spread out before him, the world "was still silent, and its soul, which is communication, had not yet come awake" ("Noch war sie aber stumm, und ihre Seele, das Gespräch, noch nicht erwacht") (I, 268, ll. 5–6). The world is still dream, but the dream is to be translated into the world's language and Heinrich will learn to converse in it. Those who are to teach him are conveyors of the "mother tongue" (*Muttersprache*) (I, 268, l. 7); they are a girl, whose kiss will strike the first chord of mutuality from world to self, and a poet, who will expand that basic theme for him in "infinite melodies" (*unendliche Melodien*) (I, 268, ll. 9–10).

The two phases of Heinrich's journey retrace the outlines of the "basic schema" for which the spheres of self and world are one. The outward journey of his travels to Augsburg is really inward since its progress is registered by an internal recognition of the self's freedom from the confining crossbars of estrangement; and the inward journey of his experiencing love's unfolding is really outward since the world is made ready through it to speak the language both world and self hold in common. Once the first word has been exchanged in the mother tongue and "thou" has been spoken, the great dialogue becomes possible to which the poet's craft bears witness. At this stage, it remains a possibility with which Heinrich becomes acquainted under Klingsohr's tutelage. The student can survey the promise of his own future in the master's example; to realize it, he must first experience the bitter loss of his beloved and learn that the world could speak to him through her only because it is she who speaks to him through the world. This final phase is the one outlined by the "*höhere Wissenschafts-lehre.*" It was to be developed in the novel's second part, whereas the first part essentially formulates its "Promise" ("Die Erwartung"), which Novalis had recognized in Fichte's *Wissenschaftslehre.*

Heinrich's initiation into that promise begins when his dream-encounter with the face in the blue flower becomes a waking encounter and that event occurs in response to his having arrived at the midpoint where the dichotomy collapses and world has become dream so that dream may become world. The theme of centricity had already been struck in the first chapter where the dream sequence takes place at dawn, when night meets day, and fulfillment of the father's dream is promised for "midsummer day toward eventide" ("am Tage Johannis gegen Abend") (I, 202, l. 9), when the daytime world is about to wane in the double sense of the annual and diurnal cycles. This promise applies not only to Heinrich's father but to everyone since it refers to the one dream of the blue flower each self dreams separately. The second chapter is even more emphatic in underscoring the same theme. In its opening statement, "midsummer was past" ("Johannis war vorbei") (I, 202, l. 32), the setting for Heinrich's future adventures is identified as daytime reality experienced under the growing influence of night. In other words, world is to become dream, and that transition has its origin and promise in the midpoint at which the dominance of day over night, of world over self, is held in check because it is also the point of mutual balance.

The dream had dislodged Heinrich from his habitual relationship to the world, which he had shared with everyone else before the stranger's arrival. Stirred by the poetic tale, the youth had undergone a change in which his world had quite literally become a dream. This change would not of itself have been extraordinary, except for his conviction that it was not peculiar to the state when sleep unfetters fancy but must pertain to waking reality as well. Since then, he had become "more inward" ("in sich gekehrter") (I, 203, l. 6), and that withdrawal from the old world is actually the precondition for a new encounter in which he is to grow aware of his changed perspective as a new world opens up before him. The dream has made him ready to see the world in a different light, a light no longer restricted by darkness because it springs from the common ground where both are joined in forming the living phenomenon of color. Novalis is very careful in this chapter to inform his readers that he does, indeed, envision color to originate at the point of tangency between light and dark:

> Wer wandelt nicht gern im Zwielichte, wenn die Nacht am Lichte und das Licht an der Nacht in höhere Schatten und Farben zerbricht; und also vertiefen wir uns willig in die Jahre, wo Heinrich lebte und jetzt neuen Begebenheiten mit vollem Herzen entgegenging.

> Who does not like to walk in the twilight, when night and light break up into higher shadings and colors as they encounter one another; and so, let us immerse ourselves willingly in the years when Heinrich lived and was, just then, about to go and meet new experiences with an eager heart.
>
> (I, 204, ll. 17–21)

This statement not only helps confirm the symbolism of the dream's color scheme but also serves here, above all, to emphasize the centricity of perspective that is necessary if the world is to be revealed in its entirety and complexity of variations, which it is by the time the author allows his protagonist to emerge from the central chapter (I, 268, ll. 4–5).

The time of twilight has its historical equivalent in the Middle Ages as the period centrally located ''between the crude age of barbarism and the modern age abounding in art, knowledge and wealth'' (''zwischen den rohen Zeiten der Barbaren und dem kunstreichen, vielwissenden und begüterten Weltalter'') (I, 204, ll. 14–15). It is a median era and it marks the same juncture for Novalis that ancient Greece did for Schiller in his *Aesthetic Letters*. Both see historical development as passing through a midpoint at which the human spirit emerges free from the bonds of nature and not yet distanced from her in prideful conceit nurtured by a false sense of superiority that all too readily tends to accompany achievements characteristic of the modern age. For example, the postmedieval abundance of art, knowledge, and wealth Novalis mentions is also an implicit allusion to the faults such riches have fostered. The wealth of goods (Novalis uses the attribute *begütert*) tends to possess the possessors, which elevates the dictate of commercial interest to the position of a categorical imperative; the abundance of knowledge (*vielwissend*) can lead rapidly to the supreme rule of discursive reason in the household of human affairs, as illustrated by the scribe's ascendancy to power in Klingsohr's tale; and even the ample endowment bestowed by the profusion of skill in all manner of arts (*kunstreich*) harbors the danger of encouraging faith in a self-created world culminating in a precious aestheticism that is sufficient unto itself and as barren in its superbity as the king's court in the next chapter's tale would have remained had not his daughter found her way beyond the palace's enclosure.

At the midpoint of the Middle Ages, dependence made manifest by want is no longer the sole criterion that determines an individual's relationship to the world. As the pressure of need lessens and the ''crudity'' of that relationship wanes, objects previously valued only for their utilitarian function may come to be appreciated in a freer context, a context that may again be threatened by the abundance of a later age:

> Die Pracht und Bequemlichkeit des fürstlichen Lebens dürfte sich schwerlich mit den Annehmlichkeiten messen, die in späteren Zeiten ein bemittelter Privatmann sich und den Seinigen ohne Verschwendung verschaffen konnte. Dafür war aber der Sinn für die Gerätschaften und Habseligkeiten, die der Mensch zum mannigfachen Dienst seines Lebens um sich her versammelt, desto zarter und tiefer. Sie waren den Menschen werter und merkwürdiger. Zog schon das Geheimnis der Natur und die Entstehung ihrer Körper den ahndenden Geist an: so erhöhte die seltnere Kunst ihrer Bearbeitung, die romantische Ferne, aus der man sie erhielt, und die Heiligkeit ihres Altertums, da sie sorgfältiger bewahrt, oft das Besitztum mehrerer Nachkommenschaften wurden, die Neigung zu diesen stummen Gefährten des Lebens. Oft wurden sie zu dem Rang von geweihten Pfändern eines besondern Segens und Schicksals erhoben, und das Wohl ganzer Reiche und weitverbreiteter Familien hing an ihrer Erhaltung.

For in those times the splendor and comforts of a prince could hardly compare with the amenities which in later times a well-to-do private individual could provide for himself and his own family without extravagance. On the other hand, the feeling people had for the utensils and possessions they gathered about them for the manifold service of life was all the more deep and tender. These things and possessions seemed more valuable and remarkable. The mystery of their nature and origin held great appeal for intuiting spirits, and people's attachment to these mute companions of life was heightened by the now uncommon art that had lent them shape, by the romantic distance from which they were received, and by the sacredness of their antiquity, since, when more carefully preserved, they often became the heirlooms of several generations. They were often elevated to the rank of consecrated pledges of a special blessing or lot, and the welfare of widely scattered families and of whole empires depended upon their preservation.

(I, 203, ll. 20–35; Hilty, 24–25)

Within this freer context, midway between barbarism and modernity, the world ceases to address the self merely as an individual defined by subjective needs, and objects begin to assume significance that may be shared with all humankind, not so much in terms of needs held in common but rather in terms of value held in common, regardless of need.

Whereas the barbarian, for all his communality, remains in subjective isolation from nature, the same danger arises for later ages at the other extreme where freedom may be confused with human self-sufficiency to the exclusion of nature. Be it governed by want or by pride, in either case the self displays a self-seeking attitude that prevents it from being receptive to anything beyond its confines. At the center, selflessness must prevail, a condition that is free from want and free from self-indulgence. Novalis calls it *"charming* poverty" (*"liebliche* Armut"*) (I, 203, l. 35), *"charming"* because the unsightly compulsion of need has given way to a more gracious mode of life, and "poverty" because it is a simple life, as poor in means of wealth as it is humble, or poor, in spirit. This aesthetic qualification of poverty indicates that the people so described have ceased to perceive nature merely as the inimical "other" whose challenging command, "survive against me as best you can!", constitutes the sole validating criterion for human action. No longer nature's bondsmen, they are able to survey their world and detect in it a significance that had necessarily remained concealed from eyes with a field of vision narrowed to the arena of physical survival.

The antagonism and one-sidedness of polar stress appears everywhere because it is the lens through which we perceive our reality. Its removal means opening "a new and higher kind of eye" ("ein neues höheres Auge") (I, 204, l. 5) and acquiring the ability to gain a view from the middle ground where the unity behind all opposition may be revealed as an economy of equal distribution that spans the range between the poles. This is the sort of economy Novalis means when he uses the term to link the distribution of light and dark to the concept of the Middle Ages:

> Eine *liebliche* Armut schmückte diese Zeiten mit einer eigentümlichen ernsten und unschuldigen Einfalt; und die sparsam verteilten Kleinodien glänzten desto bedeutender in dieser Dämmerung, und erfüllten ein sinniges Gemüt mit wunderbaren Erwartungen. Wenn es wahr ist, daß erst eine geschickte Verteilung von Licht, Farbe und Schatten die verborgene Herrlichkeit der sichtbaren Welt offenbart, und sich hier ein neues höheres Auge aufzutun scheint: so war damals überall eine ähnliche Verteilung und Wirtschaftlichkeit wahrzunehmen; da hingegen die neuere wohlhabendere Zeit das einförmige und unbedeutendere Bild eines allgemeinen Tages darbietet. In allen Übergängen scheint, wie in einem Zwischenreiche, eine höhere, geistliche Macht durchbrechen zu wollen, und wie auf der Oberfläche unseres Wohnplatzes die an unterirdischen und überirdischen Schätzen reichsten Gegenden in der Mitte zwischen den wilden, unwirtlichen Urgebirgen und den unermeßlichen Ebenen liegen, so hat sich auch zwischen den rohen Zeiten der Barbarei und dem kunstreichen, vielwissenden und begüterten Weltalter eine tiefsinnige und romantische Zeit niedergelassen, die unter schlichtem Kleide eine höhere Gestalt verbirgt.

> A *charming* poverty adorned those times with a peculiarly earnest and innocent simplicity; and in that twilight these treasures [i.e., the family heirlooms previously mentioned] gleamed all the more significantly for being sparingly distributed, and they filled the thoughtful heart with wondrous hopes. If it is true that only a skillful distribution of light, color, and shadow reveals the hidden glory of the visible world and that a new and higher kind of eye appears to open here, then it was this sort of distribution and economy that prevailed everywhere at this time; whereas the more prosperous modern age presents the monotonous and less significant monochrome scene of an all-pervasive day. During every period of transition higher spiritual powers appear to want to break through as in a sort of interregnum. And just as on the surface of our dwelling place the districts richest in natural resources above and below ground lie between the wild and inhospitable primeval mountains and the boundless plains, so between the rough and crude times of barbarism and the modern age abounding in wealth, art, and knowledge there was a reflective and romantic period concealing a higher form under its simple garment.

> (I, 203, l.35–204, l. 17; Hilty, 25)

Novalis injects these deliberations at the beginning of Heinrich's journey in order to point out the propitious historical setting that stands ready to aid the protagonist's progress and prefigures the central perspective he is to attain in his personal development.[13] Even the journey's end, Augsburg, is chosen with that centricity in mind. Like Munich of Thomas Mann's *Tonio Kröger*, Augsburg represents the median ground between north and south, but its location is indicative of polar equilibrium and not of polar stress, of "moral grace" in Schiller's sense and not of its amoral offspring in whose name Tonio must be judged a "*bourgeois manqué*." At Augsburg, as his travel companions, the merchants, report and Heinrich is to find out when he arrives there, the "freedom of aesthetic play" ("[die] freien Spiele und Erzeugnisse . . . des bildenden Tiefsinns") (I, 206, ll. 12–13) complements the workday's efforts and infuses all aspects of social life, particularly the evening's festivities, with an artistic or rather poetic spirit.[14]

Novalis's comments on the Middle Ages inform his readers that history, as the collective record of human endeavor, assumes its significance with reference to a criterion or principle that has universal applicability. Such universality can be attributed only to a principle that is the condition and not the derivative of experience. Incidental experiences may reflect more or less clearly the principle that makes them possible, but the principle itself resides with the agent rather than with the object of experience. In short, centricity is the reflection of the lens of self-consciousness through which the world is perceived and not an opportune juncture or accidental constellation among the objects of sense perception in time and space. The central perspective is removed from the determinative immediacy of experience because it includes an awareness of the self's free and undetermined state as the precondition for the self's determinability, that is to say, as the precondition for the relationship between self and world.

The remoteness of perspective in question is not simply a spatiotemporal dimension but one of disengagement from the demands of the moment. It is an attitude of selflessness, which makes a poetic relationship to the world possible, and poesy is the very topic broached by Heinrich's travel companions at the outset of the journey. At first, they do so quite spontaneously in their description of Augsburg, and thereafter in response to Heinrich's wish to hear all they know on the subject. As traders they have traveled widely and their opinions are based on what they have seen and heard. Theirs is the collective voice of experience, for which reason they do not speak as individuals but address their audience in unison. They are merchants, and this characterizes them not only as members of the social class that will rise to prominence in the postmedieval era but also — and this above all — as representatives of the commonsense rationalism that was to become the popular philosophical bias of our enlightened age, which is by no means its worst feature. Heinrich's questions concerning the arts meet with replies that are essentially the common property of informed opinion founded on observable practice. The merchants' discourse allows Heinrich to share the wealth of experience they possess as though he had himself been exposed to it. However, for Heinrich it is experience once removed, the same as theirs yet not gathered in the course of mercantile pursuits inspired by utilitarian concerns that recognize human existence only in terms of its dependent state.

The limits of this latter perspective quickly become apparent. First, its one-sidedness is made evident when the merchants declare the path of experience to be the sole avenue leading to valid judgments with regard to human affairs in the world. In contrast to them, Heinrich acknowledges two paths, the outer along with the inner: one as approaching the goal of universal validity and the other as the immediate guarantor of it. Obviously, the contours of the "basic schema" begin to emerge for him as he recognizes the complementary nature of the two paths, but his companions are not quite capable of matching his perspective. The merchants present a corrective to Heinrich's inwardness, which he is readily able to accept, and he, in turn, presents a corrective to their outwardness, which they admit "good-naturedly" (*gutmütig*) (I, 208, 1. 19) to be possible but quite foreign to their way of thinking. This is Heinrich's first step on the road of experience and it results in his first attempt to define for himself the central perspective from which world-consciousness reveals itself as self-consciousness.

The merchants' lack of central perspective and the limitations of the dogmatist position represented by the common voice of experience are illustrated not only in the discussion of the two paths but also — and even more pertinently — in the deliberations concerning the nature of art that follow. When asked to give an account of the poet's art, the merchants unhesitatingly confess that they are not acquainted with its "secrets" (*Geheimnisse*) (I, 209, 1. 9) because, unlike the other arts they cite (I, 209, 11. 12–34), it cannot be explained in terms of a mimetic principle. In their experience, words spoken by poets have an effect as though "one hears a foreign language and is able to understand it nonetheless" ("Man hört fremde Worte und weiß doch, was sie bedeuten sollen") (I, 210, 11. 10–11). It is not the language that is "foreign" — it stays exactly the same — but rather the referential context in which it is used. The poetic use of language requires suspension of the common prejudice, which is as common as are the univocally voiced opinions this prejudice supports, that the uniform ground of linguistic reference must be the self-sufficient reality of the objects referred to. To put it as succinctly as possible, the poet appeals to the self's freedom and not to its state of dependence as the uniform ground of mutual understanding. The merchants are fully aware of the appeal's negative connotation, whereas the source of its positive effect remains a "mystery" (*geheime Kunst*) (I, 210, 1. 2) for them. They simply know from experience that exposure to poetic "song" (*Gesang*) (I, 210, 1. 29) induces a disassociation from their accustomed frame of reference and transports them into a state of "enjoyment" (*Freude*), even "ecstasy" (*Rausch des Augenblicks*) (I, 210, 1. 30), free from any pragmatic concerns that would otherwise preoccupy them. In other words, they have, on occasion, been moved to occupy the poet's central perspective, but they cannot maintain it under the pressure asserted by "the continued demand of mercantile interests" ("die unaufhörlichen Handelsgeschäfte") (I, 210, l. 31).

Since the merchants are not themselves poets, they are merely able to report what they have heard concerning the extraordinary power poesy confers on its practitioners. However, no one but poets can speak with authority on this subject, so that their identity may only become apparent in a poetic rendition of the poet's function, which is exactly the sort of narrative the merchants declare themselves ready to retell. As the first one of two, Novalis has them relate the legend of Arion in which the poet proves capable of uncovering a congruent relationship between the realms of nature and humanity. In contrast to the poet, those driven by greed fall prey not only to a state of inhumanity but also to one of isolation that ultimately brings about their destruction in confrontation with a hostile environment. The tale is a clear illustration of the poet's central perspective from a midpoint where freedom has replaced the barbarian attitude of self-seeking greed as the basis for a relationship between self and world. Consequently, the poet speaks a language common to man and nature. It is the language of humanity, the language of beings free to act as moral agents, and also the language of nature no longer experienced only as the antagonist on whose terms the battle for survival must be fought.

The legend of Arion, as the merchants tell it, outlines the poet's bearing and actions against the contrasting background of benighted barbarism. Most revealing in this regard is the marked difference of attitude the two parties display toward personal possessions. The poet treasures them because they are pledges of friendship and love bestowed on him in response to his art. The sailors to whom he entrusts his person and all he has see only the marketable value of his belongings; worse yet, they want to rob him and would have no human pledge attached to their gains other than the present owner's death. Their definition of humanity is effectively restricted to the self exclusive of all other forms of being. The egocentric isolation that inspires the sailors differs emphatically from the poet's lack of possessive drive and from his ability to commune with the whole world around him, even with his hardened travel companions had they not stopped up their ears to avoid being tempted by the voice of true humanity. Ironically, only human beings are capable of such willful perversion, whereas nature corresponds in its freedom from combative opposition to the spirit in which the poet offers his song.

The poet's perspective is the same as the one Novalis specifies for the Middle Ages. It is the vantage point from the middle ground and it may be approached from the same two directions, from the materialistic egoism that characterizes primitive subservience to nature and from the postbarbarian extreme of ego inflation that sets in when freedom is mistaken for self-sufficiency. The tale of Arion shows the possibility of the first movement, which directs the self to abandon the state of nature for the state of freedom made manifest in the poet's relationship to his environment. If this first movement culminates in an initial attainment of the central perspective, the second movement marks a return to it after the goal has been overshot and the balance has tilted in the other direction. That this danger is very real has already been pointed out by Novalis's critical reference to the postmedieval era. The centricity he envisions in his definition of the Middle Ages is actually a state of mind rather than a fixed period in time and its only historical dimensions are those states of mind that differ from it, either because they have not yet reached the appropriate level of self-consciousness or because they have lost sight of it again. The poet's state of mind maintains the highest level of self-consciousness in its purest form, and where he is, there are the Middle Ages; that is to say, there is the middle ground where self and world meet in mutual freedom and extend the message of their union in both directions, to those who still have not heard it as well as to those who need to be reminded. Thus, the figure of the poet may either appear as a beacon of liberation where barbarian dependence on nature's dictates predominates or it may serve to effect a reconciliation between the realms of nature and the human spirit once they have become estranged. The tale of Arion attests to the first of these contexts in which the poet exercises his function; the second one is illustrated in the next story the merchants feel compelled to relate in order to do full justice to their task as Heinrich's informants.

"Another tale," so they tell him, "which is not quite as marvellous and also belongs to a later era . . . will acquaint you even more fully with the effects of that extraordinary art" ("Eine andere Geschichte . . . die freilich nicht so wunderbar und auch aus späteren Zeiten ist, wird . . . euch mit den Wirkungen jener wunderbaren Kunst noch bekannter machen") (I, 213, ll. 13–16). In other words, "that extraordinary art" the poets practice is now to appear in a "later" setting, one that no longer requires the bridling of nature's all-pervasive forces in order to reveal the spirit of humanity. That spirit flourishes in pure celebration of the poet's art, but it does so in isolation at a royal court whose ruler's might and ken reach far and wide yet somehow fail to extend beyond the palace walls where nature's forest grows in undisturbed profusion. Nature, however, does not constitute a realm independent of its being observed. Contained within it is a human shelter, a small clearing and a cottage that is home to an older man and his son who form a team of teacher and student engaged in deciphering the cryptic text that is their environment. At the beginning of the merchants' second tale, aesthetic refinement and science have obviously gone their separate ways, which represents a very real danger for the "later era," a danger for his own age Novalis is not alone in recognizing, long before C. P. Snow diagnosed its fully realized impact.

The schism between the "two cultures," to which we have by now actually become heir, can arise only, so the story tells us, when science is not yet understood for the poetic endeavor it is and poetic discourse is mistaken for being self-sufficient, which it is not. Individual objects and their lawful interrelation, which we collectively regard as nature, are thought to be objectively valid because we believe them to be real for everyone. That belief would remain pure fiction, unless a consensus of opinion were possible with respect to those objects and the laws that determine them. Accordingly, such ultimate consensus is the preconditional framework that allows for any and all scientific understanding, which means that the world we behold assumes its differentiated concrete reality not within a self-referential context but as communicable data. Communicability, however, presupposes an intersubjective ground of validation for which the world gains its contours, and that is the very ground Fichte had cleared by stipulating that all knowledge, or science (*Wissenschaft*), is possible only because the nonego falls within the horizon of the absolute ego. His *Doctrine of Science* (*Wissenschaftslehre*) begins with the absolute Ego as the preconscious limit of the world (*Tathandlung* or the *a priori* of self-consciousness) and it ends with the absolute Ego as the ultimate referent of individual world-consciousness insofar as every human being is capable of free moral agency. With his "*höhere Wissenschaftslehre*," Novalis lets the hermeneutic implications of Fichte's system come into full view. For him, theoretical reason, which brings world into consciousness, and practical reason, which guarantees intersubjective validation, are no longer linked by a circle of purely noumenal reality but by one immediately apparent to those who are aware of the "mother tongue" the world speaks (I, 268, l. 7). That awareness he calls *Poesie* and those who consciously employ language in this sense poets. It is this simple insight into the hermeneutic character of science, for which Fichte had opened his eyes, that inspires Novalis when he insists that science is the business of poets, as he does throughout his *Lehrlinge* and also his *Ofterdingen*. In this particular instance, he presents his view with unmistakable emphasis because he has the youth of the tale reach maturity only after love has transformed him into a poet.

With his poetic qualification of science, Novalis indicates that he understands any attempt to explain nature to be an interpretative effort for which the relationship of things to one another falls within the bounds of the self's unconditional identity with itself. Self-identity, in this sense, furnishes the ground of reference for the self's release from subjective isolation and for its potential identity with others. That potential is the unconscious premise realized in every act of communication, because communication entails the eventual possibility of a consensus for which subjective differences remain invalid. In practice, the self's unconditional identity is its identity with the communal self, not with any particular community but with the community of mankind. It is the same transcendental community to which we belong as free moral beings, only Novalis also derives from our potentially realized citizenship in it the actual possibility of language, no matter what its relative code might be. As Novalis conceives of it, language has transcendental value and therein lies not only its claim to truth but also its poetic quality. Accordingly, he does not consider that the poet speaks of the world, since this is only possible for those who employ language as though it were secondary to an experience of that world; instead, the poet hears the world speak — as Heinrich had been about to do before his dream — and when he speaks, he speaks the language he hears. What poets hear is the original language of humankind, the "mother tongue" in whose terminology everything has received its particular name, which each object pronounces for those to hear who know that there is only one language community and that its idiom silently accompanies all human speech. All language has this unspoken dimension that cannot, in turn, be codified in a language and must, therefore, be conveyed by the use of language itself. Such use of language is the "extraordinary art" poets practice, to which the merchants have referred most aptly as an ability to speak as though it were in foreign tongues and yet make oneself understood. In this sense, poets necessarily complement scientists, because poets demonstrate by their poetic use of language that the concrete observations of science derive their validity not from the object of experience but from the consensus concerning that object, which can only be obtained and verified insofar as subjective experience is also communicable.

The function Novalis assigns to the poet anticipates crucial aspects of language theory that have become focal topics of concern for philosophers of our century. Briefly stated, the most telling results to be derived from recent discussions on the nature of language have led to the summary conclusion that the concepts of consciousness can no longer be considered to be independent of their communicability.[15] This effectively means that nothing can be known, unless it can also be communicated, or that epistemology has been expanded to include a complementary theory of language. In other words, the decisive criterion for knowledge is not that it refers to autonomous objects, nor that it must refer its objects to the transcendental apperception of self-consciousness, but rather that it may occur only within the context of its potential as shared communication. Once language is no longer regarded in the traditional sense as a vehicle subordinate to a fully independent reality, be it material or conceptual, the linguistic event rather than the supposedly unaffected standards it had been thought to convey moves into the foreground. Actually, the relationship can now be considered to have been reversed and it may be argued that reality depends on language.

It is this kind of argument that has landed us in the currently almost proverbial "prison house of language," a prison of palatial dimensions that is capable of inspiring a false sense of freedom. However, it remains a prison, whether it is a prison turned into a palace, where its inhabitants may celebrate their liberation from a "metaphysics of *présence*"[16] or whether it is a palace turned into a prison, where noble spirits have fallen prey to the seductive power of pure aesthetics. The king of Novalis's tale is certainly portrayed as the victim of such seduction, even though the doctrine of *l'art pour l'art* was to evolve much later and had not yet become a part of our culture's legacy. The story is notably successful in characterizing aesthetic purism as a form of elitist self-delusion, which is a fault that is demonstrated not only in the narrative of a king's fate but also by historical events closer to our times, when this very fault was to contribute one of the sorrier chapters on art and artists in the age of fascism. The poetic use of language, in Novalis's view, opens up a new dimension that supersedes the earthbound reality of human existence; however, the poetic realm is not exclusive but inclusive of that reality, and this crucial difference may easily go unnoticed when aesthetic delight and its ennobling sense of freedom have cast their spell most strongly.

The royal court of which the merchants tell is quite definitely under the spell. Its beneficial effects are felt throughout the land, but underneath the idyllic splendor and harmony a "mysterious fate" ("geheimnisvolles Schicksal") (I, 214, ll. 31–32) threatens. This mysterious fate is rooted in the king's mistaken tendency to appreciate the poetic dimension, to which he has given up his life, as an exclusive rather than inclusive sphere. Happenstance or fate, more so than conscious intent, is to blame for his misconception, which only gains ground as his attachment to the world of poetic imagery grows ever more compelling, so that it serves not so much to enhance as to replace his relationship with the rest of mankind. The inevitable companion on this isolating path is pride, which seals off all potential exits in the name of self-sufficiency. That characteristic ultimately stands for the barren void the king is to experience before long as his steps echo through the halls of his palace where the mysterious disappearance of his only daughter, the one person he truly loves, has left him in utter despair and without any hope for the continuation of his line. His love of poetry had inadvertently turned into an esoteric conceit with social implications that moved him to deem none worthy to be her suitor since everyone seemed so far beneath the ethereal image he had come to associate with himself and his lineage. Now that she has vanished and he stands alone amid his splendor, he recognizes only the emptiness that surrounds him, an emptiness that even extends to the poets' words, exposing them for mere "mockery and delusion" ("leere Worte und Blendwerk") (I, 223, ll. 14–15).

Poetry, more so than mason's skill, had fashioned the resplendent palace that has become the king's prison, and the song of poets now merely serves to underscore the deprivation and the isolation he must suffer. There he would have languished without reprieve had not his daughter held the key for his release. She had been raised at her father's court, which caused her love of the poetic arts to flourish, until it was more than equal to his. Her love proved greater because it matured by reaching out beyond the palace walls where she and the young student of nature were to find in each other the consummation that is, in Novalis's sense, the very spirit of all poesy. After a year's absence she returns, presenting the king with a grandchild and a new son, whose lyric appeal for acceptance melts the last vestige of the wall of pride behind which the king had been held captive.

The youth's inspired composition revolves around the central theme that love of poetry remains mere self-indulgence in aesthetic delight, unless it also is love of the fellow human being in whose name the poet speaks and whom he addresses in each member of his audience. As the astonished court listens, it hears the young man tell of a poet who criticizes a state of affairs in which his words are appreciated only for themselves and for the elevating sense of self-gratification they may afford, while their real appeal goes unheeded (I, 226, ll. 5–10). The poet's plea that he be recognized for his humanity and not just for the gifts he brings is an eloquent reminder that art is not for art's sake but for the sake of calling each individual to membership in the community of humankind to which we all belong because we actually are conversant in the language that unites us and grants us the ability to behold the world in common. That language is the language of poets which is, indeed, esoteric since it appears to raise us beyond the world in which we live and to which our ordinary use of language refers. Poetry does, in effect, make the familiar seem foreign, as Heinrich had experienced at the very beginning of the novel and as the merchants have pointed out by terming it a "foreign" language; however, it does so in order to make the foreign familiar, not by absolutizing the esoteric moment and by constituting an autonomous sphere in which art replaces the world for a deified subject, as the king had come to believe (I, 215, ll. 8–26), but by revealing the common ground of our identity as human beings with reference to which this world assumes reality for us and we are to assume reality in it.

In this context, science is to be understood as a hermeneutic effort, as an attempt at interpreting a text written in the language of its intended audience. That language would have to be one we may all potentially speak, for which reason the scientist must really be a poet or: the language of science ultimately derives its authority from the language of languages. Our poetic potential, however, derives from another one that would allow us to suspend the self-centered perspective of individuated existence because we recognize the self in the other. Knowledge, art, and the normative principle of moral worth constitute an interrelated sequence. Only when this sequential circle is complete and all stages have been realized has each stage been fully realized individually. The scientist is not a scientist unless he also appreciates the spirit of the poetic arts, and the lover of poetry loves only himself in the work of art unless he is able to identify his own being with all human being, and that sense of identity, while it validates our actions morally, is experienced to its fullest as love. That sort of love marks the completion of the circle within which the separate status of science and poetry is united under the common bond that is as much prerequisite for the possibility of shared knowledge as it is for the possibility of communication.

Novalis conveys the full interdependence of this relationship through the imagery with which he has the merchants conclude their tale. Not only have the realms of science and poetry become mutually complementary in the union of the recluse naturalist's son with the princess from the castle but the example of their union sets the tone for everyone else. Love, not isolating and barren but encompassing and fruitful, pervades the land henceforth, which happy state, one is led to assume, continues to persist, except that it does so only as the promise of a possibility because the fabled land's name is Atlantis.

Atlantis has disappeared and remains as hidden beneath the surface of the world as does the self when the veil of estrangement prevents us from recognizing it in the other person and in the vast text that is nature. Whoever proves capable of lifting this veil also rediscovers Atlantis; only that part of the story the merchants cannot tell since it has to be lived in response to the very appeal with which poetry transcends its own bounds and reveals the moral foundation of human communality, as the poet of the tale had pointed out to his audience. For Heinrich, the veil of estrangement that hides us from ourselves had started to move aside ever since word of the blue flower had first reached him. It has continued to draw back steadily and is now ready to open where self stands embattled with self in the manifest estrangement of war. After that, the process is completed when the veil also disappears where self confronts nature as an apparently impenetrable mystery. The first phase occurs as Heinrich is caught up temporarily by the religious fervor that finds its expression in the Crusades. His enthusiasm is of short duration, however, because he gradually realizes that his feelings have actually far less in common with the Christian longing for conquest than they do with one of its Moslem victims' poetic longing for home. Following this episode, the final phase evolves in the fifth and central chapter, where Heinrich is allowed to glimpse nature as it appears to those for whom it is not an antagonistic power to be pressed into service but rather a text that contains the book of life.

At the old crusader's castle, which furnishes the setting for the fourth chapter, Heinrich becomes acquainted with the spirit of warfare. He proves very receptive to its poetic appeal, which is conveyed by a chorus of veterans who sing of Christ's grave as an allegorical figure pleading for liberation from cruel mistreatment under the yoke of enemy rule. One in voice and mind, they call for Heinrich to join their ranks, and he appears ready to do so in the belief that he has been called to join humanity itself. He soon realizes that this is a mistaken belief because its narrowness becomes all too obvious in his chance encounter with a young Moslem woman whose song of longing for the home her captors had forced her to leave attracts him from afar, as he wanders through the wilds outside the castle. The warriors inside had aroused his desire to come to the aid of the holy grave, which they had depicted as a captive of callous hordes who were turning a deaf ear to its universal appeal. As his inner turmoil calmed, warlike ambition with its possessive bias clarified into a pure feeling of longing (I, 234, ll. 6–7) that reached out in the direction indicated by the suffering female figure his imagination had made of the sacred site (I, 233, ll. 17–23). In this frame of mind, he hears the stranger's song and meets in her just such a figure, suffering in captivity and pointing the way home, not only to her home but to the home of homes, to the ''Orient'' as the representative home of poesy.

The Christian knights believe the holy grave to be far off in a distant land, where it is subject to desecration simply because it is in the ''wrong'' hands. Heinrich displays a much keener sense of religiosity and recognizes in his fellow human being the temple Christ had sanctified. There is Christ's memorial and it is located in the knights' midst where their prisoner's suffering dishonors the memory of the Crucified far more than the question of ownership at Jerusalem. War is a call to communal unity, and therein lies the poetic and moral appeal Novalis ascribes to it. However, that appeal is not conferred on a community of warriors who, like the crusaders, exhibit possessive aspirations and conceit resulting in blindness for human worth. They speak of territorial conquest and booty (I, 230, l. 32–231, l. 4), of a subhuman species they call ''heathens'' (I, 231, l. 24 and 233, ll, 1–4), and of pretty girls who may be brought back in bondage (I, 231, ll. 18–21). Such attitudes point in the opposite direction, away from the ultimate communality of all human beings, away from their real home that is also home to the language of poetry. The knights have, in effect, abducted the human spirit from its native home and led it into distant captivity, which is precisely where Heinrich discovers it in the person of the unhappy woman who sings her plaintive song to the rocks and trees of the forest.

Since ancient times, war has been glorified in much of our culture's most prized literature, and Novalis unquestionably perceives the poetic and moral appeal of war in reference to this tradition, which also holds definite philosophical implications for him. In his view, all divisiveness must be ascribed to the state of nature in which the self knows itself only as a physical being whose continued existence and welfare must be its primary concern. By comparison, war in the heroic tradition demands readiness to sacrifice life and fortune for a just cause and the good of others. Compliance with such a demand, therefore, represents a more advanced stage of self-awareness, because it presupposes a sense of unity that ultimately means the unity of all mankind on whose behalf the poet speaks and the moral agent acts. However, war may also be based on other than heroic motives and the two combine all too frequently in unholy marriage, as illustrated by the episode at the crusader's castle. There, Heinrich is given to understand that war may simply be a more efficient organization of the war of all against all, in which case it is an intensification of divisiveness and a form of self-betrayal. If there be any merit in it, war is to overcome war by fostering an attitude of self-denial that is incompatible with thoughts of self-enhancement and material gain at the expense of others.

From our vantage point in this century, Novalis's praise of war seems hopelessly naive and, more than that, morally highly suspect, particularly in light of the effect such notions were to have on the course of German history. Later on in the novel, his idealization of the hero in connection with nationalist and religious fanaticism (I, 285, ll. 5–21) only serves to confirm this judgment.[17] War, many of us would be inclined to say, has never been anything but organized murder, which precludes any pretense for condoning it. Very few have spoken this way in the past, however, and not many more until fairly recently.[18] These certainly have not yet been enough to obviate the occurrence of war, and there may never be enough voices to do so; but hope remains alive more urgently than ever that awareness must grow in our days of the pressing need for overcoming war in a continuing and spreading attempt at mutual understanding. We, too, it would seem, have heard the victim's song, which kindles the hope that the number of those may increase who identify with it, rather than with the chorus of crusaders. The school of war that taught us to see with Heinrich's eyes was undoubtedly far more atrocious and inglorious than Novalis had envisioned; yet the lesson was still the same and so was the school in which we learned to distinguish our longing for peace more clearly from longing for war in its pursuit.[19]

In Heinrich's case, this essential discriminatory shift of perspective regarding the self as it relates to others opens a correspondingly different view of nature. From his encounter with the knights, Heinrich gained the ability to look through the veil of war's divisiveness to the underlying unity of humankind for which all individuals long as the true home of their language and identity. The language is the language of poetry, which spoke directly to his heart in the crusaders' song and in the song of their prisoner. Each time he felt himself addressed in this manner, the confines of his individuated selfhood expanded in an awareness of his identity with others. First, Henrich felt at one with the crusaders and the aim that united them, but then his sense of unity also extended to those who had remained excluded. He did, in effect, become conscious of himself as a moral being and is now ready to learn how nature may be approached in that frame of mind.

After leaving the castle, the company of travelers makes the acquaintance of a miner who fascinates them with tales of his craft. As the story of his career unfolds, the audience is left in no doubt that he considers the profession of which he speaks more of a priestly calling than profane labor devoted to scraping a meager livelihood from the earth's innards. He describes his apprenticeship in terms of an initiation that empowers him to read the signs of hidden treasure where others see nothing but the surface on which we conduct our lives. Accordingly, the discovery of gold in the depths below is treated as the ultimate disclosure, and being witness to this revelation is the miner's reward. Once the precious find surfaces, it takes its place among the objects that comprise the world we confront in the struggle for our physical survival and well-being. Of royal rank in its own realm where solid matter blocks the sun that shines on our bustling preoccupation with the business of living, gold loses none of its regal authority when it enters the light of day. There, too, it holds a commanding position and rules over all other worldly goods since it serves as a point of concentration for our manifold proprietary ambitions with which we seek to assure our freedom from want.

No hoard of gold nor the power for which it stands, however, could possibly free anyone for whom freedom is indistinguishable from dependence on possessions. Freedom from want is only granted as freedom from wanting, which is exactly the attitude the miner displays. It is the key that enables him to unlock the earth's secrets and decipher the holy writ of its formation. Where others take the appearance of things for real and allow themselves to be governed by the unfathomable autonomy of that reality, he reads a text, and the gold he discovers is what it says to him. It is a scientific text and his discoveries do, in fact, lend themselves to pragmatic exploitation, as do all discoveries scientists make; however, as long as freedom from wanting has not yet replaced the self-seeking pursuit of freedom from want, those discoveries only retain value as commodities of power that serve to amplify, rather than abate, the pervasive battle for possessions.

Nature, so the miner explains, is free and her treasures do not allow themselves to be pressed into service for any one individual's benefit. As possessions, they tend to circulate, passing from hand to hand in their effort to belong to all, and those who attempt to hold them in permanent grasp are destroyed by the possessive aspirations that enslave the owner to the demands of ownership. The fellowship of miners spends most of the day below, and when its members emerge on top, their eyes are not clouded by habitual confinement to surface reality. They have depth of vision, which makes them all the more receptive to the bounty and beauty revealed under heaven's light, and they remain untroubled by the "dangerous lunacy" (*gefährlicher Wahnsinn*) (I, 244, l. 33) common among most surface dwellers, who perceive the world only from the narrowing perspective of the viewer's possessive ambitions. The miner does not pound at nature's gate with the demanding query: "What can you do for me?" Instead, he asks to know who nature is and will not tire in pursuing her innermost secret, no matter how formidable the wall of obstacles that protect it. The question predefines the answer, and the answer defines the person on whose behalf the questioner requested it. At the heart of this hermeneutic game is the concept of self, and as long as the questioner has not expanded that concept beyond the restrictive limits of "me," the answer will only serve to reemphasize those limits. Self limited to "me" is surface, a fleeting moment mistaken for permanence, whereas the self seeking knowledge is no longer just limited to "me," because what it seeks can be sought and found only in the name of all human beings. Mining treasure, as the miner speaks of it, is mining knowledge beneath the superficial surface of human affairs that seem to be conducted entirely on the basis of personal need and greed.

In seeking out gold beneath the earth's surface rather than on it, the miner refuses to confine his sense of self exclusively to the dimension where the summary goal of human desire, for which the metal stands in either realm, is no more than a "commodity" (*Ware*) (I, 244, l. 36). To be sure, his activity permits him to make a living, but the satisfaction of his modest needs does not exhaust the value he attaches to his craft. He practices it not to enrich himself but others, and if his gifts turn into poison in their hands, the fault lies with the recipients who think primarily in terms of private gain, unaware that such gain merely serves to underscore their lack of freedom. For the miner, gold is far more than a commodity; it is more like a bride whose favors are to be earned by faithful and unselfish service. She is the prize that gladdens his heart throughout hours of toil, and his untiring efforts are joyfully devoted to overcoming the barrier that separates them. The goal reveals the true nature of the self who seeks it, and in this case it will have to be a person who, by identifying with his fellow human beings, acknowledges his freedom from the state of utter dependence that is the foil of all egocentricity. The gold the miner brings to light is actually the golden source that underlies the formation of the world for the self, not for any particular self but for all selves insofar as they are cognitive agents. Essentially, the miner executes a descent into the same cave that had sheltered the golden jet in the earlier dream sequence. However, his is no longer a dream but rather a reading of the earth's history based on the hieroglyphs of its inner structure, and that text is written in a language comprehensible only to the free self because it addresses all of humanity in each individual.

According to Novalis's theory, language of this kind would have to be fundamentally poetic which is evidently the reason why he has the miner summarize his exposition in two songs representative of the guild's spirit. The first celebrates freedom as the primary characteristic of miners, the sort of freedom untroubled by the fetters of wanting because love rather than want governs their relationship to the world.[20] The second refers to gold as a mythic king who, in his castle, is held fast beneath hardened walls of stone. His liberation may only be brought about by human "insight" (*Einsicht*) (I, 250, l. 3), an insight that ultimately means our liberation as well because it reunites us with ourselves. Freeing the gold that lies at the earth's core means uncovering the world's reality underneath the layers that merely constitute the reality of individual experience; and, as the final lines of the last song proclaim with their imagery of ocean waves instead of stone, this means the melting of the wall of otherness that locks each self away from world and other selves.

Except for Heinrich, the audience seems to have missed the point of the recital entirely. Their dominant reaction is inspired by the desire to profit from the knowledge and experience the miner must have gathered on his sojourns. This attitude on their part is hardly surprising; they are, after all, denizens of the surface and not miners, very much kin to the merchants with whom they freely associate, as the crusaders had also done. Nonetheless, the gathering of listeners is not altogether unreceptive to the song's poetic appeal, particularly the last one's, which "entertains them in a waking state like a dream" ("[das sie] im wachenden Zustande wie ein Traum unterhielt") (I, 248, ll. 26–27). For Heinrich, the effect lingers on; he asks to copy the lyrics and feels they seem strangely familiar, as well they might since they are the objectified counterpart of his dream. The cave with the golden jet he had beheld lies buried under the firm contours of material reality, just like the king's castle of the song, which sank out of sight and came to rest beneath a surface of seemingly impenetrable rock. In hearing this song, however, he also begins to realize its promise of liberation; the dream has surfaced and comes to meet him in the miner's words, words that speak the name of things in the language common to all selves. They are poetic words whose effect is to be the one their imagery describes, namely the melting of the hardened crust that keeps self, world, and selves apart.

His audience may not be fully aware of it, but the miner has done more than just describe the intricacies and conditions of his art. In drawing forth the gold of poetry that lies hidden in the prosaic use of language, he has actually given a demonstration of the manner in which not only his but any other craft is to be conducted. All pragmatic endeavor is prosaic, and yet it possesses at least potential, if not always overt, social dimensions, so that its ultimate framework of reference is not self-serving individuality but rather self-detached communality without limit. Such communality is the equivalent of moral freedom and its communicative manifestation is poetic, or in Novalis's terms, it is *Poesie*. The pronounced utilitarianism that seems to inspire commercial enterprises, such as mining, tends to link all participants through selfish interests. However, this narrow view does not allow the horizon of common interest to shine forth, which coincides with moral freedom and within which any and all enterprise derives its human worth, even its utilitarian context of validation. Through the miner's general attitude toward his work, that very horizon of moral freedom becomes visible, as does the essentially poetic character of his prosaic world. In both these respects, he attests to the exemplary status of his craft, not as an empirical trade but as an activity that proves him capable of raising the golden treasure of freedom from a terrain where less observant eyes only detect the stony surface of the stage on which we play out our lives in physical and intellectual dependence.

Both the miner and his gold have an obviously symbolic function; only in this case, the concept of symbol does not apply in any customary sense that would have it refer to a concrete contextuality beyond itself, be that outside a given text or within it. The gold remains just what it is, namely gold, and as such it is of value; value, however, varies according to the concept of self for whom the object has worth. As a medium of exchange, gold illustrates very effectively that it has no inherent value and that the same is true of anything for which it stands. No matter how intrinsic to the object it might seem, value arises only with respect to need, and no matter how private the need, it is never experienced in a manner so singular that it cannot potentially be shared by all human beings. There is, then, no value other than one given in a communal context, which means that a highly prized object like gold pointedly links a purely private sense of self and attendant values to a sphere of objective validity selves hold in common. If that sphere is thought to extend only to the realm of things, then self-realization will be on their terms and gold may assume collective value for everyone as the one thing representative of all others. If, however, collective value does not refer to a collective thing but has its common ground in a collective self, then gold stands for this self, and self-realization means recognizing it in all objects, be that in terms of shared truth (science) or shared purpose (moral conduct) or shared pleasure in true communication (*Poesie*).

The miner's task is to open up the world by fathoming the inner core it conceals, and he has attempted to do just that for his listeners by revealing the poetic core beneath the prose of daily toil. If they are approached in the spirit of freedom, as he specifies throughout his narrative and in his songs, the walls of resistance we must continually face will become doors of perception. This promise of the old man's tale has been fulfilled in Heinrich's case, for whom the whole world suddenly appears in the strange light of a visionary reality that is an amplified extension of the dreamlike waking state into which the mining songs had put the group. To escape the public room's oppressive closeness and, incidentally, to follow up his words with a brief practical exhibition, the miner concludes his elaborations by proposing a walk to nearby caves. Along the way through the moonlit night, shortly before Heinrich is to follow his guide into the world's interior, he sees its exterior transformed into a vast cathedral to which his own modest "living room " (*Wohnzimmer*) (I, 252, 1. 16) is linked by a secret door that has just opened. Within the cathedral, cosmic past rises from beneath the floor of stone where its record lies buried in the earth's formation, and cosmic future descends from high above to meet it, streaming down clear and golden and accompanied by song. Once the barrier between self and other melts, once self and world are recognized as one, the barrier of time is also lifted and the present is no longer experienced as a mere point segregating past and future but becomes a true center whose circumference encompasses both in an eternal now.

Beginning and end also coalesce into timeless significance with respect to each individual being since every form of life enters the cathedral through a large gate and audibly pronounces in its own language a simple appeal that is the summary formulation of its "innermost nature" (*innere Natur*) (I, 252, ll. 20–23). The term "innermost nature" refers to the inherent potential all living things seek to realize in their own way by the process of their very existence.

The appeal stated in the cathedral is this selfsame process for which beginning and end are one because both are its parents, just as lack and fulfillment are united in the Greek concept of *eros*. With Heinrich's visionary image of the world, each creature stands revealed as an entity that is never just an isolated instance in the passing of time; rather, it is a participant in a chain of final causation where the ultimate goal is anticipated in the origin. Here, simultaneity has replaced the sequential order of efficient causality according to which the mechanistic model of the universe and the linear concept of history take on reality for human understanding. Those precepts guide the merchants on their way as well as all others who, like them, believe that knowledge may only be gained as the direct result of experience. Their first conversation with Heinrich, however, has already left little doubt that this point of view remains incomplete. As he gave them to understand, there is an other one that opens a vista of simultaneity where the effect is not only the final event in a sequential progression but precedes itself in the cause. The merchants could not make much of this information, but the reader was alerted to the fact that their reliance on empirical data presupposes the uniform context for which it attains the significance of just that, namely empirical data.

The anticipatory leap within which the concrete reality of an experiential world unfolds can only occur on a level that transcends the order of events and interrelations constitutive of that reality. In his vision, Heinrich gains awareness of this level, but not as the transcendent unity of a Neoplatonic deity, not as the Creator God of old who is both alpha and omega, nor as an equally noumenal qualification of human consciousness in the Kantian tradition. Instead, whole is related to part in a hermeneutic circle where every form of life renders an interpretation of being. Each does so in a peculiar language or dialect, but it is language nonetheless and as such of general communicative and communal value. Neither God nor absolute consciousness preside over the world to bind it into objective coherence; rather, the concrete contours of its reality arise within the context of their communicability and do not rest on a foundation that dissipates into noumenal fiction.

After the surface world had thus become transparent in its simplicity for Heinrich (I, 252, ll. 23–26), he descends into its interior through a maze of caves whose walls contain the record of their ancient past. There, beneath the world's exterior where gold maintains its secret kingdom, he and his companions do, indeed, come into a royal presence; however, it is announced by the musical cadence of poetic speech and not by the promise of a bright metallic gleam. Led by this message, the group descends further and encounters at these subterranean depths another self in gold's stead. The self thus discovered is clarified, detached, fully free in its absolute, all-comprehensive love, and leads a hermit's existence, even though its role in the unfolding of time is that of a king.

After welcoming his visitors, the recluse briefly relates his story and dispels all suspicion that he might be a particularly exotic representative of monkish escapism from worldly afairs who follows the common pattern of parading his weakness as virtue to the world he supposedly left. His life is too secluded to benefit from such subtle strategies for power, and his choice of abode does not correspond to the idyllic image of nature where romantic spirits have traditionally been thought to seek refuge in critical aversion to a corrupt society. This hermit has experienced life to the fullest and he did not turn his back on it in a gesture of tired disappointment or hopeless distress. His love of life — and it had given him much to love — had found its focus in the woman who became his wife and in their offspring. Death took them from him, but his love was great enough to withstand this last tug at the fetters that hold the self captive to the dictate of circumstance. Bereft of the object on which it had been nourished and concentrated, his love did not die to the world but became free to reach out and encompass all of it. That this is indeed the case can be determined from all he says and does throughout the visit, though most explicitly from his words at its beginning and conclusion. The song that announces his presence does so on the dominant theme of a loving heart's open receptivity to love from above (I, 254–55), and his parting remarks end with the exhortation to keep one's eyes fixed steadfast on heaven in order to find the path that leads home (I, 266, ll. 9–10).

It is of particular significance that this very traditional imagery of the heavenward glance for heavenly guidance is employed by an individual who spends his life far away from any glimpse of heaven beneath the earth's obstructive bulk. The traditional image invoked to characterize a reality that utterly belies it has the oxymoronic effect of linking the past's mythic sense of the world with the enlightened view that would behold this world's reality without the aid of myth. The massive reality of the world surrounds the hermit like an impenetrable, alienating wall; and yet this world is not his jail, is not a barrier, because every part of it has reality for him only as an expression of the mythic whole on whose terms the world is what it is, not for itself but for any and all possible selves. He still refers to this mythic whole as heaven, although he does not mean the traditional hypostatized realm of perfection beyond the clouds that obscure our temporal vision. As his entire bearing (I, 255, ll. 16–18) and discourse indicate, and as he explicitly states (I, 263, ll. 23-26), the world has been transformed for him long ago. He has ceased to dwell on its surface in every sense of the word, and his life's story is very much the personified sequel to the miner's revelations concerning the mysteries of that profession. Released from attachment to any particular objects, the hermit embraces them all in selfless love and has thus penetrated the world's depth; without the restricting horizon of selfish concern, he has come to appreciate every one of its aspects as a sign that gains its validity with reference to the shared consciousness of all selves, the sort of consciousness the myth of heaven and its beatific vision was meant to illustrate.

The individual in the cave no longer represents just himself but rather the self of selves, the very horizon within which any and all of the objects comprising the world assume meaning. He is the self of selves consciously realized in every moment of world-consciousness, which is what everyone potentially is and Heinrich is to become. In that capacity, the hermit is not only Heinrich's father, as will be intimated in the novel's second part (I, 325, ll. 13–14), but also the moral soul of society at large. That soul is to have its representative steward in the imperial monarch, according to Novalis's definition of this office in his other works.[21] Here, the same theme is struck when he assigns the name of Hohenzollern to the recluse, the name of the house that there serves a similar function of expressing his hope for Germany's and Europe's future. Far from being restricted to the narrow confines of German nationalistic ambition, such hopes pertain to a vision that includes all of humanity as the free citizenry to which each individual potentially belongs.

Potential and future realization are concepts that apply to the sequential order of causality and historical time, but from the perspective of the extratemporal present in which the hermit lives these differences disappear. Here, past and future merge not in a punctual reduction to momentary transcience but in the comprehensive expansion from each moment to the entire process. Accordingly, history is the main topic for extensive conversation between the miner and Hohenzollern, with each supporting the other in the view that events necessarily have to be read with the principle of their overall coherence in mind. As had been the case with science, history, too, is found to be a hermeneutic endeavor for which the same human context of interpretation must be presupposed. Just as the true scientist had turned out to be a poet in the tale of Atlantis, the true, or rather best, "historians" would have to be "poets" as well (I, 259, ll. 13–21) since they read and speak the "mother tongue" in which not only each thing but also each occurrence is assigned its name.

Hidden beneath the immediacy of the event is the context in which it gains meaning. To have the event appear within this contextuality is to have it appear as meaningful in relation to other events, and the trace thus reflected is history. Like *Poesie*, history is not reducible to any particular statement or defined circumscription. No matter how apt or inclusive the formulation, the last chapter to the book of history will always be missing because it would have to contain the source of its own possibility. That source is the human context of interpretation within which events may take their shape and gain historical significance. History's last chapter would, therefore, require that interpretation be recognized for the authorship it is and that may occur when the erstwhile interpreter of the world becomes its poet. That Heinrich is about to undergo this transition is evident from the form of self-discovery he is permitted to make at the end of his stay in the cave. There he finds the book of his life in a Provençal manuscript that depicts his past, his present, and his future. The final chapter, however, is missing, which leaves the outcome in doubt and causes readers to wonder whether one had ever been written. There is very little doubt, though, that Heinrich's future career will have to supplement the incomplete document. It is written in the language of troubadours, a language still foreign to Heinrich, even though the concrete images that accompany the poetic text seem to refer him to the familiar world of his experience. Once he learns to speak the language of poets, so it would follow, he will not only be able to read the text of his life but also discover himself as its author. That is the last chapter, which will never be written because it will have to be lived. It would seem that this is the task awaiting Heinrich, who has at this point completed the first movement of his journey in which the world has been transformed into the reality of a dream. He is now ready to embark on the second half in which dream-reality becomes world. In other words, he is to be readied for experiencing the world as though it were a poetic text, and when he is able to read it, read it so that the poetic principle of interpretation is also demonstrated in poetic practice, he might just find that the missing chapter will have fallen into place.

Chapter 10
Journey's End

With Heinrich's arrival in Augsburg, he enters a world that seems strange compared to the one he had left behind, and yet he belongs there as much as to the other. His reactions to the new environment correspond to those the merchants described in their effort to define the effect of poetry. Novalis had them employ the paradoxical formulation of "words in a foreign language that are familiar, nonetheless" (I, 210, ll. 10–11); here he uses analogous terminology when he refers to the impressive houses of the city as leaving his protagonist with simultaneous feelings of "estrangement and pleasure" ("'die großen, steinernen Häuser befremdeten ihn angenehm'") (I, 268, ll, 16–17). Heinrich is obviously about to complete his transition from the world in which he used to live (I, 195, l. 15) to the world in which the blue flower is real.

By birth Heinrich may claim citizenship in both, in the prosaic world where the clock's measured beat alters with the set rhythms of daily industry and in the poetic world where time and industry derive their worth from the free communal sphere of festive celebration. It is just such a circle of celebrants that greets the travelers as they reach Schwaning's house. Schwaning is Heinrich's grandfather and the very person mother and son had come from so far to see. The host joyfully embraces his kin, and the others join him with great animation in welcoming the unexpected guests, whom they accept quite effortlessly in their midst. The poet Klingsohr and his daughter are among those present. They lend a special grace to the occasion, and in them Heinrich actually encounters what had to this point been real only as a dream. The girl's features are those the blue flower had shown him, and both she and her father seem already familiar from images glimpsed in the mysterious book with which the waking dream of Heinrich's descent into the cave had reached its climax and conclusion.

Dream becomes world, becomes reality in which all share, and this shared consciousness also underlies the social bond of festive play as Heinrich experiences it on the evening of his reception. Only now does he realize what it means to participate in true celebration and his entire stay at Augsburg would seem to be conditioned by the progressive intensification of that realization; it was to be, just as he assured himself, "the first and only festivity of his life" ("das erste und einzige Fest meines Lebens") (I, 277, ll. 14–15). The merchants had already sung the praises of Augsburg at the journey's outset (I, 205, l. 28–206, l. 36). Now their claims are supported in every detail, and the poetic interlude with which Schwaning and Klingsohr accent the tenor of the entire evening substantiates the merchants' characterization of Southern sociability as "free play" ("freies Spiel") (I, 206, l, 17).

The author introduces this terminology quite consciously in Schiller's sense. Here as there, play means release from the day's toil, release effected from the world we think holds us in common, and this release is gained because we recognize that world as one to which we lend significance in common. Accordingly, the feasting at Schwaning's house is a celebration of community in the prosaic acts of eating and drinking and in the equally prosaic concerns that may govern relations between the sexes. Taking up the latter theme, the host composes a poem teasingly directed against the rules of marketplace propriety that must customarily be observed in matters only the heart should sanction, whereas Klingsohr sums up the festive spirit singing the praise of wine as the divine agent most effective in liberating the self from the walls of self-seeking isolation.

If play, as Schiller would have it, is to be the effortless coincidence of bondage to the world and freedom from it, of personal inclination and the individual's validation in terms applicable to all humankind,[22] then the graceful sociability over which Schwaning and Klingsohr preside is certainly in accord with this definition. However, it is not only a definition of play but also a philosophical circumscription with moral implications for the social condition that gives rise to any form of aesthetic qualification. This qualification of the gathering's festive playfulness is brought out most conspicuously by the lyrical banter with which the host and his partner in poetry crown the evening's entertainment. Thus, it is the spirit of poetry that knits the communal bond, and Heinrich realizes its full impact in Mathilde, to whom he feels drawn as though the gap of separation stretching from individual to individual had ceased to exist. Effectively, he has experienced that the bonds of self-identity are not exclusive but inclusive of the other, and this awareness is emphatically underscored by the recognition that his vision of the blue flower has come to confront him in the person of Mathilde, whose features are those of the face at the flower's center. In this sense, more than any other, it is, indeed, his first and only festival since henceforth everything he does or says will be in celebration of the truth that the immediacy of his dream's reality is the reality with which the world stands ready to meet him.

Dream becomes world in that truth, and Mathilde is its guarantor; its celebration, however, entails far more than love for a specific individual. This love will have to grow along a path on which the first delightful liberating step cannot remain the last one. The first step leads beyond the self; the second must lead further in the same direction, even beyond the other individual with whom the loving self identifies, and that step entails pain and separation. Of these trials Heinrich has as yet merely a premonition. After retiring for the night, he has a dream in which the evening's encounter unfolds for him with foreboding images of death and loss; however, they are followed by more reassuring ones that relegate his painful separation from Mathilde to the level of a temporal necessity through which the permanence of the bonds underlying their union is made evident. Dream becomes world, and that applies to this dream as it does to the first one. The process begins with an initial awakening to the reality of a familiar expression in the foreign expanse beyond the self's limits, and it is brought to completion in the full realization that not only one but all expressions comprising the world's vocabulary are couched in the language the merchants had defined as poetic. Mathilde is the first such unveiling of the world for Heinrich, and he duly acknowledges his debt to Klingsohr by referring to him as "the father of love" ("Du bist ja der Vater der Liebe") (I, 287, l. 27). In this capacity it is quite fitting that Klingsohr is also the one to whom he will owe his initiation into the "mysterious art" (I, 210, l. 2) poets practice.

The lessons begin promptly on the next day, during a picnic on a scenic hillside overlooking the town's attractive surroundings. The beautiful day and the impressive view cause Heinrich to rejoice and reflect on the effect the beholder's intent or mood invariably have on the manner in which nature is perceived and appreciated. Implicit in these deliberations is the truth that every aspect of objective reality always reflects a human feature and, conversely, that the very status of objective reality arises only with reference to a consciousness whose subjective differences may be shared as humanly valid. Klingsohr lends summary expression to these implications by comparing the human mind (Gemüt) and the world it confronts to the power of light in its encounter with the dense obscurity of matter. According to his exposition, light allows the objects of the world to appear. This it does to differing degrees, depending on its relative strength; objects may seem to have their own radiance when struck by light, or they may seem translucent if it equals the power of their darkness, or they may conduct luminosity to all other bodies if the power of light is superior.

The analogy is quite clear in its intent. It specifies that the objects comprising the world appear in the light of self-consciousness. If the self is not aware of this, they seem to be independent of it; if, however, the self discovers itself in the other, then the object becomes transparent as a medium of self-consciousness, and if the self is fully conscious of itself in its freedom, the entire world will reflect this assurance. Nature, the impenetrable other, becomes transparent when we recognize it as a self in another human being. This is exactly how Heinrich understands Klingsohr's remarks, to which he replies: ''I understand you, dear master. Human beings are like crystals to our minds; they are transparent nature'' (''Ich verstehe Euch, lieber Meister. Die Menschen sind Kristalle für unser Gemüt. Sie sind durchsichtige Natur'') (I, 280, ll. 19–20). And with a backward glance to the color symbolism of the first chapter, Novalis has Heinrich speak of Mathilde as ''a precious, clear sapphire'' (''einem köstlichen, lautern Saphir'') (I, 280, l. 21). With this formulation, the reader is to be made aware of the full significance the author attaches to the figure of this girl. In her, nature's infinite otherness becomes familiar and reflects back on a point of tangency where other is equal to self. At that point the black impenetrability of limiting estrangement gives way to the light of freedom, which would cause the dark sphere to radiate a transparent tint of blue in the direction of the light one, according to the Goethean scheme of colors; in other words, the point of tangency appears as blue transparency, or, in Heinrich's words, as a clear sapphire that is to be his crystalline lens through which the world will stand revealed. Here as before, and throughout the entire novel, blue is the color that emerges when the darkness of self-estrangement begins to appear in the light of self-identity, just as that light manifests a golden sheen where it prevails beneath the alien exterior.

As Klingsohr has put it, light and dark stand opposed as mind does to matter, as inner to outer world, and it is within the light of this inner reality that the outer world assumes its concrete outlines. Inner reality has an immediacy about it that differs markedly from the reality of objects presented to consciousness. The difference is equivalent to the one we associate with the reality of our feelings as compared to reality validated in terms of discursive reason. However, just as light and dark constitute a balanced continuum in the crystals of which Heinrich speaks, feeling and rational understanding are to be coordinated functions and not, as is falsely believed, functions that mutually exclude one another.

That which is felt cannot be taught since feelings are experienced as an immediate presence in and for the self. The telling difference, however, is whether a person insists on attributing feelings to dependence on sensual variability, from which human need arises, or whether a person looks deeper and comes to recognize that sensual variability depends, in its turn, on an unvarying constant, that is to say, on the immediacy of the self's presence to itself in all acts of consciousness, from which the concept of the self's identity as a free moral agent arises. Compared to that which is felt and cannot be taught, that which falls in the province of rational understanding may be learned. The entire world stands ready to be explored in this manner, and whatever insights into nature may thus be gained can then be employed for its purposive use. To possess such knowledge, which means the ability to have nature serve the given purpose one might wish to pursue, is art in the sense of craftsmanship. This is the only aspect of any art that may be learned and taught, and this is also the extent and limit of what Klingsohr can teach Heinrich.

The unmediated reality of self-consciousness is a "felt" reality because its immediacy is very much like the immediate presence of sensation, or, as Novalis puts it: "The self feels itself, as content" ("Das Selbst fühlt sich selbst, als Gehalt") (II, 105, l. 12). This felt reality is the light in which the objects comprising the world appear to the mind, and discursive reason allows the mind to understand their relationships to one another so that it might employ them to pursue its ends. The question is, of course, whether the world determines those ends for the self or whether it is the self who determines them for the world. In the former case, skill and craftsmanship cater to human need, in the latter, to human purpose. It is in this latter sense that all human individuals may stand united as free beings, united in the ability to determine their fate in terms of human significance and united in the capacity to understand the secret language that lets each thing pronounce its human name. It is also in this latter sense that feeling and understanding are properly coordinated, so that the self's felt identity with itself is made manifest in the freedom of human purpose that constitutes the ultimate referential context within which the conditions nature seems to impose may be recognized; this is the equation that allows nature to equal mind in crystalline transparence, as Heinrich envisions.

For the free moral agent, fate is what he declares it to be in the name of humanity, and Klingsohr refers to this person's attitude as the "serene certainty" ("heitere Gewißheit") (I, 281, l. 17) of "faith in the human government of fate" ("Glaube an die menschliche Regierung des Schicksals") (I, 281, ll. 13–14) that is in sharp contrast to the "anxious uncertainty" ("ängstliche Un-gewißheit") (I, 281, l. 17) and "the blind fear of superstition" ("blinde Furcht des Aberglaubens") (I, 281, l. 18) with which those who are unaware of their freedom tend to anthropomorphize the power that rules their destiny. The individual who is conscious of his or her freedom is also impervious to the clamorous demands with which the world asserts its claim to be served as the validating authority for every form of existence. This is the "hardness" that Klingsohr attributes to the poet, when he insists "the poet is pure steel" ("der Dichter ist reiner Stahl") (I, 281, ll. 32–33); however, he also stipulates that an equal degree of sensitivity must accompany such hardness (I, 281, ll. 33–34), with which stipulation the position outlined by the "*höhere Wissenschaftslehre*" has once again been confirmed as the poet's vantage point.

Heinrich has, by this time, reached a level of consciousness at which he begins to experience the world as viewed from the poet's perspective. Ever since the tale of the blue flower had worked its effect, "the spirit of poetry has been [his] friendly companion" ("der Geist der Dichtkunst [ist sein] freundlicher Begleiter") (I, 283, ll. 29–307), and what he needs now is guidance in careful and selective observation, so that he will not be swept up by aimless enthusiasm; furthermore, he must learn to assemble what he experiences with skill and design, so that the poetic language he hears is effectively made audible to all others. Selecting the material and assembling it artfully are activities that pertain to the poet's craftsmanship, and that is precisely what Klingsohr offers to teach when he tells Heinrich: ''I shall gladly instruct you in all craftsmanship pertaining to our art'' (''Ich will Euch mit Freuden in dem Handwerksmäßigen unserer Kunst unterrichten'') (I, 282, ll, 34–36). Were Heinrich to become an artisan, like his father, skill and craftsmanship would still cater to human need. In his case, however, skill and craftsmanship will have to serve human purpose, and that purpose cannot be taught; it can only be outlined in contrast to human need, and that exhausts Klingsohr's curriculum, short of his furnishing the actual example of his art, with which part I concludes.

When need rules our actions, nature appears in a guise of pervasive hostility that gives no quarter and fails to extend any aid to her struggling creatures. She manifests, as Novalis puts it, ''blunt desire,'' in this case the desire that would inspire a self-indulgent ruler, ''and . . . dull lack of sensitivity and indolence'' (''dumpfe Begierde und . . . stumpfe Gefühllosigkeit und Trägheit'') (I, 284, ll. 22–23). Nature reflects the mind that perceives it, so that the spell of the same unholy trinity is even more evident in people, only with them the appearance of nature's hostility stands revealed as human self-centeredness: self-centeredness in self-seeking desire that recognizes others not as fellow beings but only as agents to be employed for its gratification. Blunt desire and its allies suffer nothing to contest their dominance; and yet they are constantly endangered by a force that does not acknowledge their power, a power that derives from the self's belief in its state of dependence.

In that state, the given realities on which the self depends define it; those realities are material, so that the self tends to define its worth in terms of possessions. In the narrowest sense, they may be personal possessions on whose terms individual status is determined; in a wider sense, they may be shared, like the land of the tribal or national society on whose terms the self relates to others, or like the common objects of worship, the holy places, the divine symbols and images of an institutionalized religious doctrine on whose terms the self relates to the world at large. However, when it happens that the relative social or religious frameworks of definition are challenged by alternative versions, the self's very identity is at stake. Such insecurity may, if sufficiently acute, result in war, and this is also the reason why wars seem to be fought for territorial gains or, as were the Crusades, for a sanctified site; in reality, though, neither land nor any given object is at issue. What is at issue is the self's identity, and that really cannot be in terms of something other than the self, that is to say, it cannot be in terms of possessions.

In wars that are fought for a national or religious cause, the true motive is laid bare, and while the combatants still believe they are contesting a piece of land or some other possession, they would be hard put to justify their actions on that account alone. In these situations there is a purpose involved that cannot be entirely reduced to desire for bounty or territory, even if the latter were to contain Christ's grave. These are just things without any value in themselves, except that they have been validated by common ambition. It is common, but not common enough, because this sort of ambition fails to realize that its true source and aim is the ground common to all humanity from which any value derives and in terms of which the self must ultimately seek to identify its world and thus also itself.

"True war is religious war," Novalis has Klingsohr instruct Heinrich, because, he continues, "it aims directly at extinction, and the insanity of human beings appears in its fully revealed form" ("Der wahre Krieg ist der Religionskrieg; der geht geradezu auf Untergang, und der Wahnsinn der Menschen erscheint in seiner völligen Gestalt") (I, 285, ll. 13–15). Human insanity consists in the error of mistaking the part for the whole, the validated for the source of value, which becomes most drastically evident when a religious institution is thought to be religion itself. In that case, the basis is laid for the religious wars of which Klingsohr speaks as those that bring out the insane principle of war's origin most clearly. They may be characterized in this manner since they are openly fought in obedience to the absurd claim that part of humanity must be excluded, and thus extinguished, in the name of Him who is simultaneously proclaimed the common ground of all humanity. Such wars are "true" ("*wahr*") because they seek to define the absolute terms of the self's identity, which is the underlying but hidden motive in all struggle, even that which seems to be conducted entirely for ends determined by need or greed; such wars are also "insane" for precisely the same reason, only in reverse, that is to say, because what they seek cannot possibly be realized so long as the very concepts of the relative nation or religion for which they are fought persist.

They will persist, of course, but — and this is the sane or "poetic"[23] qualifier amid the insanity — in war the validity of such preformed parochial concepts is put to the test. This test is not one of martial skill or craftsmanship but one of purpose independent of the war's actual outcome. First and foremost, the warring factions are forced to have their case tried in a court other than the battlefield since they must each have a unifying purpose that claims to be superior to the other one. Battle may decide superiority of arms, but superiority of purpose can be decided only by a judge who has jurisdiction over human purpose at large. That judge is the voice of humanity and its language is the imperative of the free moral agent. As Klingsohr depicts it, war is a process that tends toward its own extinction since the basic motivation that fuels it runs counter to the parochial interests it was meant to serve.

That the dynamics of war are, indeed, anchored in its elimination only becomes explicit later on, in the tale Klingsohr tells of Eros' delivery from error under Fable's guidance. There, when all walls of divisiveness have fallen and Eros has been united with Freya, who stands for peace, Perseus enters and brings the new king "the remains of his enemies" (die Reste deiner Feinde") (I, 314, l. 16); these enemies are all the manifestations of opposition itself, of the "non" that pervades the nonego, here hardened into the black and white of a petrified chessboard with figures of the same material over which Sophie pronounces the concluding formula: "all war has been banished onto this slab and into these figures. It is a memorial of the gloomy old times" ("aller Kreig ist auf diese Platte und in diese Figuren gebannt. Es ist ein Denkmal der alten trüben Zeit") (I, 314, ll. 19–21).

Unhappily, the "gloomy old times" are not yet past; instead, they are the existential present in which each individual stands embattled with the nonego. While that battle lasts, the collective battles termed war will also not cease, or as Novalis remarks in a note to *Heinrich von Ofterdingen*: "On earth *war* is at home — on earth there must be war" ("Auf Erden ist der *Krieg* zu Hause — Krieg muß auf Erden sein") (I, 346). The wall of estrangement that locks in each individual may, however, be overcome and the principle of opposition may be banished whenever the voice of humanity issues its unifying call to freedom and is heard.

The active person hears it, and with each morally free act the principle of opposition is suspended, never conclusively but categorically, nonetheless. The contemplative person also hears it, and in response the veil of estrangement dissipates to reveal the world in a poetic vision. Just as the moral agent represents the categorical suspension of the state of permanent embattlement, so does the hero, in Klingsohr's eyes, represent the categorical elimination of the state of war on earth. Opposition and war will always constitute a challenge to human agency since human purpose must be inscribed anew on the ever changing surface of circumstance with every moral act. The contemplative poet, on the other hand, attaches meaning to the world from a perspective that is removed from this challenge since what he beholds already carries a human inscription for him. Accordingly, Klingsohr punctuates this part of his discourse with the conclusion that a poet who would also be a hero transcends the bonds of human limitation since his actions would have to be as unrestricted by the world's continued opposition as is his vision; such a condition would be "god-like" (*göttlich*) (I, 285, l. 20) and for this reason also beyond the power of human language to describe (I, 285, ll. 20–21).

There is no need to point out that Klingsohr's all too facile praise of war and his equally ill-conceived glorification of the hero are far more suited to obscure rather than to illustrate his argument. War has, throughout history, led to more war and not its end, and heroes with sword in hand have proved to be singularly inadequate models of moral conduct. Given the unparalleled barbarism that was nourished in Germany by pseudoromantic ideologues, sentiments such as Klingsohr's have become most suspect. That well-founded suspicion ought not to prevent contemporary readers, though, from recognizing that Novalis is not so perverse as to have Klingsohr advocate the horrors and doubts we have in the meantime learned to associate with the terms ''war'' and ''hero.'' We may no longer speak as naively and unhesitatingly of heroes as does Novalis, but we still insist on a standard according to which we judge human behavior more or less praiseworthy. Opinions differ as to what that standard might be, but there we are in the realm of philosophy, and on this ground Novalis's position is quite clear. It is also on this ground that I have already identified the agent-hero of Klingsohr's description as the representative of the morally free agent. Furthermore, the concept of war, as Novalis employs it, is quite unsuitable for use in nationalistic ideologies that have inspired Germans since the beginning of the last century; this concept may have been used as a building block in the confining edifice of the nationalist spirit Heinrich Böll describes so well in his ''Wanderer, kommst du nach Spa . . .'', but it certainly was not assigned that use here.

War, and this is the fundamental point of Klingsohr's elaborations on the topic, dissolves the frozen forms the self employs to capture a sense of reality. This reality may be in terms of material goods, in terms of God or king or country or anything else; whatever the terminology, the reality it is to reveal will always remain hidden behind it. It is in this sense that ''war is at home on earth'' as the necessary momentum that keeps the relative formulations of human reality in flux, suspended between the reality they fail to hold and the reality they seek to capture. It is also in this sense that the hero is not ''god-like''; incapable of bringing about the golden age that would mean the end of history, heroes, unsung for the most part, must continue to trace out its text with their lives. Novalis's words may have a less forbidding and more antiquated ring to them, but this is what they convey, almost against the author's will, as it were. Throughout the novel, the poetic has been qualified as a positive movement constructive of human reality, only to culminate now in the insight that it must also destroy the formulations of reality it constructs, that it may be identified with the purely negative momentum of war. In other words, Klingsohr's poetics of war would imply that the thing in itself will remain as elusive as the golden age, when Eros and Freya are no longer separated by the veil of estrangement, and that the terms of our existence constitute our only reality, the reality of an infinite chain in which each formulation can only be replaced by another of its kind.

It would seem as though Novalis had arrived at a point in his work that lets him anticipate the Derridean argument. Not only does he lay his text open to deconstruction but he appears to deconstruct it himself. The whole dream of the blue flower and its unfolding in the succeeding chapters can now be read to demonstrate that our dream of reality remains just that, a dream or rather literature.

It can be read to speak of no immediate *présence*, other than the differentiating flow of our varied terminology with which we seek to capture reality, even though it mocks our efforts. The beautiful coherence in which world and self is being revealed to Heinrich appears to have reality only in the poetic product with which Klingsohr concludes his disciple's initiation but not for the poet himself. He, too, like the hero who is locked in war, composes the reality of life in terms that cannot contain it and that lend themselves, therefore, only to formulations that stand under the continual threat of having to give way to reformulations, which are subject to the same threat, ad infinitum.

In a striking confession, one that sounds as though Nietzsche rather than Novalis were its author, Klingsohr continues his comments and informs Heinrich that "in each poetic statement, chaos must shimmer through the veil of regular order" ("das Chaos muß in jeder Dichtung durch den regelmäßigen Flor der Ordnung schimmern") (I, 286, ll. 6–7); that is to say, it shimmers through the same transparent veil of Apollonian form behind which Nietzsche has his pre-Socratic tragedians hide the meaningless void of Dionysian reality. The negative moment of poetic endeavor that Novalis recognizes in these lines constitutes a rare and most explicit acknowledgment on his part of the concept of "romantic irony." Rare as such an acknowledgment may be in his poetic practice, it serves to substantiate his apparent proximity to the Derridean sphere in this instance since that concept has found its niche in the armory of literary analysis from the perspective of deconstruction.[24]

Novalis apparently cannot sustain his romantic poetics without finding himself on territory cultivated by those who have come to believe in the autonomy of art. This observation is hardly novel; on the contrary, it has become almost commonplace, and a Derridean context could easily be added to the others in which it has been made. Such readings of Novalis are undoubtedly justified since his concept of *Poesie* and his practice of it are not based on the premise that our thoughts and their expressions refer to an extraconscious reality. This type of a metaphysics of presence is as foreign to him as it would be for Derrida and, one should add, for Fichte as well. Novalis, the Fichtean, is far more thoroughly aware than later romantic authors that the naive belief in the objects of consciousness as things in themselves is not tenable. Like the autonomist theoreticians and writers of today, he, too, has transferred the ground of reality from a world that is thought to hold us in common to the capacity for language, which enables us to share this thought with all its implications in common. Novalis calls this shift in awareness consciously practiced in acts of perception and use of language *Poesie*.

From the contemporary point of view, the last vestiges of our culture's false belief in metaphysics could finally be shed once language was recognized as the self-referential field of organization for the communal valence that attaches to any and all objects presented to human consciousness with a claim to objective reality. It is an autonomist argument, and critics frequently point to Kantian philosophy as its intellectual ancestor. If one considers primarily those aspects emphasized in the first *Critique*, that relationship seems obvious. By denying the contents of human consciousness access to a thing in itself, Kant does indeed clear the ground for an autonomous sphere within which such contents may relate only to one another. From that vantage point, later theories of semiotic, linguistic, or literary autonomy would certainly appear as though they have come to settle on that ground, even if they were developed quite independently. However, Kantian philosophy has a safety feature against the solipsist danger that accompanies his "Copernican Revolution." That feature has largely been neglected, whereas the danger has by now been realized, and contemporary critics of autonomism must bewail their imprisonment in language. Only recently has this feature been rediscovered,[25] and it remains to be seen whether it will prove as effective now as it did then.

The feature in question is Kant's concept of morality, which is central to his entire critical philosophy, even though it remains merely implicit in his first *Critique*. It may have been overlooked because it was Fichte, a philosopher not as well known outside Germany as Kant, who carried out the implications of the first *Critique* by removing the thing in itself entirely as a possible common ground of reference in order to relocate this ground in the common sphere of the moral imperative. Within this context, the objects presented to consciousness have universal validity only insofar as they may potentially be included under the validating comprehension of the moral or human idea. As formulated by eighteenth-century thinkers, the idea of humanity seems to be a noumenal abstraction that offers a common ground of reference no less precarious than the one offered by the thing in itself. Derrida may be cited as having stated such doubts quite succinctly, when he says, "contrary to what Phenomenology — which is always the phenomenology of perception — has tried to make us believe, contrary to what our desire cannot fail to be tempted into believing, the thing in itself always escapes."[26] Since he refers to Husserl's phenomenology, he means to deny *présence* altogether, not only the presence of things but also self-presence, which is the very presence that furnishes the ground of morality in the Kantian and Fichtean scheme.

With his, in my opinion, most consequent arguments in favor of freedom from metaphysics, Derrida is able to secure a realm of pure semiotic autonomy. This realm can refer to nothing but itself in an ever differentiating movement of consciousness for which objects are never immediately present but always already voiced *(Speech and Phenomena)* or, better yet, written *(Of Grammatology)*. If anything, I understand this differentiating momentum *(différance)* to mean a progressive text that is bound neither by a common beginning *(arche)* nor by a common end *(telos)*. Such a concept may well succeed in guaranteeing freedom from all previous overt or covert tendencies toward metaphysics and with that freedom also the nonreferentiality demanded by autonomists; however, the communal nature of this voicing, writing, or literature, even within a supposedly autonomous context, presupposes a sense of community for which voice, writing, or literature may be voice, writing, or literature, unless these terms, as well as all others, are to be bereft of any meaning whatever. In other words, if signs or language are to communicate at all, there can be no autonomy since the very concept of sign or language already means something other than itself, namely sharing.[27]

Regardless of the variety within a language or the variety of language games, language already has a meaning or referent outside itself, and that referential ground is human community. This community cannot be a particular community or sense of communality, since that would merely beg the same question, namely the question on what ground or with reference to what any particular community or communities may be formed as such. One may ascribe communal formations either to accident, in which case metaphysics in the pre-Kantian sense is reintroduced, or to human authorship, in which case a perspective must be established from which a regulative principle may be sighted that applies to all human beings. Kant's moral philosophy has opened up this perspective and with it a vantage point that would allow not only Novalis but, I believe, also contemporary thinkers to envision a referential context for language to account for its communicative function.

As I have tried to point out, Novalis, the student of Fichte, has always linked his concepts of language and literature to the human capacity for moral freedom. If the poetics he has Klingsohr voice refer only indirectly to this point, it is left in no doubt when he returns to the topic in Heinrich's last dialogue, which is conducted with the sage Sylvester. The full revelation of the central importance conscience *(Gewissen)* holds for the poet is made only after Heinrich has had to overcome Mathilde's loss and is ready to transfer her mediating function to all he encounters. That learning process would in all probability have been explored if the novel had been continued. As it is, Novalis was merely able to establish the concept of moral freedom as the firm foundation for the poet's further development.

But even in part I of the novel, before Heinrich is ready to be enlightened by Sylvester, the moral foundation of all poetic endeavor becomes apparent in the concluding remarks he exchanges with Klingsohr. There, Heinrich observes that language constitutes a little world constructed by human freedom of expression, which he defines further as the ability "to reveal what is outside the world in it" ("das, was außer der Welt ist, in ihr zu offenbaren") (I, 287, ll. 14–15). This, of course, describes the same movement that characterizes the free moral act. Accordingly, Klingsohr acknowledges Heinrich's statement by replying that the term poet should actually not be employed to designate a select guild of individuals because all human beings are really poets (I, 287, ll. 17–21), only, one might add, few are as conversant in their craft as Klingsohr already is and Heinrich is still to become.

IV: The "Basic Schema" in Historical Perspective

This overcoming of all the usual barriers between the individual and the Absolute is the great mystic achievement. In mystic states we both become one with the Absolute and we become aware of our oneness. This is the everlasting and triumphant mystical tradition, hardly altered by differences of clime or creed. In Hinduism, in Neoplatonism, in Sufism, in Christian mysticism, in Whitmanism, we find the same recurring note, so that there is about mystical utterances an eternal unanimity which ought to make a critic stop and think, and which brings it about that the mystical classics have, as has been said, neither birthday nor native land. Perpetually telling of the unity of man with God, their speech antedates languages, and they do not grow old
William James *(The Varieties of Religious Experience)*

Mystischer Dogmatism des Orients — (entstanden aus *Trägheit* und *Ahndung*) höhere Mittheilung der Erkenntniß — intellectueller Quietismus — System des Wissens, wie System der Gnade — Bassives System — indirect thätiges System.

Mystical dogmatism of the Orient — (composed of *passivity* and *intuition*) higher impartation of knowledge — intellectual Quietism — system of knowledge, as a system of grace — passive system — indirectly active system.
Novalis

Thätige Unthätigkeit, ächter Quietsmus ist der kritische Idealism. Du wirst leicht einsehn wie sehr Fichtens W[issenschafts] L[ehre], nichts als Schema des innern Künstlerwesens ist.

Active passivity, true Quietism, that is what Critical Idealism is. You will have no difficulty in realizing that Fichte's *Wissenschaftslehre* is nothing else but a systematic exposition of the mentality required for being an artist.
Novalis

Chapter 11
Georges Poulet's *Metamorphoses of the Circle:* A Critical Reading

Throughout the recorded history of our culture, thinkers and poets have relied on the basic structural pattern of the circle in order to convey their respective views of being. Dietrich Mahnke's treatise traces that history from Greek antiquity to Novalis in whose work he recognized evidence of the same pattern.[1] The historical survey is not only the most valuable but also the most ambitious part of the book since the chapter on Novalis is very short and leaves the complexity of his schema unexamined. Meyer H. Abrams refers to the concept of the circle very extensively in his classic *Natural Supernaturalism*,[2] and Marshall Brown has recently presented his perceptive study of circular and elliptical configurations he considers to be characteristic for romanticism in general.[3] Their arguments leave little doubt that circular imagery is, indeed, prevalent in romantic literature. Finally, there is Georges Poulet's structuralist analysis in which he traces the "metamorphoses of the circle" from the Middle Ages to our century and shows the drastic shift in self-comprehension they reflect.[4] Since it is the legacy of this shift with which Novalis and his contemporaries must contend, I should like to be more explicit about Poulet's work and the work of Goethe, the most representative of those contemporaries, in order to provide the appropriate background against which the "basic schema" must be judged.

For the self exposed to the meaninglessness of existence, the circle is an orientational pattern that can impose coherence on the infinity of being: it transforms the infinite into unity, either through the beacon of a center, with reference to a potentially inclusive whole, or through the comprehensive totality of a circumference, with reference to a center thus potentially defined. As Poulet points out, the thinkers whose influence gave direction to the Middle Ages tended to draw an absolute circle with the divine both at its center and at its circumference; their views essentially represent an interpretation of the widely accepted definition that states "God is a sphere whose center is everywhere and whose circumference nowhere" ("deus est sphaera cujus centrum ubique, circumferentia nusquam").[5] Rather than repeat what Georges Poulet has cited in his expert summary exposition, I should like to deal with the implications of his presentation in a more general and independent fashion better adapted to the intellectual issues that are important within the context of those concerns that find their focal expresssion in such works as Goethe's *Faust* and in Novalis's "basic schema."

The divine sphere, the circle in an absolute sense, is difficult to imagine. It may be easiest to think of it as describing the simultaneity of an outgoing motion from the center and the same movement in reverse. The infinity it encloses reflects, then, an ordered coherence insofar as each of its parts relates positively to the center, as one of its emanations, and negatively to the circumference, as lacking in its perfection. For the medieval worldview either the centricity or comprehensive capacity of the divine could be emphasized. The formula "deus est sphaera cujus centrum ubique, circumferentia nusquam" summarizes very succinctly this dual function of absolute unity, that is to say, of unity when that concept applies to all of being, which it does in its capacity as beginning, or uniform source, for everything, and end, or inclusive plenitude, the perfect whole. If God is conceived as center, the image is one of a point infinitely expanded, an ever creative source, so that it is entirely true to say "God is a sphere whose center is everywhere"; but then, conversely, anything created is external to the productive center, and from its perspective the same motion is seen in reverse. Consequently, for everything created the infinite center becomes an infinite periphery, an infinity of being where the individual would drift in hopeless confusion if not for the point of orientation in the center, in the common ground of origin.

Within this context, each mode of being can be perceived as a positive manifestation of the divine, but only once the Creator God has been revealed in equally positive terms. When Faust, for instance, spurns medieval reliance on revealed truth and turns, instead, to the powers of the human intellect in his attempt to fathom "what holds the world together at its innermost core" ("was die Welt / Im Innersten zusammenhält") (11. 381–82),[6] he has to admit defeat, and despair over the meaninglessness of existence takes possession of him, until he sees no alternative but suicide. Faith in the revealed divinity is at the heart of established orthodoxies like the medieval Church; accordingly, Poulet finds many passages where God is depicted as the center radiant with infinite creativity, and he seems tempted to consider this construction the one most characteristic for the manner in which a person would experience living as a meaningful enterprise during the Middle Ages.

There is, however, the other half of the original formulation, which defines God as circumference, and that relationship is equally important, even though its exposition may not have been as prevalent in an age securely ruled by only one ecclesiastic orthodoxy with catholic claims to authority. The divine circumference can be imagined only in flux, as was the case with the center, because a static enclosure constitutes limitation, which would imply a force other than the center's expansive power. But there is nothing other than God: God is the fountainhead of all being and all of being is contained in God. Whereas the individual self assumed its position on the periphery with respect to the divine center, its relationship to the divine circumference can only be maintained if it were to function as that sphere's center: not in the absolute sense as source of the fullness of being but rather as its relative lack, as a point that exists only with reference to the comprehensive totality of being from which it is, however, separated by that same being's infinity. From this perspective, the universe surrounding each individual is not regarded as a positive manifestation of its origin; instead, it is a realm, of which the self is a part, that must be transcended if it is to be apprehended in its wholeness and perfection. The view from the circumference offers the ultimate vision, and there is no vantage point for it from within. No human acquisition of knowledge and experience can ever match the expansion of the divine center, unless the self were to become that very center and thus also the circumference, that is to say, unless it were to become God. Then the self could behold all things as they really are and become conscious of its own place within a true immutable order where, previously, it only ascertained the enigma of existence without direction or purpose. Since the self is not God nor able to leave the realm that cannot itself contain God who contains it, there would seem to be only one answer to the ever repeated question that underlies the Faustian theme and that each person asks merely by being alive: "Is it for your sake I live, are you the moment to which I say 'stay, thou art so beautiful'?" That, or something similar, is the unvarying refrain, and the inevitable reply inherent in anything the world has to offer is a resounding "no!" Many pretend to hear a "yes" instead, but that is a delusion more or less temporary and unfailingly dispelled, at the latest by death's final "no," which reaches far beyond any particular individual because it applies wherever time holds sway. Thus, the human quest for final comprehensive insight would appear to be hopeless from the start were it not for the very feeling of insufficiency that initiates it and furnishes the criterion of negation against which nothing short of the transcendental goal can prevail. In other words, the divine as perfection, as absolute unity and comprehension, is only negatively present, present only through its absence; however, negative presence is presence, nonetheless. It is a presence made manifest in a twofold fashion: first, by the self's sense of privation, of lacking what is most essential, which is at the core of all human motivation, and second, by the self's ability to say "no," to recognize the goal not for what it is, since that is precluded by its absence, but very definitely for what it is not.

Implicitly, this means that the positive reality of things, concepts, and words must ultimately be bypassed or rather negated since nothing they convey will prove adequate to reality itself. It cannot be revealed at all because the only reality we know is one that is forever replaced by another, except for the consciousness of self, the unmediated awareness of our own being. Oddly enough, however, the self, which seems to be the most immediate object and therefore, the least likely to elude us, remains unknown and refuses to be conclusively identified with any one or any sum of objects, with anything, in short, that can possibly be grasped by human knowledge. The self is experienced only through its thoughts and actions, which appear to it as a continual process of expansion toward a circumference that is the fullness it lacks. The center of individuated being is thus akin to the center of all being, and that relationship, once reassembled within the absolute pattern of the divine circle, results in an alignment where the essential self, the core of the soul, is the relative center and God the circumference that encompasses the infinity of being converging and extending with reference to this particular individual; or, the center can now also be considered the negative presence of the fullness that is God, God's concentration or reduction, and that lack serves as the directive toward the soul's final goal, the soul's personal encounter with God, the beatific vision, which is the end of every human life, according to the Church's teachings.

This intensely personal, even subjective, relationship with the divinity is the necessary corollary to its institutionalized and objective version, just as, within the divine sphere, any given point representative of the self necessarily assumes the position of both relative center with reference to the absolute circumference and relative circumference with reference to the absolute center. These two interdependent conceptions of the individual's position in the universe find their overt manifestation throughout the Middle Ages.

The simultaneity of the self's being as both relative center and relative circumference had its distinct theological implications. From the self's position as relative circumference, all objective reality is an outflow of the divine center and, therefore, a manifestation of it. For this reason, the Church has placed doctrinal emphasis on positive, external formal aids — such as a priestly hierarchy, sacraments, scriptural exegesis, and so on — to insure the believer's orientation toward God. However, from the self's position as relative center, all objective reality is a deprivation of the whole that is the divine circumference or divine all-inclusiveness. This position has also been reflected in the Church's doctrine, insofar as it insists on the ultimate efficacy of a purely internal, personal relationship to the divine by way of prayer, spiritual attitude, and grace, without which the external aids would remain ineffective.

The imagery employed during the Middle Ages to illustrate a person's relationship to God would appear to reflect the same dualism because, judging by the samples Georges Poulet cites in his initial chapter, references to God as center of the universe seem to predominate, complemented by some taken from the mystical tradition, that claim the divine is harbored within the human soul. As the positive, institutionalized aspect of this worldview began to wane, only the personal one, which was represented most emphatically by the mystics, could prevail, and Poulet points to mysticism as preparing the way for the Renaissance, for the change in intellectual attitude that initiated our own age.

During this period of leave-taking from the Middle Ages, which occurred at different times in the various regions of Europe, the self and its powers assume central importance with respect to a world that must be ordered anew. It is entirely true that the self moves into the center of the divine circle, whether that image arises from the mystic's vantage point or from the perspective of Renaissance humanism, but there is also a distinct difference in the functional relationship between these respective centers and their circumferences. As Poulet suggests, in the one case, the powers of the self are attributed to God's presence in the soul, which establishes the individual in a position of correspondence to the all-inclusive divinity on high, whereas in the other, the self is the active center from which it embarks on the conquest of the universe in an effort to reach the outer limit of its comprehension. Even though it is not expressly stated, this conquering, expansive self has effectively moved into God's place at the center, which initiates the possibility of replacing the divine sphere altogether with a human one.

Once the cosmos can no longer be regarded within an absolute sphere, unity becomes a relative concept applicable to any aspect of being contained by an infinity of being for which there is neither unity of origin nor unity of comprehension. Accordingly, Georges Poulet's chapters depicting subsequent metamorphoses of the circle reflect the loss of its absolute contours, which can be translated, for the individuals he cites, into confusion, despair, and lack of orientation mitigated by varied attempts to redraw the line that would again wrest meaning from the chaos of infinity. Foremost among the few who prove capable of reenvisioning human existence within a coherent framework are those whose thoughts betray a tendency reminiscent of intellectual attitudes that were characteristic of the mystical tradition. Poulet's failure to distinguish clearly between a positive moment in the divine sphere and a negative one, which latter marks the mystic's path to God, unfortunately prevents his readers from recognizing distinctly those aspects of our medieval and pre-Christian heritage that continued to furnish a basis for orientation long after the dogmatic assurance of established religion had ceased to offer unquestioned guidelines.

Poulet's chapter on romanticism, in which a great number of European authors are named — among them in prominent place Fichte and Goethe as well as Novalis — records an astonishing restablization of circular imagery. He perceives in the literature of the period a trend conveying a sense of the individual's function that represents a renewed appreciation of the self's true centricity or, in a paraphrase of his own words, of that centricity's inherently religious nature[7] These features of similarity in self-conception are particularly conspicuous when they pertain to thinkers and writers of entirely different eras; not only are the Middle Ages several centuries removed from the "Age of Goethe," but the first is still steeped in the metaphysical security a living God could grant to people as diverse in time, place, and temperament as Meister Eckhart and Pico della Mirandola, whereas the second is without any such shelter against the cosmic void. This remarkable parallelism can occur in such diverse historical and cultural settings because it refers to a common tradition, the one I mentioned under the rather vague label of mysticism. In order to clarify what this term means, I propose to furnish a brief exposition of some major tenets underlying Western mysticism, with the added intent of tracing their applicability to a secular framework. As a result, I also hope Novalis's place in history of ideas and letters will become more clearly apparent.

It is no simple task to determine what mysticism connotes with reference to our Greco-Judeo-Christian culture, and I do so without any claim to render an exhaustive theory or definition; rather, my intention is to indicate points of orientation that serve to guide the mystic and, as I have already implied, can also do the same for those who must find their way bereft of metaphysical protection. Since this postmedieval dilemma has found its most succinct expression and best-known symbolic representative in the figure of Faust, I shall, later on, also direct my discussion toward Goethe.

Chapter 12
A Short Survey of Western Mysticism's Principal Tenets

First, to dispel any misleading notions that might be entertained whenever I refer to mysticism, it is necessary to remember that the term definitely does not imply the nebulous, ambiguous irrationalism quite rightfully distrusted by those accustomed to the rigors of reason.[8] Evelyn Underhill, probably the best-known English authority on mysticism, offers this definition: ''Mysticism is the art of union with Reality. The mystic is a person who has attained that union to a greater or less degree; or who aims at and believes in such attainment.''[9] Essentially, she states nothing more complicated than the fact that the polar opposition of human reality and absolute reality allows for a reciprocity she refers to as union. Three basic aspects would have to characterize such a relationship: first, the interpolar stress, the field of energy, so to speak, created between poles; second, the path that must be traversed from one pole to reach the other; and third, the fundamental equality of opposites on which all relationship rests, even that of opposition.

Plato's is the best-known description of the dynamic stress between the world of mortals and eternal reality. In his *Symposium* he has Socrates speak of it as the realm of Eros, whom he defines as love expressive of lack, as presence through absence, by means of which he is able to establish a relationship between the relative reality of human experience and the absolute reality it lacks. Eros's realm extends from the mortal to the immortal or, in other words, Eros is the name for the dynamic stress that links the world of privation with fulfillment, the world of beings with Being itelf, the world of realities with the Real, our world with the perfection it lacks. The seemingly prosaic insight that love is expressive of lack is the gateway to our mystical tradition.[10]

Love, if seen in this light, can become the soul's sure guide to its final fulfillment, which can only be experienced as longing, that is to say, as lack, before it is attained. This ultimate goal, the goal of all human strivings, cannot be defined in positive terms because we can know it only as a sense of lack and insufficiency. Final fulfillment is merely another name for what Evelyn Underhill calls Reality, with a capital R, and we know of it only insofar as we lack it. All endeavors throughout our lives owe their enactment to our unceasing search for final fulfillment; all our endeavors would thus be fathered by the spirit of love, yet few indeed show their heritage. Obviously a criterion must exist that would allow us to discriminate between all actions in general and those that lead to the desired goal of all activity. This latter possibility would constitute a path to absolute reality, and Plato depicts love as rising along such a path, the path of beauty, to the vision of the incorporeal reality of beauty that is reflected in all things beautiful. It is important to note in this context that the relative terminology of empirical experience can circumscribe its absolute criterion only negatively; that is, absolute beauty cannot be described so much for what it is but rather for what it is *not*, as may be determined from the following passage:

> Whoever has been initiated so far in the mysteries of Love and has viewed all these aspects of the beautiful in due succession, is at last drawing near the final revelation. And now, Socrates, there bursts upon him that wondrous vision which is the very soul of the beauty he has toiled so long for. It is an everlasting loveliness which neither comes nor goes, which neither flowers nor fades . . . Nor will his vision of the beautiful take the form of a face, or of hands, or of anything that is of the flesh. It will be neither words, nor knowledge, nor a something that exists in something else, such as a living creature, or the earth, or the heavens, or anything that is — . . .[11]

The end of the journey lies beyond the way stations but, at the same time, the order and sequence that might constitute stages along a path originate from incoherent multiplicity only with reference to the goal beyond. Accordingly, the criterion of relative beauty, or rather absolute beauty's relative lack, enables Plato to organize the entire realm of human experience into three distinct spheres of gradual ascent toward the ultimate vision. First, the realm of physical appearances must be traversed leading from the love for one beautiful person to the appreciation of phenomenal beauty unrestricted by the limits of particularization. From there, love may advance further toward an attachment for the beauty of soul, the inner harmony that can be equated with goodness, and, again, the road leads from one to all, from one virtuous person to the virtue of social institutions. Finally, the coordination of nature reflects a beauty that is the fitting object for the intellect whose love aspires after that insight of comprehensive unity commonly referred to as truth, and, once more, particular sciences must point to an all-comprehensive science of sciences, which must be equated with philosophy since it holds that elevated rank for Plato; at this stage the proper state of receptivity for beholding Reality or pure beauty has been attained, no further medium may stand between Eros and his object, and lack can now be transformed into ultimate fulfillment.

Although everyone may be supposed to love beauty, most individuals do not ascend along the stages just described and therefore fail to establish direct communication with the divine. They labor, instead, under the erroneous assumption that satisfaction may be found in a particular object or a particular set of temporary circumstances. The fatal error arises from an all too narrow concept of beauty. Plato extends that concept far beyond the limits within which it is generally understood. He speaks of beauty as the visible reflection of absolute reality within the realm of relativity. If anyone mistakes the relative instance of the reflected image for that which it reflects, his path will no longer be one of ascent, it will rather be one of stationary circularity.

In order to understand the unique function ascribed to beauty in the *Symposium*, we must think of it as harmony, as the law that unifies without disproportion or clash. Only then does the seemingly arbitrary intermingling of aesthetics, ethics, wisdom, and absolute reality become meaningful. Aesthetics, ethics, and wisdom are all manifestations of the absolute reality of absolute unity; aesthetics manifests Unity as the harmonious proportion of form, ethics manifests Unity as the harmonious proportion of human interaction, and wisdom manifests Unity as the harmonious proportion of all phenomena.[12] Each constitutes a stage on the ascending path that love traverses from the relative reality of isolated multiplicity, and its corresponding lack of unity, to the absolute reality of Unity, and its corresponding sense of fulfillment.

An interpretation of the *Symposium* that centers around the concepts of unity and multiplicity has actually already left the Athens of Agathon for the Alexandria of Plotinus and Porphyry. The school of Neoplatonism represented by these two men furnishes the intellectual background for the fifth-century writings of a Syrian monk who chose to ascribe his works to Dionysius the Areopagite, an Athenian convert of St. Paul's mentioned in Acts 17:34. This Syrian monk, known to posterity only under his assumed name, was one of the first great Christian mystics who attempted to furnish a detailed record of his experiences in the communicable terms of the philosophical and theological framework that was available to him. John Scotus Erigena, probably the most renowned of the many eminent scholars under Carolingian patronage, translated the Areopagite's works in the ninth century, and their influence throughout the Middle Ages was enormous.[13]

An element essential to the mystical way is its negativity, and the Areopagite's outline of the path leading to union with absolute reality emphasizes just this element, that is to say, the negativity of all stages with respect to the final goal. The same negativity was already implied in the passages from the *Symposium*, because the entire concept of an ascent in stages is based on the comparatively negative value of each stage with respect to the stage that follows it. Aside from the relative negativity encountered on the stages of ascent in knowledge, the Platonic dialogue also makes it quite clear by its negative definition of pure beauty that absolute reality transcends the comparative reality of all the stages. Nonetheless, it is sameness, or rather similarity, that Plato underscores, whereas the element of negation remains an implication. With Dionysius, the negative momentum of mystical ascent is clearly stated. An emphasis on God's transcendence, the complete otherness that separates creator from creature, is central to his "negative theology."[14] All of creation, either in part or as a whole, is therefore that which God is not. No predicate at our command can possibly apply to God, not even a name. All concepts, words, and knowledge at human command can merely render a negative circumscription of the divine; they can merely state what God is not. If absolute reality constitutes the complete opposite of the relative reality of human experience, the stages of mystical ascent will be marked by a gradual disengagement from relative values. However, it is not enough to define the entirety of our physical and mental realms as the negation of absolute reality. In order to reach the Absolute, abstract definition will have to be replaced by total commitment. The main stations on the road to God are now called: purgation, illumination, and union.[15] Purgation refers to the process of disengagement from the controls exercised by the physical realm. The physical realm has no longer any power over the spirit who recognizes that realm as negation of absolute fulfillment. Illumination refers to the process of disengagement from the controls exercised by the realm of knowledge. That does not necessarily mean knowledge must not be pursued at all; on the contrary, knowledge should be pursued, but this should be done in the right spirit of humility that may ultimately lead to the fully comprehended insight of human ignorance.[16] This stage must not by confused with despair. It is the positive realization of human limitation that prepares the soul for its ultimate experience, the experience referred to as union because all mediation between the human individual and absolute reality has been removed.

If all sensual faculties as well as all mental ones lead toward nothing but negation, there seems to be no faculty left with which to behold the divine. The resolution to this apparent problem is the central insight that inspires the mysticism of Meister Eckhart, the German Dominican who lived during the late thirteenth and early fourteenth centuries. His influence on German philosophy is inestimable and reached far past the Middle Ages into the nineteenth century.[17] As was the case with Dionysius the Areopagite, Eckhart's name is not mentioned in order to point to a specific phase in the historical development of mysticism within the Western cultural realm, but rather in order to illustrate a particular aspect common to mysticism as such. I specified three such aspects, two of which have already been discussed: the force between relative and absolute reality has been defined as Eros, and the road love must travel has been identified as a path of negation; the underlying unity between the realms linked by Eros's intercession remains to be examined, and this is best accomplished with reference to Meister Eckhart's concept of the human being's innate divinity.

The concept of divine transcendence was essential to the negative theology of Dionysius; God, however, cannot only be transcendent, because in that case there would be no link between God and creation, which means that the latter could not exist. God is also immanent.[18] For Plato, as the author of the *Symposium*, such immanence of pure reality was most strikingly manifest in the harmony of beauty, and also Dionysius's path of negation can actually lead to God only if it stands in a definite relationship to the divine.

Meister Eckhart locates the key to the relationship between divinity and man in that part of the soul which can attain union with God. Its presence is guaranteed not so much by the statements on the part of a great number of people who claim to have reached the ultimate stage on the mystical path, but rather by an experience immediate to each and every person. All individuals are more or less keenly aware of the limitations imposed on their existence. An awareness of limitation as limitation must be based on a criterion that transcends the limit. In order to judge something inferior, a standard derived from something better must be applied. If the standard of judgment were equal to the thing to be judged, inferiority could never be predicated. The sense of lack that accompanies all human experience throughout life can only be produced against the background of a standard of fulfillment. Since nothing the world has to offer can grant the absolute gratification desired, the criterion for fulfillment must necessarily transcend the realm of empirical existence, which means that it is divine. The element of divinity each person must harbor in order to recognize his or her mortal plight has many names because, like God, it is essentially nameless. Meister Eckhart considers this mysterious power of the soul to be its very essence, and he never tires of pointing this out in his sermons and treatises. In the sermon entitled "God Enters a Free Soul,"[19] he mentions among other names the one of "vünkelin," which in English means "sparklet" or "little spark," whereas its Latin equivalent would be "scintilla animae." Let us accept that terminology for the present purpose in the same noncommittal spirit Eckhart suggests in his own effort to describe our divine endowment:

> I have said that there is one agent alone in the soul that is free. Sometimes I have called it the tabernacle of the Spirit. Other times I have called it the Light of the Spirit and again, a spark. Now I say that it is neither this nor that. It is something higher than this or that, as the sky is higher than the earth and I shall call it by a more aristocratic name than I have ever used before, even though it disowns my adulation and my name, being

far beyond both. It is free of all names and unconscious of any kind of forms. It is at once pure and free, as God himself is; and like him is perfect unity and uniformity, so that there is no possible way to spy it out.[20]

The last words, "there is no possible way to spy it out," are merely intended to signify that we cannot recognize our absolute nature as absolute. This absolute nature manifests itself as a negative criterion only; it enables us to recognize *lack* of perfection, and more than that the comparative *degree of lack* of perfection, but nothing more. As one progresses along the road of gradual disengagement from the imperfect and unreal, that absolute nature, the divine spark, is able to shine forth with ever increasing freedom and splendor, until the final negation when all the encumbrance of imperfection is shed and nothing but radiant divinity remains. At that instant, as Eckhart puts it, "God is born in man."[21]

Meister Eckhart's *scintilla animae* combines two seemingly opposite qualities. Insofar as it can behold the divine it is divine, and insofar as it is man it is not divine. If this seems to be a contradictory statement, Eckhart's words, which convey a concept originally found in Platonic doctrine, may vindicate its feasibility:

If I am to see color, I must have that in me that is sensitive to color; but I should never see color if I did not have the essence of color already.[22]

Eckhart uses this example in order to clarify the function of the soul spark. His intention is to communicate to his audience that the soul, as the spiritual eye, must have the essence of God already if it aspires to behold God, yet the soul is also as different from God as the eye is different from the object it sees. If modern optics disagree with this analogy, let us just say that the ultimate fulfillment we seek is already potentially present in us insofar as we seek it, yet it is also absent for the same reason. Inadvertently, it seems I have returned to the topic of Eros, since this very same absence, this lack of fulfillment, was also the cause of Eros's dynamic force. Lack of fulfillment is nothing but the negative presence of fulfillment, which is what Plato actually tries to imply when he cites Poverty as Eros's mother and Abundance as his father.[23] A concept like the negative presence of fulfillment or divinity points directly to the negative theology of Dionysius who only admits to a negative definition of God in the finite realm. It is now easy to see that the three aspects of mysticism that were discussed are completely interdependent and quite inseparable. If they were, nevertheless, presented separately, it was an artificial separation produced for the sake of a more comprehensible presentation.

Evelyn Underhill's definition of mysticism as the art of union with Reality can now be envisioned to entail a systematic pattern of relationship with love pointing the way from lack of affluence along stages of negation. What has been shown is only a rough outline of the basic intellectual framework as it applies to the mystic tradition of the West. In order to illustrate the fundamental aspects under discussion, I mentioned names that span the years from ancient Greece to the Middle Ages, but the tradition does not stop there; it continues in one form or another to our days. I have intentionally avoided any references to this historical development of the mystic tradition, because mysticism represents far more a basic human attitude than a historically conditioned phenomenon. The historical garb of the travelers may vary, but whether they wear the robes of Greek philosophers or the cloth of monks or the attire of our secular age, their path remains the path of negation.[24]

Chapter 13
Mysticism in a Secular Context and Goethe's Metamorphoses of the Circle: An Illustration with Reference to *Faust*

In the Germany of the late eighteenth and early nineteenth centuries, the Germany of Kantian philosophy, of "Storm and Stress," romanticism, and the "Age of Goethe,"[25] the mystic's temperament was strongly represented. Once again, in the pronouncements of Weimar classicism, notably those made by Schiller, we encounter beauty on an equal footing with ethics as humanity's guide to freedom;[26] once again, from the great thinkers of German Idealism, we hear of concepts (*Vernunftbegriffe* or *Ideen*) ungraspable by human understanding that, paradoxically enough, determine or regulate the realm of experience;[27] and Meister Eckhart's favorite thesis of man's inherent divinity finds an especially resounding echo. As is well attested in most histories of culture and literature that deal with the epoch, the influence of Pietism is widespread, and hardly anyone of note escapes exposure to this doctrine of inwardness at some point in life. It is not only this religiously inspired attitude in Protestant circles of testing all experiences against the divine criterion harbored within the soul that is reminiscent of Meister Eckhart's teachings; inner reality comes to furnish the standard for evaluating the outer world quite generally, and Kant's "Copernican Revolution," whereby he redefines the laws of interaction and coherence for all phenomena as laws of the mind's operation, reflects and determines the intellectual trend, quite aside from strictly theological concerns, for many years to come.

Kant's internal relocating of the focus for reality was occasioned, as he himself says, by Hume's skepticism that awakened him from his dogmatic slumbers in which it appeared as though the solid ground of general validity was to be found out there, among the things themselves. In the same manner, the firm outlines of all established, positive values, rules, and frameworks, be they theological, political, legal, sociological, or aesthetic, had become ever more indistinct under the onslaught of critical questioning and reexamination that arose once the Reformation no longer allowed for one basic systematic order within which each individual's function could be defined. As the outside world ceased to offer reliable points of orientation for human existence, the stage was being set for the typically "modern" sense of personal isolation. Goethe's *Werther* best illustrated the negative impact of such a condition,[28] and the chorus of alienated voices has grown remarkably since then. However, there is also a positive aspect to this alienating effect, because the less the self is defined in terms with which it circumscribes the realm outside, the more it is reduced to its innermost core and made aware of its own creativity in formulating the very positive, objectively binding reality that had previously seemed to be the independent source of all certainty. Consequently, this is a time of true rejuvenation, Germany's "Golden Age" and much-delayed Renaissance, when the concrete givenness of external reality loses its dead remoteness with respect to the individual who no longer feels dependent on the structures without and, empowered by the discovery of the self's freedom, imbues them, rather, with a new or, at times, completely altered life. That process of revivification undergoes many mutations and a number of stages, comprising the enlightened belief in human progress, the "Storm and Stress" cult of genius, the classicist faith in the delivering grace of aesthetic form, and the romantic vision of the self as activity bridging the span between the initial and final congruence of subjective and objective reality. Awareness of inherent powers furnishes the foundation for each of these varied attempts to gain a new sense of orientation in a strange new world that lacks the guidelines of divine order made relevant by a doctrine held in common; however, to the exclusion of such externally directed concerns, only the prerequisite turning inward has generally been recognized — either in praise or derision — and has become proverbial for being a typically German trend away from the realities of the world.[29]

Actually, the very opposite is true: far from withdrawing into its encapsuled interior, the individual must look outward and experience the world in order to realize the self's innate potential to the fullest extent. This process can be envisioned as a journey[30] from an undefined beginning that is being defined along the way to an undefined goal, and this is exactly the "personal development and education" ("Entwicklung und Bildung") for which Goethe's novel *Wilhelm Meisters Lehrjahre* became the accepted literary paradigm.

Wilhelm, however, is undeniably a kin to Faust, if in no other way but that both find themselves in a world where they must seek out their respective ways toward the place they are to hold in it since there is no preconstrued framework from which such an assignment might be determined. In each case, the pattern of progress is marked by the same characteristics that made it possible for the mystic to advance toward his goal along a negative path where all positive criteria prove insufficient to guide him. For Faust's struggles, medieval theology and its attendant mythology still furnish the background but, significantly enough, quite unbeknownst to him; neither the "Prologue in Heaven" nor his ultimate salvation affect his actions. Mephistopheles seems to be the only emissary from the unknowable realm, and he turns out to be the principle of negation with which Faust must ally himself if he is ever to encounter the "Yes" that supersedes it. This ultimate affirmation cannot be addressed to any particular aspect of being; it cannot be, to paraphrase Plato's definition of absolute beauty, "yes" here and "no" there. Ultimate affirmation must apply to being itself in its totality, which can only occur from a vantage point of the Whole and not the part, not from the perspective of the mortal but the immortal. Accordingly, only angels are in a position to sing the unqualified praise of creation, which they do in the "Prologue," whereas man may merely aspire toward arriving at the ultimate vision that would permit him to join his voice to theirs; its actual attainment has traditionally been called salvation, the very state into which an angelic choir of attendants transports Faust's soul after his death, proclaiming that they are empowered to do so as long as love from above has duly been met by continual striving on the mortal's part (ll. 11934–41).[31] This, then, circumscribes the human sphere of endeavor and it seems a simple enough request, except that we are not told what to strive for.

The individual, who must judge from the viewpoint of the part, can only affirm the Whole by negating its parts. This is a positive negation, quite different from negation that is equivalent to despair. It is negation affirmed, an acceptance of negation that extends not to any particular but over the entire range of partiality itself. Simultaneous affirmation and negation is at the heart of the dialectic process Goethe refers to as striving, a process that does not allow for a goal implicit of cessation in its attainment. Faust affirms this type of negation with his last words: the moment to which he says "yes," the moment he wishes to eternalize entails a vision of humankind active on behalf of its common well-being but never without the threat of disaster, so that there is no room for idleness, neither that of despair nor that of permanent attachment to the impermanence of worldly achievement (ll. 11563–86). He says "yes" to his and every individual's fate that had previously only elicited curses from him when he had still been unable to translate human confinement into containment.

Confinement is the experience of human limitation with reference to the self only; it is an experience of pure negation that stamps individuated being as an exercise in futility arising from nothing and returning to nothing along a path of continual frustration. With the term "containment," on the other hand, I wish to signify the experience of human limitation with reference to the totality of being, and the only way Faust, or any person, can refer to it is by actively affirming his place in it, which means the active acceptance of the negation that arises from the limits imposed on human existence. No matter how limited an individual's sphere of activity, as long as it is not permitted to confine its agent to inaction through inducing either a false sense of final accomplishment or the conviction of ultimate futility, striving, that is to say, free agency affirming the self within its limits as an integrated and interrelated part of the universe, is possible. For Faust, being is a mystery that offers no clue to its potential resolution, other than the "no" of his limitation, a "no" he finally learns to interpret as an indicator pointing to the field of endeavor where the "yes" becomes possible. There is no positive formulation for his place in the order of things, but there is a negative one that can be determined only by the full exercise of all his powers, through which he discovers their limits and through their limits their true potential that comprises his assigned sphere of activity. In this manner, dissatisfaction becomes Faust's guide to satisfaction, so that he travels a path of negation toward his undefined goal, just as the mystic traversed his *via negationis* guided only by lack, by his soul spark, by his inherent potential for fulfillment in the vision of absolute reality.

Aside from this similarity, the difference that unquestionably exists between medieval mysticism and the modern quest for orientation also becomes quite evident in Goethe's dramatic poem. The religious spirit feels itself drawn to the absolute source of attraction that is its God, who may be hidden from human recognition but whose reality is not in doubt. For that matter, the same certitude, and thus the same dynamic relationship, is introduced by Plato insofar as he assigns absolute reality to beauty. That kind of initial assurance is exactly what is unavailable to the Faustian individual; consequently, he has to set out on his journey propelled by the force of his own powers, driven by his insatiability, compelled by what Goethe calls his "dark" urge (*dunkel*), where the term "dark" means blindness occasioned by the absence of a goal. Meister Eckhart's inner criterion of orientation remains, only the soul spark has become a volcanic source of energy as well, and in the course of its eruption into human action, into striving, the negative way stations no longer appear in a predetermined hierarchical order but must be discovered through error (317). Faust needs Mephistopheles to experience the entire range of all the Lord of Negation has to offer in order to assure himself, and us, that human existence without a fixed metaphysical point of orientation is not necessarily framed by futility. Faust is the individual magnified to his or her utmost potential and stands, in this capacity, as a collective expression for all humanity.

Wilhem Meister, on the other hand, is humankind's individual expression, the inclusive poetic symbol's counterpart in prose, illustrative of the same truth, as it is lived by one person rather than by one for all. Since Wilhelm does not have to explore the outermost limits of humanity's potentials and deals merely with those of his own, the shadow of despair does not hover so heavily over his path and its negativity is toned down by a sense of positive accomplishment.

Nonetheless, the principle of his education differs in no way from Faust's, except that the unknown taskmaster is not God and his host but rather a secret society headed by an Abbé, a cleric entirely devoted to the unusual pedagogical enterprise of having his charges come to the full realization of their powers by allowing them to follow their respective drives, urges, or inclinations — and commit mistakes. The basic premise, here as was the case with Faust, is that human motivation essentially heads in the right direction, which is only possible if its source prefigures its goal; however, since neither goal nor source are known, the relative sense of dissatisfaction with any particular accomplishment furnishes a painful but trustworthy guide to the true course and its mark. Evidently, the setting must be such that it offers ample opportunity for action in which a person's given talents and aptitudes might be tried, trained, and fully developed, until there is no longer any doubt about the active part that individual is to play in human affairs. In Wilhelm's case, this journey leads from a vague discontent with the confinement the circumstances of reality impose on him to an ever greater involvement with the theater. This is his school, real yet unreal, an aesthetic education, where he may test and foster all his powers, learn to use them, come to recognize his relative strengths and weaknesses, and finally, after he has mastered all levels of theatrical practice, gain the self-assurance he needs in order to realize his future is not on the stage and that he must begin to assume his role in life. What that role might ultimately be remains unclear; after all, Wilhelm is merely finishing his apprenticeship and is still far from being a "master" of life.

However, the direction in which he goes is quite clear; as an apprentice he learns that the lurking conflict between the dictates of circumstance and individual freedom, between pragmatic necessity and self-affirmation, cannot be resolved by attempting to substitute fantasy for reality or, rather, art for life. Through his acquaintance with the theater, which had initially attracted him because it seemed to set no bounds to anything imagination could conceive, he learned that even art is anchored in life's mire and that a vast array of utilitarian detail awaits the mastery of craftsmanship before the image is formed for the audience's appreciation. Form, the result of craftsmanship, of mastery, of sovereignty over the object's obstinacy, is the key that endows art with life and, conversely, it can also transform life into art, that is to say, living into an expressly human act in which the imprint of the free spirit's directive is joined to the given material nature provides. The effortless juncture of those demands originating from man's physical estate, insofar as he is part of nature, and those derived from his capacity to act freely in an ethical fashion, in a context that is significant only in human terms,[32] *that* is the ideal, the potential that slumbers in each person. At the end of his apprenticeship, Wilhelm is married to an individual in whom this ideal is realized, and if we were to project the trend of his development, there is little doubt that ultimately he must attain to similar unity of self in order to assume his rightful role in the great cosmic drama. Once this stage has been reached, it means continued action, but now as a full-fledged participant in mankind's common striving. So Wilhelm, too, will cast his "yes" in the teeth of futility by realizing his individual talents and powers as the tools with which he can exercise his craftsmanship in forming life on human terms.

Striving would mean, then, the unending but never futile task of translating the idea of humanity into concrete situations in an effort to stem the ever-threatening tide of nature that would engulf us and reduce what was or could be human to a state of animallike dependency. With this imagery, my thoughts on Wilhelm Meister's eventual mastership rejoin Faust's last vision of a free people united in their common effort against the waves that gnaw unceasingly at the dams by which their realm is secured. Thus, within our modern, nontheistic setting the mystic's path toward union with Reality is still traveled, only its name is self-realization; self-realization into what Goethe calls a "person," into a free, that is to say, a human or moral, agent, is the gateway through which each individual may rejoin the order in the unity of being.

True wisdom ("der Weisheit letzter Schluß") (l. 11574), as Faust acknowledges with his last ecstatic words, is the realization that being human means being an individual with the unremitting obligation to transform existence by chance into life by choice and design. "Freedom" is the key word to that final monologue with which Faust concludes his own sojourn on earth in the affirmative, and the freedom he means cannot be procured by a magical command over nature, be it by the devil's power or by technology's. Nature will always rule supreme in her own domain, because no matter what accommodations human beings might require of her, they require them according to nature, according to demands that arise only insofar as human beings are her creature. The desire for freedom, however, springs from our claim to citizenship in a realm where the decrees of nature, even the certainty of death that is decreed with every life, have no value other than the one we give them.

In this context, freedom means determining one's own sphere, which may be envisioned as extending from the self at its center to the reality of the world "out there" that is bounded by the self at the periphery. Conversely, in the unfree state of nature the objective sphere is experienced as determining the self, and since there is no discernible periphery, the self cannot function as center but functions merely as point of impact for a succession of events that remains unfathomable because their comprehension would only be possible from the center. In order to be free, the self must be active; it must change from a point delimited by forces external to it into one that expands, one that is center and circumference inclusive of all limiting "otherness," so that everything appears only in terms of the self, and all limits other than those set by the self disappear. The isolated point of individuated being must go outside itself, become the other, an object in terms of objects, before it can cast the circumference and establish itself as center thus returning from "out there" as self objectified, as self with general rather than merely subjective validity. Moral conduct in the Kantian sense is the only action that can attach objective human authority to individual behavior, and every time the self determines a sequence of events ethically, it moves into a central position from which even the endless unfolding of all being could assume meaning, as if it were beheld within the scope of an absolute and final circumference.

Whenever people act morally, they act freely; they act from a zone that is subject to the determinative force of nature only if they were to permit it, just as the territory Faust envisions for human habitation must constantly be safeguarded against the encroachment of the sea, against the element most representative of nature's power, according to Neptunist theories, which repeatedly furnish the ideological background for Goethe's work.[33] That happy land of freedom cannot be wrested from the onrushing waves with spades: the work of spades is by the dead and for the dead. Faust is blind when he sees it rise from the ocean before his inner eye, and there, in the innermost recesses of each person, the demands of nature can be brought to halt by a decision for freedom, by a decision to assume responsibility for one's action, to have the self act and to have it act in the name of all selves rather than permit it merely to react on its own direct or indirect behalf, submissive to the law of nature that governs the flow of life and death. From this perspective of free agency the positive, concrete realities of physical existence are superseded by a sphere within which their independence must be negated evermore in favor of human significance.

The moral path, like the mystic's way, is a *via negativa* since it entails the steadfast denial of anything that would exercise power over the self. In contrast to the mystic, though, such denial is not accomplished by means of ascetic withdrawal but rather through continual active engagement in the world of physical, circumstantial, social, and historical conditions with only one purpose: to have every act, even the slightest motion, reflect that its origin and purpose cannot be fathomed in terms of those external givens. Under these auspices, human behavior breaks the determinative independence of physical reality and transforms its self-sufficient validity into an openness, a readiness to be completed within a more comprehensive sphere, one that is no longer drawn by death but includes it. The world and its values do not complete the self; they merely furnish the general complement to subjective isolation or rather the realm through which, not in which, the self may assume general validity, be subject and object, beginning and end, of its own activity and draw, for the moment, the circumference to its own sphere. True, the periphery must always be drawn anew, but insofar as it can be drawn at all, the self becomes aware of its own centricity, of itself as potentially absolute sphere, which is exactly that aspect of post-Kantian moral philosophy Fichte's concept of "Ego," of the self's tendency toward absolute objectivity, attempts to convey.[34]

For those who subordinate their freedom, death, each individual's steady companion, is a constant threat of the inevitable final limit nature will impose; a free agent, however, sets limits to nature, and the readiness to do so also entails in its most extreme form a preparedness to die, not in resigned despair, nor in a mood of scornful withdrawal from a futile game, but in the spirit of affirming life as a decidedly human enterprise, which could not be continued if it required abdication, the forfeiture of freedom, a settling for the expediences of nature where human values ought to prevail. Death, anticipated in each moral act, is the concluding way station on the moral path, the last "no" with which the world of concrete physicality is denied its claim to exclusive reality. This last negation, already incipient in the mere realization that being human means being free, completes the move to the center, and man, the potentially absolute sphere, or, in this case, mankind's representative, Faust, can go no further: he has assumed his place in the order of all being and entered into an unmediated relationship with its unity, with the comprehensive sphere our tradition refers to as the divine.

Moral action constitutes a twofold movement. On the one hand, it is a disengagement from the world, until the self stands all alone, free to decide, and on the other, it is a reengagement in which the world must never serve as end, but ony as medium that leads from the pure subjectivity of free agency to its general validity. The moral act, therefore, cannot be justified by its effect on any given situation; it has its own merit and constitutes, essentially, an openness, a never-finishedness, that has its complement in the all-comprehensive unity within which each and every aspect of being is absolutely defined. In other words, God is the complement of man, exactly as the sphere of immutable Reality is the aim and completion of the reality with which the sphere of human significance can endow merely the moment. As a free moral agent the individual is able to cast a circumference around a segment of objectivity and make it meaningful in human terms; however, all of objectivity will never be captured, no matter how far the line is flung, because the movement from one to all is infinite and can only be completed if it is met by a reciprocal movement from all to one, from the absolute objectivity of Reality, the infinite circumference of all-comprehensive Unity, to the relatively real, the relative center from which it is approached.

Goethe portrays those two movements and their encounter very clearly when he has angels from the heavenly host descend to carry off Faust's immortal self, proclaiming that the coincidence of human striving and love from above are the conditions under which admission among the blessed is vouchsafed.[35] After his death, Faust is conducted on an ascent that leads from the point of contact on earth to ever higher spheres and corresponding clarity, until he has reached the position that grants a view from the perspective of perfection, from the absolute circumference that encompasses the unity and fullness of all being.[36]

Once Faust has fought his way into freedom,[37] he has moved into the center from which he enters into a direct relation with that comprehensive unity he had sought all along. The focus for Faust's eventual ascent had already been set in the "Prologue," where the archangels praise all of creation; beginning with the majestic movement of its outermost spheres, they narrow the circle to the rapid turning of earth between day and night, only to close in further describing the clash of elementary forces raging over its surface, after which they end abruptly on a note of peace and harmony, showing unmistakably that even the most fearsome discord and the pinpoint of a planet so remote from the imposing Whole have their place and remain contained within the unity of their origin whose name is God. As for humanity, it is not mentioned by the angels in the scheme of things. It is left to Mephistopheles, the devil, to present our case, which he does by characterizing us as creatures so pitifully disoriented that we are irretrievably lost; God, on the other hand, claims we know the way aided by our urge toward something we cannot perceive and, in the case of Faust, our representative, God specifically declares Mephistopheles, the "Spirit of Negation," to be his helpmate, thereby characterizing the protagonist's course through life as a *via negationis* from the very outset.

Even structurally, the human drama, Faust's drama, unfolds from the central position, in between the metaphysical prologue and epilogue; both, in turn, depict the divine sphere exactly in Poulet's sense as infinitely comprehensive circumference and ubiquitous center; the first moves from the absolute periphery toward man, who must be defined as its center, and, once that task has been accomplished, the other describes the same motion in reverse. However, the divine sphere, from either perspective, remains unseen by mortals who are exposed to the infinity of being with nothing but their own powers to guide them. That is the essential human problem for Faust as humanity's representative, and Goethe has him resolve it along a negative path, a path that constitutes a move to the center.

The stages on this journey could still roughly be classified under the headings of "purgation," "illumination," and "union," only most of it up to the last moment in life is basically purgative, a disengagement from thing-relatedness through engagement, through an active pursuit of knowledge since the contemplative stance of the scholar is dismissed as futile at the very beginning. Love is the difference that separates the world of books from living experience and, once again, in a manner for which Plato had set the pattern, Eros leads his follower. He conducts him through the various phases of an aesthetic education that continues after death but pauses briefly beforehand in the illumined state wherein the self discovers its ethical nature and declares its freedom from the physical bonds with which it had confused its nature all too long. However, from the emphatically engaged point of view, from the thing-orientedness with respect to which action, even moral action, must take place, the effect will never show freely defined human significance, except for the individual who acts in the knowledge of ethical freedom. Without such clear awareness, the maxims of human agency will remain couched in terms of pragmatic efficacy and would consequently lack distinct criteria that might prevent any endeavor, even one "morally" intended, from assuming criminal dimensions. For example, Faust has committed murder in his blind pursuit of obtaining a neighboring piece of property he deemed necessary for his land-clearing enterprise that was to benefit others. Now, physically blinded, he learns the last lesson, that he must look inward for the true criterion of reality and not become captivated by the reality of things, because external land is not the issue but the inner creation of significance through deeds is. Once this insight has been attained, the move to the center has been completed and the next stage, that of union, can only be reached insofar as death has cut the tragic dualism between the individual's freedom in his moral attitude and his incapacity to effect this same reality externally where he remains bound to the conditions imposed by his physical nature.

Faust becomes conscious of his freedom at the end, when he finally recognizes that the tragic discrepancy between human desire and human reach need not necessarily result in the tortures of Tantalus.[38] The entire history of Faust's striving is rescued from its sense of futility in the last moment when he finally hears the "yes" that had furnished the summary background for every "no" with which life had countered his demands. Faust dies when the knowledge of his and every person's inherent freedom dawns on him because with it the sphere of human activity as a meaningful enterprise has been defined.

Chapter 14
Goethe and Novalis

It would have been far simpler to mention Georges Poulet briefly in a note and let readers who wished to pursue the history of the structural pattern that serves as Novalis's "basic schema" do so on their own. However, it was my intention to furnish more than a mere indication that there is historical continuity for the imagery Novalis employs. Poulet succeeds very well in tracing that continuity and in proving its history of metamorphoses to be a useful index of cultural change, yet there is an important variant he fails to appreciate in its full implication. The neglected variant is the specific version of the medieval spheral pattern indicative of mysticism's negative theology. It has been my intention to show that this particular pattern is one in which the self may come to understand its relationship to the world even outside the religious context of an established orthodoxy like the medieval Church.

Of prime importance in this regard is the path, the *via negativa*, traversed by the mystic, rather than an eventual state of union and ecstatic vision, which may or may not be granted at its conclusion. In the short survey of Western mystical tradition I have attempted to demonstrate the three essential features characterizing that path. Summarily, they circumscribe an activity devoted to a progressive shift in perspective that affords the self an ever more inclusive and meaningful view of its own reality. Even though mystics are the ones referred to as being engaged in this process, there is nothing mysterious about it. Any act of learning may be thought of as a process involving the same moments that typify each advance on the mystic's path. If, for example, a person is to acquire new information that would expand the horizon of that individual's knowledge, the precepts to which previously held knowledge had been limited must be suspended in order to create the state of receptivity necessary for new information to be received. In effect, learning is not so much a passive response to imposed data as an effort directed at freeing the self from error, from the confines within which habit and complacency of thought tend to hold us captive all too easily. From this point of view, human comprehension may be expanded only if it does not remain limited to its current content; in other words, any given state of comprehension must first be negated before it can be expanded. Negation, in this sense, means using what we already know to formulate a question, which is equivalent to making ourselves receptive to an eventual answer. Without this questioning attitude, this readiness to receive, we may be exposed to all manner of experience, but we would be incapable of absorbing it meaningfully.

For the mystic there is an ultimate stage of receptivity at which the self is totally free from adherence to partial knowledge, from identifying with partial reality, and in that state it may be granted the final answer, the vision from the perspective of the whole that is with God. In terms of the structural pattern of spheral imagery, the mystic's course toward freedom is equivalent to having the self assume its place at the center from where it can only be complemented by an all-comprehensive sphere. Centricity of self also seems to be most characteristic of postmedieval attitudes with which our own secular era is ushered in during the age of the Renaissance. There is a telling difference, however; the self moves to the center not to be complemented by an all-inclusive sphere but rather in order to draw that sphere on the self's terms. In this central position the self is also considered to be free, but freedom now means the right and power to draw a sphere that bounds the universe and lays it bare to human knowledge and practice, a concept best expressed in all its ambiguity and naive vigor by the ideal of the *uomo universale*.

The *Faust* drama harks back to the age of the Renaissance and its protagonist most definitely displays the ambitions that would inspire the *uomo universale*. He also displays the limits to which those ambitions are subject and exposes the problematic nature of human existence in modern, postmedieval times. Human freedom from metaphysical bondage to the revealed truth of a divinely ordered universe, so Faust must learn, is useless, unless that freedom proves itself capable of bestowing meaning on existence itself. It is this very meaning that could be derived in the Middle Ages from the divine sphere, which originates and comprehends all of being; without it, the human spirit in its freedom would either have to encompass the universe within a sphere of total knowledge, a task Faust attempts and forswears in suicidal despair over its futility, or that same freely active spirit would have to project its own sphere of generally valid meaning, if not for all of being then at least for human being. The latter alternative is the one corresponding to the Kantian concept of free moral agency and — as I have argued — to Faust's last vision of human freedom as well.[39] Amid the aimless back and forth between water and land, a motion as much a part of nature and as meaningless as the endlessly evolving tapestry of life and death, amid this existential void Faust plants his colony. It is a circular space, bounded by mountains on one side and dams on the other, specifically carved out against the forces of nature in order to support life on human terms, life lived not as a pointless enterprise that terminates in death, which is the only meaning nature gives it, but as a process conducted according to values that identify the interests of each person with those of every other person. Such values are ethical values and they are the product of the human spirit free to overrule nature's only decree of self-assertion and self-maintenance in favor of the law of humanity. Its enactment projects a sphere of generally valid meaning for human beings into a universe that holds no answer to our persistent query why it or anything it contains should exist.

Goethe's *Faust* serves to illustrate not only the existential dilemma of the "Renaissance man,"[40] but also its potential resolution, which emerges for German poets and thinkers acquainted with the new direction offered by Kantian philosophy.[41] Of particular interest and pertinence is his use of spheral imagery, both to symbolize the sphere of human freedom within nature and to indicate its divine complement. For the latter purpose he makes use of traditional motifs taken from biblical and medieval heritage, but he does so by removing the heavenly sphere from the *Faust* drama itself and by portraying it with parodistic overtones since it is this very framework of metaphysical certainty that is no longer an assured reality for the modern individual. Only death gains Faust access to the divine realm from which the entirety of being becomes discernible as meaningful, as divine creation.

Love from above must complement Faust's striving if the sphere emanating from the self as a free agent is to be joined by the all-comprehensive sphere from above. The same reciprocal movement is envisioned by Novalis, with spheral imagery far more complex and diversified but basically representative of the same fundamental pattern within which the self in its capacity of free moral agent is capable of assuming a position that functions as the potential center for the "absolute sphere" ("absolute Sphäre"). This secular version of the mystic's momentum toward freedom and centricity is also a negative path since the divine sphere is just as categorically removed from human reach as it was for the negative theologian. If anything, it has moved away further, as Goethe's parodistic frame would indicate, because the mystic set out on his journey supported by faith, a support Faust (1. 765) and those who follow in later ages can no longer claim. The revealed yet hidden God could inspire faith, but once God's singular revelation in the institutionalized canon of medieval Christianity became increasingly open to doubt, faith in the divinity proved to be an unreliable staff, still available to some, not available for all too many. Bereft of faith in God, the individual is now offered the alternative of faith in human freedom, a faith that calls for its justification through constant enactment and holds no promise of reward or punishment, neither on earth nor beyond. But even the moralistic rigor of the categorical imperative may be supported by a revelation. Goethe hints at it by having Gretchen, who had inspired Faust's lust and his love, welcome his immortal self in the heavenly sphere.

Novalis, however, is far more explicit in his insistence that the absolute sphere comes to meet the individual already on this earth in the figure of the beloved. This is what he had experienced when he encountered Sophie and, again, it turned out to be a revealed yet hidden Absolute insofar as Sophie was soon taken from him. Only after her death was the conscious enactment of his moral freedom accompanied by a loving outlook that proved receptive to all aspects of the world as potential media of revelation, as points where his being, centered in its freedom, could be complemented by the absolute sphere. This final version of the "basic schema" presents an exact replica of the mystic's pattern independent of any religious orthodoxy. Instead, it outlines the entirely secular concept of an improved or advanced *Wissenschaftslehre* within which ethics is complemented by love and activity, that is to say, the enactment of freedom, by passivity, by the ability to behold the world from the perspective of freedom.

V: Concluding Remarks

Nachdem ich dieses weiss, weiss ich, von welchem Puncte, alle Bildung meiner selbst und anderer ausgehen müsse: von dem Willen, nicht von dem Verstande. Ist nur der erstere unverrückt und redlich auf das Gute gerichtet, so wird der letztere von selbst das Wahre fassen. Wird lediglich der letztere geübt, indess der erstere vernachlässigt bleibt, so entsteht nichts weiter, als eine Fertigkeit, ins unbedingt Leere hinaus zu grübeln und zu klügeln.

Now that I know this: I also know from what point all cultivation of myself and others must proceed — from the will, not from the understanding. If the will is steadily and honestly directed toward the good, then the understanding will of itself apprehend the true. If the understanding is exercised only while the will remains neglected, there can arise nothing whatever but a dexterity in groping after vain and empty refinements within an absolute void.

Fichte (Vocation of Man)

Künstler aus Sittlichkeit.

The precondition for being an artist is moral capability.

Novalis

Das analog moralisch Sichtbare ist das *Schöne*. Das analog moralische Denken macht den Philosophen. D[as] anal[og] m[oralische] sprechen — den Redner und Dichter.

That which is in an analogically moral sense visible is the beautiful. Thinking in an analogically moral sense characterizes the philosopher. Speaking in an analogically moral sense characterizes the orator and poet.

Novalis

Chapter 15
Novalis in Contemporary Context

After nearly two centuries, during which the methodology of the exact sciences has gained unquestioned prominence in the guidance of human affairs, romantic theorists like Novalis, who proclaim instead the preeminence of poetry, seem oddly out of tune with reality as it confronts us today. His insistence that natural as well as social sciences, if rightly understood, must be regarded and conducted as poetic endeavors could, at best, be considered a pious wish in an era dominated by the ever growing estrangement of the ''two cultures.''

Attempts at closing that gap have apparently only succeeded in widening it. Contrary to the promise positivism seemed to hold for the humanities, the discipline of literary scholarship never did attain full scientific legitimacy under the old school's or the neopositivists' tutelage. Having been excluded from the real world scientists could explain, the study of literature was left to foster its isolation as a virtue. The ideological lineage that is commonly assigned to this separatist movement predates the demise of positivism in our century and is generally traced to idealist or, more specifically, to Kantian aesthetics, which declared art to be independent of any purpose external to it. With this declaration, art came into its own and no longer needed to be justified as a medium in the service of church, state, or popular entertainment; however, art had also potentially lost its immediate referential ground in the actual pragmatic and moral contexts within which human beings conduct their lives. That loss, only potential at the time, has been fully and intentionally realized by now, and the chorus of isolationist fervor insisting on the nonreferentiality of the artistic statement has become so pervasive and persuasive that the possibility of integrating life and literature seems more remote than ever.

These remarks on the present situation and its background are meant to indicate in bare outline the scope of the problem I wish to address. Since the chapter in the history of ideas to which they refer is quite familiar and well documented, there is no need to review it here in greater detail, at least not for the purpose at hand. That purpose is to show how Novalis's views might prove to be quite useful in overcoming some aspects of the dilemma they, along with those of other Kantians and romantics, supposedly helped initiate.

The ideological link between French symbolism and Novalis has been established since Werner Vordtriede's study on the subject appeared,[1] and others have recently extended that relationship to include modern theories on semiotics and language.[2] From there, it would not be difficult to make the connection with New Criticism, structuralism, and poststructuralism. Scholars have done as much by citing, for example, "romantic transcendental philosophy" as the source of the categorical "relativism" associated with literary autonomy, be it the more narrow, "formalist" version of the New Critics or the expanded, "visionary" one of the structuralists and poststructuralists.[3]

Whether the romantics are hailed or decried as forerunners of modern theoreticians and practitioners of art, the fact remains, as Meyer H. Abrams[4] and René Wellek[5] among others, have pointed out, that neither Kant's Copernican Revolution nor its romantic offshoots were meant to clear the path that inevitably leads to the prison walls of language behind which we may triumphantly declare our freedom from the metaphysics of any external presence. Transcendental philosophy, even Fichte's, does not deny the dogmatists's, or realist's, ground of reference for the objects of knowledge that lies outside the subject. It does not deny the real world; it merely questions by what right realists may assume that our minds are mimetically attuned to the world so that independent objects correspond to our knowledge of them. Since there is no basis for this assumption in the objects themselves, transcendental philosophers turned their attention to the operations of consciousness. They recognized that the ground of external reality objects refer to could not be real for the subject, unless it constituted the subject's potential range of receptivity, which is equivalent to saying unless it constituted the subject's potential range of expansion. Consciousness of anything the subject is not is, therefore, also always consciousness of the subject, and that permanent feature of consciousness Kant called "transcendental apperception." The same insight gave rise to Fichte's concept of *Tathandlung*, on which he based his primary axiom for the entire *Wissenschaftslehre*, whereas Novalis developed his "basic schema" for the simultaneity of the outer and inner paths from it. For these transcendental philosophers, the coincidence of subject and object may be found nowhere, except in the "fact" — Fichte's and Novalis's term is "*Factum*" — of self-consciousness, and this "fact" guarantees the correspondence of consciousness with its object, which realists take unquestioningly for granted.

The primacy of self-consciousness does not imply that everything has been withdrawn into the individual's interior and that a retreat to solipsism has been sounded. To put it as succinctly as possible, transcendental philosophers essentially point out an oversight on the part of realists who are not aware that consciousness is receptive to objects only insofar as the self is always one of them. If, as realists believe, there could be simple consciousness of autonomous objects, then, such consciousness could only be considered a subjective fiction since the criterion for the object's validity, its autonomous being, would remain entirely independent of the object's being known. This is exactly the problem Kant circumscribes with his concept of "thing in itself." Thus, paradoxically enough, the realist insistence on consciousness as knowledge of things in themselves also provides the theoretical foundation for the very absurdity of solipsism and its derivative forms of relativism this dogmatic insistence on the realist's part is meant to combat. The assumption that the content of consciousness simply refers its reality to external objects would leave the question unanswered how that same content could be a reality for any and every consciousness, as we presuppose in all acts of communication. It is therefore understandable that the realists' concept of reality has come under progressively persistent attack in the fields of literary and linguistic scholarship. Unfortunately, however, the realist concept seems to have been replaced by an equally misconceived point of view — actually the same one reversed — that assigns reality to language or *écriture* exclusively. In effect, the prison wall of things has merely been exchanged for one of words, and the only difference is that the former makes the world into a prison, whereas the latter pretends to make the prison into a world.

I believe the transcendental approach offers a possibility for avoiding the mutual exclusion of the consciously real and the reality referred to, because it provides a perspective that can account for both spheres of reality. Once self-consciousness is recognized as the focal criterion for all consciousness, consciousness of any object can no longer be thought to occur without consciousness of self and vice versa. The objective moment of consciousness is never without its subjective moment and the subjective moment never without its objective counterpart, so that every moment of consciousness may be understood to refer to two spheres of reality simultaneously. In one respect, the self is consciousness of itself in terms of objects, and that entails its "being in the world" or its physicality; in another, but concurrent, respect, the self is conscious of objects in terms of self, and that entails the subject's claim to universality as a conscious being and moral agent.

In his first *Critique*, Kant established the universal validity of conceptual thought by showing that its referential ground is not only the "thing in itself" but also the self in itself, or consciousness in itself, which he characterized as "transcendental apperception." Since the objects that comprise our world assume their valid contours with reference to the self's noumenality, the physical self's being in the world, that is to say, the individual's conduct, would have to receive its validation from the same source, and that form of validation furnished the topic for Kant's second *Critique*. "Theoretical" and "practical" reason imply each other, but Kant did not quite see it this way and treated their respective areas of competence separately. Fichte realized that their mutual interdependence derives from the noumenal self and was therefore able to move them closer together. For Fichte, the world that takes form for reason is also already the potential object of moral action, or, to put it more succinctly, practical reason circumscribes the horizon for theoretical reason. The same would also have to hold true in reverse, but that did not concern him since he was essentially only interested in defining the reality of the self's autonomy as a moral agent. It was left for Novalis to add the complementary half of the formula and to expand the *Wissenschaftslehre* at a higher level. Basically, Fichte's philosophy traces the configuration of a hermeneutic circle in which all science, taken in the comprehensive sense of *Wissenschaft*, is potentially self-knowledge, and that is exactly the point Novalis's *"höhere Wissenschaftslehre"* makes explicit. As a morally authentic being, Novalis argues, the self not only acts but also perceives as a consciously free agent, and that sort of perception is accompanied by a keen awareness of its communicability, which characterizes such perceptions as poetic visions or simply as *Poesie*.

Poesie means recognizing the object as referring not merely to its own but also to the self's ground of reference, recognizing it not merely for an object but for what it really is, an object for consciousness. That consciousness is shared, not because it is absolute in its uniformity, as it is for Kant, nor because the self is absolute in its freedom to act upon the evidence of consciousness in order to acknowledge the self in the other, as Fichte proposes, but because theoretical reason and practical reason are mutually interdependent functions, which interdependence manifests itself in that every object of consciousness carries the intersubjective valence of its communicability.

The reality of the world as it presents itself to us is therefore a meaningful reality, and it is that for a romantic like Novalis as it would be for any realists. There is a difference, though, since the realist can only make this claim as an article of faith, whereas Novalis is able to substantiate it. From the realist point of view the object's identity guarantees the referential context of concept and, once removed, of language, but Novalis takes a wider perspective and refers the common ground of language to the horizon with respect to which that identity is defined. For him, the objective reality that comprises the world is meaningful because all of it falls within the horizon of self-consciousness, that is to say, within the horizon of consciousness capable of attending every possible variation in which the world may become experience. Since the self is continually affected by experience and thus in a constant state of change, it actually never becomes an unmediated object of consciousness; in its stead, that to which the affect is attributed appears and constitutes the world in which we live. This world is real, but its reality speaks the language pre-scribed by consciousness. The language of consciousness does not apply merely to a limited segment of the world but rather comprehends all of the world's reality; it is not merely the language of my consciousness or yours but rather of everyone's. In short, the objects of consciousness assume their identity as language in which the hermeneutic dialogue is conducted that refers to the world for its text.

"World-consciousness is self-consciousness" could be the motto inscribed on each of Novalis's two novels since either essentially represents a demonstration of that insight. Self-consciousness, however, entails both the "transcendental apperception" of theoretical reason and the moral "categorical imperative" of practical reason. In the former context, self-consciousness functions as the conceptual horizon for the world with reference to which the object assumes its identity in its relation to others; in the latter context, self-consciousness functions as the conceptual horizon for the self with reference to which it assumes its own identity in its relation to others. From the perspective of theoretical reason, world-consciousness prevails, behind which the self remains hidden from view; but it is brought to light and world-consciousness reveals itself as self-consciousness from the perspective of practical reason. Thus, for Novalis, world consciousness always entails a moral dimension, even though it may not be immediately apparent. To be aware specifically of this dimension would, then, be the critical indication that a position has been attained from which the reality of the world may be understood for what it is. That awareness occurs when world appears as *Poesie*, that is to say, when it appears in its essential communicability with reference to all selves, not because the world is but because they are. In this sense, some of Novalis's more outlandish statements might seem less strange and fantastic, such as, for example, his repeated assertion that "nature" will have to become "moral," which is equivalent to his even more frequently voiced call for the "poetization of nature," a call that culminates in Klingsohr's prophetic vision of its fulfillment.

If one were to translate Novalis's antiquated romantic dialect into ours, then *Poesie* is, indeed, *écriture*, if that term is meant to signify the horizon of all possible language games; but it is also not *écriture* since that horizon of poetic, literary, or linguistic intersubjectivity coincides with the one Kant had uncovered as pre-scriptive for human, that is, "moral" purpose as it applies to the concrete reality of each individual's existence in the world. Kant's authority, it might appear, would hardly be acknowledged by today's critics and theoreticians caught up in the currents of poststructuralist trends. The mere mention of his name could, thus, easily be taken for sufficient evidence that the romantic concept of *Poesie* cannot be translated as I suggested and may only be appreciated within its own historical context. After all, much has happened since Kant. His alleged ahistorical formalism has been overcome by Hegelians, and poststructuralists invoke such non-Kantian, or even anti-Kantian thinkers as Heidegger and Nietzsche to buttress their positions.

A horizon of pre-scriptive universality based on moral self-identity is pointedly absent, for example, from the concepts of language and writing Derrideans profess, for whom they essentially constitute the conscious retracing of an interplay in which neither self nor other have an identity of their own. It is a pre-scriptive relationship of mutual representation in which the self appears only in terms of otherness, or in terms of infinite differing, and the other only in terms of identity infinitely deferred. This mutuality with a negative momentum, for which Derrida has coined the term *"différance,"* may be regarded as language spoken without words and writing inscribed without benefit of an alphabet. Its basic tenor is not the universality of unity but one of "violence" since the self is not permitted its own identity in which it believes — a belief Derrida unmasks as metaphysical fiction — and which it seeks either to maintain or to attain. Communal ethos is, therefore, wrought by power, by an insistence on the individual's subjugation under the "other," either by open suppression or by more subtle means that allow for the fiction of selfhood to be maintained within the context of some codification of equality. The Nietzschean resonance is unmistakable and openly admitted by reference to "the genealogy of morals" (*Of Grammatology*, 140, passim; see also "Translator's Preface"). In this context, ethics constitutes an attempt to bridge the gap of violence or differentiation, whereas immorality exploits it; either is possible only with reference to the interplay for which the concepts of "self" and "other" constitute ideal limits or, as Derrida says: "The arche-writing is the origin of morality as of immorality. The nonethical opening of ethics. A violent opening" (*Of Grammatology*, 140).

Despite Derrida's disclaimer, his *"différance"* is as metaphysical a concept as "self," or "nature," or "God," or any other of the many designations traditionally employed to convey the identity of the nonidentical; it is certainly not a qualitative difference if Derrida chooses to emphasize the nonidentity of the identical, and that is all he does, because the concept of *"différance"* includes identity insofar as it pertains to a relationship, even if it be a purely negative one expressed by such terms as "differing" and "deferring." The Derridean position has the advantage of clearing the human panorama of all false idols, of allowing no refuge to be constructed in honor of identity as long as the builders have but the shifting sands of constant change at their disposal. However, not all who affirm identity over difference — whether it be spelled this way or any other — are given to idolatry. They know quite well that the name of God is unspeakable, that nature is a term for the thing in itself beyond the comprehensive reach of reason's design, that Being is and is not being and nonbeing, that the self is present to itself in all acts of consciousness but never as a self-identical object, and so on. Those ideal concepts function as regulative principles and for that reason cannot be enclosed within the realm they regulate. Since that realm is the one comprising the extent of our physical experiences and their integration into a conscious order, these ideal concepts are regarded as "metaphysical." However, such nomenclature is not necessarily synonomous with the category of erroneous fiction. Without reference to a metaphysical idea of unity, no experience to which we could lend conscious expression would be possible at all since it would lack any referential context beyond its own incidental occurrence.

The idea of humanity, or rather self-identity in the Kantian sense, is not only the essential regulative principle of moral validity for human action but also the conceptual horizon for the contiguity of thought and the contextual framework of its communicability. As an idea, it is as foreign to "closure" as is *différance* since its attainability is equally deferred and its executability infinitely differentiated; however, the moral implications are quite different from those of the will to power Derrida seems to favor when he speaks of ethics and violence. If freedom be the measure of morality, as both Kant and Nietzsche contend, then the former's ethics has the edge over the latter's. Nietzsche's "aristocrat" is supposedly free from compassion as a sneaky form of superiority and only deals with those who are his equals as equals; Kantian ethics requires the same freedom from "inclination" as a moral motive and goes one step further: all human beings are as such the moral individual's equal, whether they demonstrate that equality — which they all have potentially — or not, and that sort of generosity, from power and not from need, Nietzscheans lack. The Nietzschean creates his own world in the void — and that seems much admired by antimetaphysicians like Derrida — but the Kantian does the very same in the same void, only his creation is not effected at the cost of falling prey to the metaphysical trap of self-idolatrous solipsism antimetaphysicians of Nietzschean heritage mistake for freedom, be that in the form of morally isolated supremacy or monologic pantextuality.

It is not very surprising, then, that Kant's name is heard again, pronounced not merely by those who mourn the loss of metaphysics but also by those who most certainly have incorporated post-Kantian thought in their work. In critical recognition of their own position and that of their intellectual forebears, voices from the poststructuralist camp in France, which have not yet been widely included in critical and theoretical debate over here, have been raised in appreciation of Kant. Of particular interest in this respect is Gilles Deleuze, who sought to meet the enemy when he wrote his book on Kant but emerged with an ally instead. The record of this encounter has just become available in English and reveals a comprehensive understanding of Kantian thought that recognizes the interdependence of the first two *Critiques* from the perspective of the third.[6] It is this very perspective that is necessary in order to avoid the epistemological fallacy[7] from which the philosophical vantage point for current literary debate suffers all too markedly, in my opinion. Another set of voices that refer to the *Critiques*, with primary focus on the second one and this time in the straightforward effort to address the question of ethical practice after deconstruction, belongs to Jean-François Lyotard and Jean-Loup Thébaud whose *Au juste* (1979) has just appeared in English translation.[8] Here, too, the same fault in philosophical perspective is quite consciously identified, and the corrective seems to have been drawn from the same source that lent direction to poets and thinkers reared in the tradition of transcendental philosophy.

In the country of its origin, that tradition's hidden continuity has surfaced again in some of the more recent pronouncements from the Frankfurt school. Foremost in this respect are Jürgen Habermas and Karl-Otto Apel, both of whom rely on language theory to make the connection, and particularly on developments in Anglo-American philosophy that have led to the present concern with speech-act theory.[9] Of the two, Apel offers the more explicit and detailed argument in support of the need for a renewed transcendental approach to philosophy.[10] His central thesis is that Kant's philosophy contained the foundation for a philosophy of communication and language, a potential that was not initially exploited by Continental philosophers but rather by the American Charles S. Peirce, for whom the abstract noumenality of the subject disappears and the mutual interdependence of theoretical and practical reason is realized in the concept of a supraindividualistic community of interpreters, "a *Community*, without definite limits, and capable of a definite increase of knowledge."[11] Peirce's "semiotic transformation" of Kant's philosophy replaces the transcendental subject with a community of communicants, whose discourse is, however, limited to the sciences. In order to complete this transformation, Apel relies on Wittgenstein's theory of language games, which allows him to arrive at a concept of community that is not restricted to any game in particular.[12] The community of communicants he envisions is one whose members are engaged in the game that comprehends all possible games. Since its membership is limitless and includes all of humanity, this community represents the state of perfect mutual understanding or the completion of the dialogue that functions as the normative horizon within which all communication takes place. The fulcral concept that accomplishes the transformation of Kantian philosophy into the transcendental language game Apel proposes is the concept of language as developed by the Anglo-American schools of thought whose representatives are shown to parallel and complement in many, "generally more effective" ways the insights gained in the field of hermeneutics by Heidegger and Gadamer.[13] The latter are credited with uncovering the hidden transcendental premises that underly the logic of science and with establishing the "hermeneutic circle" as the dialectic pattern that resolves the mutually exclusive opposition between *a priori* and *a posteriori* acts of understanding.[14] However, Apel is not alone when he also criticizes "Hermeneutic Phenomenology" for its historical relativism,[15] which his own "transcendental hermeneutics" is designed to correct.

The corrective is the normative principle inherent in the communal nature of communication. The unlimited community of communicants is the necessary ideal premise for every communicative act, and every such act is, at the same time, to be valued according to its relative contribution in the unbounded historical progress toward the realization of that community. There is still relativism, historical as well as cultural and personal; in short, there is still the relativism of the various language games, but it occurs within a normative rather than neutral context that allows for a criterion of validation. Communicating simply means breaking through relativistic isolation, and the task of doing so has been accomplished for better or worse according to the degree to which that goal has been approximated. This task is never finished, but the direction of its progress has been marked out with its inception, and its performance within the concrete setting of world and society comprises the actual course of human history. Since the normative regulative principle derives from the ideal community of mankind in which all relativism is suspended, it is fundamentally an ethical principle, so that a normative logic of science, which explains the world, presupposes not only a normative hermeneutic, which generates mutual understanding, but also a normative ethic.[16]

The prison walls of language, it would seem, are walls erected for and by players of a particular language game but not of *the* game, as its participants believe. The rules for it are those of the hermeneutical circle; however, this version of it remains to be superseded by a more inclusive sphere from which the normative criterion for consensus derives that *écriture* lacks but presupposes on its infinite progression of interpretative differentiation. Science, it is true, relies on hermeneutics as its prerequisite, but this does not eliminate the reality with which science deals; it merely means that the very "objectivity" of scientific research already constitutes an interpretative context relative to the self and its kind. Hermeneutics, in turn, presupposes the possibility of total consensus, which is the precondition for any consensus at all; since total consensus is a communal idea, hermeneutics is ultimately based on the ethical premise of human equality in a possible community of communicants without limit that is progressively realized to the degree in which communicative acts prove successful. Language, in the sense of the transcendental language game, does have a key function, but it is not exclusive of the world's reality nor of a normative criterion for human conduct; rather, it is the mediating ground for both and thus truly beyond the dualism of object and subject, of dogmatic materialism and dogmatic idealism, beyond any form of this schism that has bedeviled Western thought from the beginning, "beyond," not in a new realm of metaphysics but on this side of heaven on the concrete ground of historical reality.

The "house of language," so it turns out, is not the hermetic edifice for which it is currently still hailed and decried.[17] Neither exclusive palace nor confining cell, it stands wide open to the world on which it rests and is host to the spirit that unites its inhabitants. Nearly two centuries ago, Novalis had already referred to that house with his concept of *Poesie*. It is the same house with the same features and he quite clearly considered it his task to call attention to this abode as the "house of the truth of being" that is not only for but also of and by humanity.[18] It seems to me that it is now time for us to take Novalis seriously in this respect, to forget our misconstrued romantic notions concerning the theoretical origins of artistic autonomy, and to focus our attention on the long-neglected implications for practical reason inherent in all forms of communication but demonstrated most effectively in that privileged form of artistic expression we call literature.

Notes

Notes

Foreword. Do We Need a Revival of Transcendental Philosophy?

1. Jürgen Habermas, *Knowledge and Human Interests*, trans. Jeremy J. Shapiro (Boston: Beacon Press, 1972), vii. Henceforth cited parenthetically in the text.

2. For a socio-historical assessment of German romanticism, see Jochen Schulte-Sasse, "Der Begriff der Literaturkritik in der Romantik," in *Geschichte der deutschen Literaturkritik*, ed. Peter U. Hohendahl (Stuttgart: Metzler, 1985), 76-128. The book will soon be available in English from the University of Nebraska Press.

3. See Jürgen Habermas, *Legitimitätsprobleme im Spätkapitalismus* (Frankfurt: Suhrkamp, 1973), 110. Habermas's theoretical assessment of the function of art in modernity has changed over the years, or, to put it more bluntly, it has swerved. But the reason for this swerving is precisely his refusal to reflect on the transcendental status of language in his system.

4. I quote Novalis within the text as N plus volume and page numbers according to the standard historical-critical edition cited in von Molnár's bibliography.

5. See my remarks on the effect this development had on the function of art in modernity in my afterword to Jay Caplan, *Framed Narratives* (Minneapolis: Univ. of Minnesota Press, 1985), 97-115.

6. Paul de Man, *Blindness and Insight, Essays in the Rhetoric of Contemporary Criticism*, 2nd, revised ed. (Minneapolis: Univ. of Minnesota Press, 1983), 56.

7. Oscar Fambach, ed., *Ein Jahrhundert deutscher Literaturkritik* (Berlin/GDR: Aufbau, 1963), V, 206.

8. Immanuel Kant, *Kritik der Urteilskraft*, ed. Karl Vorländer (Hamburg: Meiner, 1924), 168. See also 82-83.

9. Friedrich Schlegel, *Kritische Ausgabe*, ed. Ernst Behler et al. (Munich et. al.: Schoeningh, 1958-), II, 319.

Preface

1. Some attempts have been made in the past that might be classified as comprehensive presen-

tations, but those published before the present critical edition of Novalis's works had become available are no longer reliable within the context of current scholarship. Friedrich Hiebel's *Novalis: German Poet, European Thinker, Christian Mystic* (Chapel Hill: Univ. of North Carolina Press, 1954) has been enlarged and revised but is available only in German (*Novalis: Deutscher Dichter, europäischer Denker, christlicher Seher* [Munich/Bern: Francke Verlag, 1972]). This impressive compendium, to which all subsequent references to Hiebel refer, brings valuable insights in many respects; however, it still suffers too much from an overemphasis on Novalis's religious mysticism, for which Hiebel fails to offer an adequate philosophical foundation. An excellent introductory text, less detailed but also more balanced and perceptive, is John Neubauer's volume, no. 556 in the "Twayne World Series," *Novalis* (Boston: Twayne, 1979).

2. Philosophical endeavors that take their orientation from the perspective introduced by Kant's *Critiques* are commonly referred to as "transcendental" or "critical" philosophy.

3. Stanley Fish, *Is There a Text in This Class? Authority of Interpretive Communities* (Cambridge, Mass.: Harvard Univ. Press, 1980).

Introductory Remarks

1. For details on the early Novalis cult, consult Leif Ludwig Albertsen's essay, "Novalismus," *Germanisch-Romanische Monatsschrift* 48 (1967):272–85, and Hans-Joachim Mähl's essay in Benno von Wiese's *Deutsche Dichter der Romantik* (Berlin: Erich Schmidt Verlag, 1971), in particular pp. 190–92. Hans-Joachim Mähl also sheds light on the dire effects of Tieck's editorial policy in his article on Goethe's opinion of Novalis, "Goethes Urteil über Novalis," *Jahrbuch des Freien Deutschen Hochstifts* (1967):130–270; further information can be obtained by comparing the various editions from Tieck to Kluckhohn.

2. *Novalis Schriften*, eds. Paul Kluckhohn and Richard Samuel, 2nd ed., 5 vols. (Stuttgart: Kohlhammer Verlag, 1960–); abbreviated: Kl². All references to this edition will simply be designated by volume number, page number, and — if applicable — line number.

3. (Notes 3 through 7 furnish a survey of the most notable contributions to the various areas of research cited in the text and are not intended as an exhaustive documentation of the bibliography pertinent to the field.) Theodor Haering's *Novalis als Philosoph* (Stuttgart: Kohlhammer Verlag, 1954) was a valuable first attempt to survey the entire collection of fragments, whereas Manfred Dick, in *Die Entwicklung des Gedankens der Poesie in den Fragmenten des Novalis* (Bonn: Bouvier, 1967), confronts the same task with less prejudice and a more systematic approach. In a more selective fashion, Manfred Frank unravels the philosophical complexities that comprise the notion of "magic idealism" ("Die Philosophie des sognennannten 'magischen Idealismus'," *Euphorion* 63[1969]:88–116) and in his later book, *Das Problem "Zeit" in der deutschen Romantik* (Munich: Winkler, 1972), Frank reexamines Novalis's concept of time. My own work, *Novalis' "Fichte Studies." The Foundations of his Aesthetics* (The Hague: Mouton, 1970), which deals with the "Fichte-Studies" exclusively, furnishes an outline of Novalis's initial concepts on aesthetics, whereas Richard W. Hannah, *The Fichtean Dynamic of Novalis's Poetics* (Bern/Las Vegas: P. Lang, 1981) and Stefan Summerer, *Wirkliche Sittlichkeit und ästhetische Illusion* (Bonn: Bouvier, 1974) offer comprehensive expositions and analyses of the impact Fichte's philosophy had on the entire range of Novalis's intellectual development. Another attempt to determine Novalis's aesthetic theory and practice, but without specific emphasis on the philosophical notebooks in general or on the "Fichte-Studies" in particular, is Josef Haslinger's *Die Ästhetik des Novalis* (Königstein/Taunus: Hain, 1981). Dennis F. Mahoney's *Die Poetisierung der Natur bei Novalis* (Bonn: Bouvier, 1980) allows aesthetic, or rather poetic, theory to appear within the framework of Novalis's philosophy of nature. Novalis's theory of the symbolic has also received attention, specifically in Klaus Ruder's *Zur Symboltheorie des Novalis* (Marburg: Elwert Verlag, 1974). Even Novalis's philosophy of formative education, to which the German concept of *Bildung* refers, has been made the subject of a separate

study by Klaus Geppert, *Die Theorie der Bildung im Werk des Novalis* (Frankfurt/Bern: Peter Lang, 1977).

4. Kl^2 contains a collection of previously unpublished material with explicit commentary in the introduction by Richard Samuel.

5. Among the numerous contributions, the most representative are Heinz Ritter's painstaking research to establish the chronology of Novalis's major poems (*Der unbekannte Novalis* [Göttingen: Sachse & Pohl, 1967] and "Die Datierung der 'Hymnen an die Nacht'," *Euphorion* 52 [1958]:114–41); Lawrence O. Frye's insightful articles "Spatial Imagery in Novalis's 'Hymnen an die Nacht'," *DVLG* 41 (1967):568–91 and "Prometheus Under a Romantic Veil: Goethe and Novalis' 'Hymnen an die Nacht'," *Euphorion* 61 (1967):318–36; Winfried Kudszus's analysis of the use of history in "Geschichtsverlust und Sprachproblematik in den 'Hymnen an die Nacht'," *Euphorion* 65 (1971):298–311; and Friedrich Hiebel's pertinent chapters in the second, revised edition of his monograph.

6. Novalis's pronouncements on history and society, particularly in *Die Christenheit oder Europa*, gave rise to Ursula von Mangoldt's interpretation of his concept of Christianity (*Novalis: Europa oder die Christenheit: Utopie oder Wirklichkeit: Versuch einer Antwort* [Weilheim: Otto Wilhelm Barth-Verlag, 1964]) and to Wilfried Malsch's study of his political statements, which, he contends, are visions poetically conceived as an ideal historical imperative rather than prophecies of utopian reality (*"Europa" Poetische Rede des Novalis* [Stuttgart: Metzler, 1965]). Ulrich Gaier has devoted an entire book to the study of *Die Lehrlinge zu Sais* that brings fascinating insights into the work's kinship with mystical tradition, especially that of the cabala (*Krumme Regel: Novalis' "Konstruktionslehre des schaffenden Geistes" und ihre Tradition.* Untersuchungen zur deutschen Literaturgeschichte 4 [Tübingen: Max Niemeyer, 1970]), whereas my own article approaches this prose fragment from the perspective of idealist philosophy ("The Composition of Novalis' *Die Lehrlinge zu Sais:* A Reevaluation," *PMLA* 85 [1970]: 1002–14). *Heinrich von Ofterdingen* has also received a good share of scholarly interest; some of its most recent manifestations since Gerhard Schulz ("Die Poetik des Romans bei Novalis," *Jahrbuch des Freien Deutschen Hochstifts* [1964], 120–57) outlined the poetics of the novel are Johannes Mahr's careful chapter-for-chapter study, which arrives at the conclusion that Novalis presents the poet as a person capable of translating the subjective realm's vague infinity into concrete objective reality (*Übergang zum Endlichen. Der Weg des Dichters in Novalis' "Heinrich von Ofterdingen"* [Munich: Fink, 1970]); Helmut Schanze's computerized *Index* along with his demonstration of its use (*Index zu Novalis' Heinrich von Ofterdingen* [Frankfurt: Athenäum, 1968] and "Zur Interpretation von Novalis' *Heinrich von Ofterdingen:* Theorie und Praxis eines vollständigen Wortindex," *Wirkendes Wort* 20 [1970]:19–33); Charles M. Barrack's article on the instructions Heinrich receives from Sylvester in the second part of the novel ("Conscience in *Heinrich von Ofterdingen:* Novalis' Metaphysic of the Poet," *Germanic Review* 46 [1971]:257–84); Elizabeth Stopp's important essay, in which she also directs attention to the novel's second part, "'Übergang vom Roman zur Mythologie.' Formal Aspects of the Opening Chapter of Hardenberg's *Heinrich von Ofterdingen*, Part II," *DVLG* 48 (1974):318–41; and several authors' pertinent references to the novel in their respective books, those for example by Armand Nivelle (*Frühromantische Dichtungstheorie* [Berlin: Walter de Gruyter, 1970]); Hannelore Link (*Abstraktion und Poesie im Werk des Novalis. Studien zur Poetik und Geschichte der Literatur* 15 [Stuttgart: Kohlhammer Verlag, 1971]); Ernst-Georg Gäde (*Eros und Identität: Zur Grundstruktur der Dichtungen Friedrich von Hardenbergs* [Marburg: Elwert Verlag, 1974]); and Friedrich Hiebel.

7. Richard Faber's rather unconvincing attempt (*Die Phantasie an die Macht* [Stuttgart: Metzler, 1970]) to align Novalis with the forces of modern socialist revolution constitutes a contemporary reply to the age-old accusation that the early romantics lacked the will and practical ability to become engaged in the realities of life, an accusation that has been voiced consistently in one form or another, beginning with the Heidelberg romantics up to Dieter Arendt who, in 1972, diagnosed this supposed romantic default as "poetic nihilism" (*Der "poetische Nihilismus" in der Romantik*, 2 vols.

[Tübingen: Max Niemeyer Verlag, 1972]); after Hans-Joachim Mähl's exhaustive presentation (*Die Idee des goldenen Zeitalters im Werk des Novalis* [Heidelberg: Carl Winter, 1965]), the concept of the "Golden Age," its real or ideal nature, its individual, historical, or cosmic eventuality, still furnished topics for consideration in the books by Malsch (*"Europa" Poetische Rede des Novalis*), Frank (*Das Problem "Zeit" in der deutschen Romantik*), and Eckhard Heftrich (*Novalis. Vom Logos der Poesie*. Studien zur Philosophie und Literatur des neunzehnten Jahrhunderts 4 [Frankfurt: Vittorio Klostermann, 1969]), who definitely sees in Novalis a chiliastic thinker, as does Hans Wolfgang Kuhn (*Der Apokalyptiker und die Politik. Studien zur Staatsphilosophie des Novalis*. [Freiburg im Breisgau: Rombach Verlag, 1961]). The most insightful and detailed conceptual analysis of early romantic chiliasm and utopianism has, however, been supplied by Hans-Joachim Mähl in his recent essay, "Der poetische Staat. Utopie und Utopiereflexion bei den Frühromantikern," *Utopieforschung* 3 (Stuttgart: Metzler, 1981), 273–302. Of interest in this connection is also Peter Berglar's essay "Geschichte und Staat bei Novalis," *Jahrbuch des Freien Deutschen Hochstifts* (1974), 143–208, in which he attempts to substantiate his claim that Novalis ought to be counted among the historians because of his unique sense of historical consciousness. Novalis, the artist, has been linked to modern trends arising from French symbolism by Werner Vordtriede (*Novalis und die französischen Symbolisten* [Stuttgart: Kohlhammer Verlag, 1963]), Marianne Thalmann (*Zeichensprache der Romantik* [Heidelberg: Lothar Stiehm, 1967]), Lilian Furst ("Novalis' 'Hymnen an die Nacht' and Nerval's 'Aurélia'," *Comparative Literature* 21 [1969]:31–46), Silvio Vietta (*Sprache und Sprachreflexion in der modernen Lyrik*, Literatur und Reflexion 3 [1970]), Margaret Mein ("Novalis, a Precursor of Proust," *Comparative Literature* 23 [1971]:217–32), Hannelore Link (*Abstraktion und Poesie im Werk des Novalis*), and Friedrich Strack (*Im Schatten der Neugier* [Tübingen: Max Niemeyer Verlag, 1982]), whose book represents the most circumspect scholarly achievement of recent date. At the other end of the historical spectrum, many questions relating to the ambivalence that characterized the relations between Goethe and the Jena Group have been answered on the strength of careful research by Hans-Joachim Mähl's articles, "Novalis' Wilhelm-Meister-Studien des Jahres 1797," *Neophilologus* 47. 4 (1963):286–305, and "Goethes Urteil über Novalis" (contested, in part, by Andreas Wachsmuth) and by Ernst Behler's excellent study in which the differing concepts of literature that inspire Goethe's *Meister* and Novalis's *Ofterdingen* are clearly stated ("*Wilhelm Meisters Lehrjahre* and the Poetic Unity of the Novel in Early German Romanticism," in *Goethe's Narrative Fiction*, ed. William J. Lillyman [Berlin: Walter de Gruyter, 1983], 110–27). Even further back, Helmut Schanze's *Romantik und Aufklärung. Untersuchungen zu Friedrich Schlegel und Novalis* (Erlanger Beiträge zur Sprach-und Kunstwissenschaft 27 [Nürnberg: Hans Carl, 1966]) and Gertrude B. Pickar's "Elements of the Enlightenment in Novalis' Poetics" (*Rice University Studies* 55 [Houston: Rice Univ., 1969], 185–95) trace the ties between romanticism and the Enlightenment. Also, in this connection, special mention must be made of Klaus Peter's *Stadien der Aufklärung: Moral und Politik bei Lessing, Novalis und Friedrich Schlegel* (Wiesbaden: Akademische Verlagsgesellschaft Athenaion, 1980). His superb analysis of the dialectic progression comprising the moral ideology that inspired the Enlightenment and remained crucial for romanticism is the only study, to my knowledge, in which the central importance of the concept of morality is fully recognized with reference to Novalis (82–138). Within the context of his argument, which seeks to demonstrate the relative political significance and efficacy of the concept of morality, he arrives at the conclusion that, in Novalis's case, this concept's radical nature precluded any immediate political applicability and caused it to be identified rather more intimately with the realm of aesthetics and with the poet's task.

Chapter 1. Early Years

1. Friedrich von Hardenberg assumed this name from his ancestors who occupied an estate called "Rode," signifying newly cleared land, and accordingly signed themselves "von Roden" or, in the latinized version, "de Novali." Although he was not known by this pseudonym until

1798, when his contributions to the *Athenäum* began to appear under it, the name has come to be so thoroughly identified with his person that a reenactment of the chronological division into Friedrich and Novalis would seem highly artificial; for my purpose, I consider the names interchangeable.

2. The entire episode is covered in Max Preitz's edition of Schlegel's and Novalis's correspondence; there are references to it in the section entitled "Vorspiel" and in the first nine letters, of which the eighth is signed "Albert von Hardenberg," apparently with reference to Werther's rational counterpart (*Friedrich Schlegel und Novalis: Biographie einer Romantikerfreundschaft* [Darmstadt: Gentner, 1957]).

3. The plan to join the military is carefully supported by rational argument in a long letter to the elder Hardenberg, who obviously needed a great deal of convincing (IV, 104–112).

4. Letter to Erasmus (IV, 122–23). Also, Karl Salomo Zachariä reports about the lighter aspects of Novalis's life at Wittenberg (IV, 576–77); the more serious ones are described in a letter to Schlegel (IV, 124–26).

5. Preitz, *Schlegel und Novalis*, 31–32.

6. The editorial comment (IV, 24*), "Hardenberg nahm an dem Bruch der Schlegels mit Schiller keinen Anteil" ("Hardenberg did not take part in the quarrel the Schlegels had with Schiller"), suffices to characterize the relationship. The battle with Woltmann is reflected in letters 33–36 to which Preitz adds extensive commentary (Preitz, *Schlegel und Novalis*, 189–92).

7. "Goethes Urteil."

8. Preitz, *Schlegel und Novalis*, 9.

9. I, 500; also I, 512; the poem "Zufriedenheit" (526–27) bears a similar message.

Chapter 2. Apprenticeship to Schiller

10. Italics are mine.

11. See his letters to Schiller and Reinhold, IV, 89–98.

12. *Schillers Werke: Nationalausgabe* 22, ed. Julius Petersen and Hermann Schneider (Weimar: Hermann Böhlaus Nachfolger, 1958), 256.

13. Ibid., 22, 260.

14. Gerhard Schulz, *Novalis in Selbstzeugnissen und Bilddokumenten*, Rowohlts Monographien 154 (Reinbek bei Hamburg: Rowohlt, 1969).

15. I have discussed Novalis's intellectual relationship to Schiller in "Die Umwertung des moralischen Freiheitsbegriffs im kunsttheoretischen Denken des Novalis," *Erkennen und Deuten: Essays zur Literatur und Literaturtheorie: Edgar Lohner in memoriam*, ed. Martha Woodmansee and Walter F. W. Lohnes (Berlin: Erich Schmidt Verlag, 1983), 101–18. Arguments I have presented there have influenced my presentation of the topic in this chapter and of relevant aspects in part II, chapter 6.

Chapter 3. The Encounter and Novalis's Twofold Love: Love of Sophie and Philosophy

1. Refer to the text and discussion of the poem entitled "Beginning" ("*Anfang*") in the third chapter of this section.

2. The spelling of this name varies since orthographic usage was not firmly established at the time. Novalis uses both "Sophie" and "Sofie."

3. All references to Fichte's works pertain to *Fichte, Johann Gottlieb. Sämmtliche Werke*, ed. I. H. Fichte, 11 vols. (Berlin: Veit und Comp., 1845–46), abbreviated to *SW*, followed by the volume and page numbers. My references to Fichte pertain to this edition, rather than to the historical-critical edition now being prepared under the editorship of Reinhard Lauth and others,

because references in Kl[2] are made to *SW*. Translations of the German text are mine; when warranted, I have added brief explanatory comments in brackets.

4. II, 29–103.

Chapter 4. The "Basic Schema" as It Evolves from the "Fichte-Studies"

5. Fichte adds this explanatory note in the second edition of the *Wissenschaftslehre*:

Dies Alles heisst nun mit anderen Worten, mit denen ich es seitdem ausgedrückt habe: *Ich* ist nothwendig identität des Subjects und Objects: Subject-Object; und dies ist es schlechthin ohne weitere Vermittelung.

All this means in different words, which I have employed since the book has first appeared: Ego [or rather the concept of "I"] is necessarily the identity of subject and object: [it is a] subject-object [in one]; and this it is without any further mediation.

6. All translations of quotations from Novalis's philosophical fragments and notebooks are mine; since his private jottings are often difficult to understand without commentary, I have added explicatory remarks in brackets whenever I thought such additions might prove to be of help to the reader.

7. In his instructive and perceptive study "Von der Poetik zur Linguistik — Wilhelm von Humboldt und der romantische Sprachbegriff," *Universalismus und Wissenschaft im Werk und Wirken der Brüder Humboldt*, ed. Klaus Hammacher (Frankfurt: Klostermann, 1976), 224–40, Kurt Mueller-Vollmer traces the modern concept of "generative" linguistic theory to its Fichtean origins in Wilhelm von Humboldt's thoughts on language. On an even broader scale, the same author has more recently shown how extensively Fichte's philosophy has contributed to the formulation of theories concerning language and poetics on the part of others, even outside of Germany, as the example of Coleridge serves to illustrate: "Fichte und die romantische Sprachtheorie," *Der transzendentale Gedanke: Die gegenwärtige Darstellung der Philosophie Fichtes*, ed. Klaus Hammacher (Hamburg: Felix Meiner Verlag, 1981), 442–61. For the most extensive treatment of Novalis's semiotic theory with reference to Fichte's philosophy, refer to Richard W. Hannah's excellent study, *The Fichtean Dynamic of Novalis' Poetics*, particularly the fourth chapter entitled "Zeichen," 103–57, from which I have profited greatly for my own deliberations on the subject.

8. Novalis deliberates the question in these words:

Was verstehn wir unter Ich? Hat Fichte nicht zu willkührlich alles ins Ich hineingelegt? mit welchem Befugniß? Kann ein Ich sich als *Ich* setzen, ohne ein anderes Ich oder Nichtich — / Wie sind Ich und Nichtich gegensetzbar / Das Ich hat eine hieroglyphystische Kraft.

What does ego mean? Was it not too arbitrary on Fichte's part when he used this term in order to subsume everything under it? By what right did he do so? Can an ego [now taken in Fichte's absolute sense of Ego] posit itself as *ego*, without positing another ego or nonego [i.e., does Fichte's concept of Ego not subsume under it both concepts of ego and nonego, and would it not, therefore, be a misnomer] — / How can ego and nonego be posited in opposition to one another / Ego [as Fichte employs the term] has hieroglyphic power [i.e., Fichte employs the term not in its own right but as a symbolic inscription that approximates that for which it stands].

(II, 107, ll. 24–29)

Chapter 5. Death and the "Decision to Live"

9. Novalis refers to his "decision" throughout the diary he kept after Sophie's death. The

meaning scholars have customarily attributed to this formulation is one that emphasizes Novalis's death wish exclusively. As the title of this chapter indicates, I disagree with this view.

10. The title may have been added later (I, 377 and 617).

11. The German original on which my translation is based appears here in full:

Es kann kein Rausch sein — oder ich wäre nicht
Für diesen Stern geboren — nur so von Ohngefähr
   In dieser tollen Welt zu nah an
      Seinen magnetischen Kreis gekommen.

Ein Rausch wär wirklich sittlicher Grazie
Vollendetes Bewußtsein? — Glauben an Menschheit wär
   Nur Spielwerk einer frohen Stunde —?
      Wäre dies Rausch, was ist dann das Leben?

Soll ich getrennt sein ewig? — ist Vorgefühl
Der künftigen Vereinigung, dessen, was
   Wir hier für Unser schon erkannten,
      Aber nicht ganz noch besizten konnten —

Ist dies auch Rausch? so bliebe der Nüchternheit,
Der Wahrheit nur die Masse, der Ton, und das
   Gefühl der Leere, des Verlustes
      Und der vernichtigenden Entsagung.

Womit wird denn belohnt für die Anstrengung
Zu leben wider willen, feind von sich selbst zu sein
   Und tief sich in den Staub getreten
      Lächelnd zu sehn — und Bestimmung meinen.

Was führt den Weisen denn durch des Lebens Tal
Als Fackel zu dem höheren Sein hinauf —
   Soll er nur hier geduldig bauen,
      Nieder sich legen und ewig tot sein.

Du bist nicht Rausch — du Stimme des Genius,
Du Anschaun dessen, was uns unsterblich macht,
   Und du Bewußtsein jenes Wertes,
      Der nur erst einzeln allhier erkannt wird.

Einst wird die Menschheit sein, was Sophie mir
Jetzt ist — vollendet — sittliche Grazie —
   Dann wird ihr *höheres Bewußtsein*
      Nicht mehr verwechselt mit Dunst des Weines.

I, 386–87)

Even though pages and line references pertaining to the poetic works and attendant commentary refer to the second and enlarged edition of K1², vol. I, published in 1977, I have kept the modernized spelling of the texts found in the first edition of that volume, published in 1960.

12. The classic treatises on the subject are his *On Grace and Dignity* (*Über Anmut und Würde*) and *On the Aesthetic Education of Man in a Series of Letters* (*Über die aesthetische Erziehung des Menschen in einer Reihe von Briefen*). An exemplary English edition of the *Aesthetic Letters* is furnished by Elizabeth M. Wilkinson and L. Willoughby, trans. and eds. (Oxford: Clarendon Press, 1967).

13. This terminology is not intended as a reference to Buber, although it might well have been justified; however, that would be a topic for an entirely separate discourse. I should merely like to point out that Novalis employs the terms "Ich" and "Du" somewhat later in his life in the sense of perceiving nature, the outside world, creatively, from an inward perspective, so that it appears within a relationship of "Thou and I" (I, 101).

14. "Klagen eines Jünglings" ("A Youth's Compaint"), 1791.

15. I use the terminology "state of moral grace" intentionally to express both, not only a condition of harmonious interaction between duty and inclination but also the aspect of its givenness that lies beyond the reach of conscious effort.

16. Within his instructive essay "Die 'göttliche Kunst und ihre Sprache'," *Romantik in Deutschland*, ed. Richard Brinkmann (Stuttgart: Metzler, 1978), 386, Friedrich Strack ventures a similar supposition regarding the gist of the conversation at Niethammer's house. He believes that the concept of "conscience" (*Gewissen*) may well have been viewed by the poet-participants as the center not only of moral but also poetic efficacy. This seems likely, given the restriction that, for Novalis, it is primarily a matter of linking a world revealed through love to one that may be fashioned according to the moral imperative. For an impressive attempt to extend the line from this conversation and the topic of "Offenbarung" (*revelation*) to Novalis's concept of "Mittlertheorie" (*mediation*) and the poet's function as outlined in *Heinrich von Ofterdingen*, see J. J. White's recent article in *Publications of the English Goethe Society*, 52 (1983):90–119.

17. II, 30–31. Essentially, Mähl states here that it is safe to assume Novalis had been familiar with Fichte's work from the beginning and must, therefore, have been following all his publications since 1794. In the "Fichte-Studies" there is evidence that Novalis had read these works: *Über den Begriff der Wissenschaftslehre oder der sogenannten Philosophie* (1794), an introductory rendition of the perspective from which Fichte's philosophy arises; *Grundlage der gesammten Wissenschaftslehre* (parts 1 and 2, 1794; part 3, 1795), his main work, simply referred to as *Wissenschaftslehre; Einige Vorlesungen über die Bestimmung des Gelehrten* (1794), implications of Fichte's philosophy for defining the academician's or scholar's function; *Grundriß des Eigenthümlichen der Wissenschaftslehre, in Rücksicht auf das theoretische Vermögen* (1795), an elaboration on the basic text; "Von der Sprachfähigkeit und dem Ursprung der Sprache" (*Philosophisches Journal*, vol. I, 1795), Fichte's theory of language, which appeared in the journal Niethammer edited and also furnished the basis for the first fragments in Novalis's "Fichte-Studies" (I, 43–44), so that the meeting at Niethammer's house may well have been seminal in more ways than one; finally, for later passages in the "Fichte-Studies," an acquaintance with Fichte's *Grundlage des Naturrechts nach Principien der Wissenschaftslehre* (part 1, 1796), his treatise on the concept of law, must be supposed. For the most astute analysis of this last work and its political implications, implications which, the author shows, Novalis was fully aware of and rejected, see Klaus Peter's *Stadien der Aufklärung*, 82–103, passim. As for the style of the "Fichte-Studies," it has definitely been acknowledged as resembling a conversation without a partner, a dialogue conducted by the self with itself for itself, a "*Selbstgespräch*" (II, 93–94; IV, 249, l. 1).

18. In a letter, dated 12 November, Novalis refers to his preoccupation with philosophy as "urgent studies in preparation for my entire future life" (IV, 159, ll. 8–9).

19. "Mein Lieblingsstudium heißt in Grunde, wie meine Braut. Sofie heißt sie — Filosofie ist die Seele meines Lebens und der Schlüssel zu meinem eigensten Selbst" ("My favorite study actually bears the same name as my future bride. Her name is Sophy — Philo-Sophy is the soul of my life and the key to my innermost self") (IV, 188, ll. 8–10).

20. Novalis had been granted a position in the administration of Saxony's saltworks where he had been working under the direct supervision of his father since February.

21. A renowned leader of Pietism at the time, with whose movement Novalis and his family were quite familiar.

22. To forestall any misunderstanding, I should like to point out that the term "practical" relates to human agency as free moral action throughout this study, whether it occurs with specific reference to the Kantian school or not.

23. In the third axiom (*Grundsatz*) of the *Wissenschaftslehre*, Fichte establishes the following sentence as the foundation for the "Theoretical Part," that is to say as the basis for his analysis of human consciousness: "*The Ego posits itself as determined [i.e., limited] by the nonego;* in this sentence the next sentence is contained: *the nonego* (actively) *determines the ego*" (*SW* I, 127).

24. In this connection, it is noteworthy that Fichte's explanation of the Ego's self-limiting action is the weakest part of his system; it seems to be a matter of renewed concern for Novalis at a crucial time for him, later on in his life, and Schlegel also remarks on it critically in his notebooks (II, 305–06). The problem, it appears to me, arises because Fichte supposes activity, whether it be thought of as absolute or relative, to have an expansive momentum, which makes it impossible to derive also a limiting counteraction from the same source. He attempts to overcome this contradiction by introducing a "push in the other direction" (*Anstoß*) that has the absolute activity turn on itself, so that it becomes a self-limiting activity through which the Ego establishes itself as an ego, limited or acted upon by the nonego and, as a free agent, acting on it in return. Where the "push" comes from remains a mystery since there is no activity other than the absolute activity, and therefore the change from pure activity to self-limiting activity remains unexplained. If, however, absolute activity is not understood in terms of the expansive, outgoing tendency, which characterizes action in the relative world of concrete phenomena, but rather in terms of an implosion from all-inclusiveness to all-exclusiveness, from the infinite and all-containing circumference to a point, from infinity to the finite, if, in other words, one understands absolute activity to *be* Self-limiting, then the entire problem raised by the introduction of an extraneous "push" could not arise.

25. The reciprocity of both movements, the simultaneity of activity and passivity that I have tried to convey with the concept of "encounter," is also most emphatically demonstrated in the following lines from a poem Novalis composed for Sophie's fourteenth birthday:

> Was ich sucht, hab ich gefunden,
> Was ich fand, das fand auch mich,
> Und die Geißel meiner Stunden,
> Zweifelsucht und Leichtsinn, wich.
>
> Liebes Mädchen, deiner Liebe
> Dank ich Achtung noch und Wert,
> Wenn sich unsre Erdenliebe
> Schon in Himmelslust verklärt.
> Ohne dich wär ich noch lange
> Rastlos auf und abgeschwankt
> Und auf meinem Lebensgange
> Oft am Überdruß erkrankt.

> What I sought for, I have found now,
> What I found has found me too;
> Gone are scourges of my past now,
> Doubt and thoughtlessness, from view.
>
> Dearest maiden, I'm indebted
> To your love for all I am,
> Even when our bond's transfigured
> And we're rapt in heaven's realm.
> Had we not found one another

I'd have drifted aimlessly
In life's course of bliss and bother
Sick with loathing apathy.

(I, 395, ll. 9–12 and ll. 21–28)

Ernst-Georg Gäde's book, *Eros und Identität: Zur Grundstruktur der Dichtungen Friedrich von Hardenbergs* (Marburg: Elwert Verlag, 1974) contains the most comprehensive exposition of the importance Novalis attaches to the concept of love in his philosophy and poetics. Gäde perceives the great Neoplatonic cycle of movement from Unity to Unity as the basic pattern for Novalis's entire work. This schema is far too general to do more than circumscribe an overall context within which a reciprocal movement of the kind I describe can take place. How the individual comes to partake of this universal movement, which is the most decisive question to be answered, and what role the ethical moment might play in such an event, as indicated in the letter to Schlegel and by the concept of "moral grace" in "Anfang," Gäde unfortunately fails to specify. For his specific interpretation of the latter poem see 179–81.

26. On 9 November 1795, Sophie had fallen seriously ill of an ailment that was diagnosed as an inflamation of the liver. She improved quickly, though, so that Novalis could consider her to be on the way to full recovery eleven days later. There were occasional relapses, yet the overall interpretation of the illness's course was that of a patient's regaining her health slowly but steadily. When Novalis received news on 10 July 1796 that, five days before, Sophie had had to undergo an operation, the seriousness of her condition could no longer be denied and from that date, it continues to be a steadily growing source of concern until her death.

27. Rudolf Unger's pronouncements are exemplary in this respect: "Nicht nur objektiv, als Dichtung, interessierte ihn damals das neue Werk Goethes, sondern vor allem als Lehrbuch der höheren Lebenskunst: er bezog, wie mehrere Stellen des Tagebuchs dartun, Wilhelms Bildungsgang und Erlebnisse auf sich selbst, auf sein persönliches Geschick und sein Verhältnis zu Sophie. Mußte aber unter diesem Gesichtspunkt auf den in tiefster Seele durch den Verlust der Geliebten Verwundeten, der eben im Begriffe stand, diese Geliebte zu seiner Madonna zu apotheosieren, nicht Mignons geheimnisvolle und rührende Gestalt — diese Lieblingsfigur der Romantik, die Friedrich Schlegel in seinem von Novalis (Raich S. 76) gerühmten Meister-Fragment im Athenäum von 1798 (Jugendschriften, hg. von Minor 2, 169) als das 'heilige Kind' bezeichnet, 'mit dessen Erscheinung die innerste Springfeder des sonderbaren Werks plötzlich frei zu werden scheint' — mußte nicht ihr Verhältnis zu Wilhelm und ihr tragisches Geschick auf Novalis besonderen Zauber üben? Mußte seine Romantikerphantasie sie nicht, wie die eigne tote Geliebte, zur Beatrice verklären?'' ("At that time, Goethe's new novel interested him not only objectively, as a poetic work, but above all as a textbook on living as a higher form of art: he related Wilhelm's education and experiences to himself, to his personal fate and to his relationship with Sophie, as a number of entries in his diary indicate. Is it not evident that, from this vantage point, Mignon's relationship to Wilhelm and her tragic fate had to hold Novalis especially spellbound, Novalis who had been wounded to the very depth of his soul by the loss of his beloved and was just then preparing to apotheosize this beloved to his Madonna. No doubt it was Mignon whom he singled out in this manner, the mysterious and touching person of Mignon — this favorite figure of the romantics, whom Friedrich Schlegel called the 'sacred child with whose appearance the hidden spring of this unsual work suddenly seems to come into the open'; Schlegel's critical fragment on *Meister* appeared in the *Athenäum* of 1798 and was much appreciated by Novalis. Was it not natural for his romantic imagination to transfigure her into a Beatrice just as he had done with his dead beloved?'') Quoted from *Herder, Novalis und Kleist* (Darmstadt: Wissenschaftliche Buchgesellschaft, 1973), 60. This is a reprint of the 1922 edition.

28. Hans-Joachim Mähl, "Novalis Wilhelm-Meister Studien des Jahres 1797," *Neophilologus* 47. 4 (1963):286–305.

29. In his letter to Friedrich Schlegel, dated 1 January 1797, Novalis implies that he has read

Wilhelm Meister and was prepared to comment on the work, possibly even review it (IV, 193, ll. 19–23).

30. 290, ll. 4–6. All references to *Wilhelm Meister* pertain to the Trunz edition: *Goethes Werke* (Hamburg: Christian Wegner Verlag, 1948–64). The last clause of my translation is to convey the sense of the Goethean term "dunkel," which I found impossible to translate in any other way. The significance of "dunkel" in this context corresponds to the one Goethe attaches to it in *Faust*, where the human drive toward an indefinite goal is termed "dunkler Drang," a drive that will lead along the "right path," even though its final aim remains "obscure," i.e., "dunkel."

31. 68–72; in particular 72, ll. 8–13.

32. 235, ll. 17–36. Hans-Joachim Mähl believes Novalis refers to the only other monologue in book 4 (276, l. 22–277, l. 25). However, Novalis thinks so consistently of Sophie as a prefiguration of that which is to come, particularly at the time, that the passage I cited would undoubtedly have caught his attention. Hans-Jürgen Schings's very insightful analysis of this first encounter and of the figure of Natalie in general would further substantiate my argument since he recognizes in her "the most 'blissful assurance' of the world's responsive character, of its responsive openness" ("die 'seligste Versicherung' vom Antwortcharakter, von der Erschlossenheit der Welt"), 65: "Agathon — Anton Reiser — Wilhelm Meister. Zur Pathogenese des modernen Subjekts im Bildungsroman," *Goethe im Kontext*, ed. Wolfgang Wittkowski (Tübingen: Max Niemeyer Verlag, 1984), 42–68.

33. The wording of the passage is also easily associated with Schiller's "Das Ideal und das Leben" (*Musenalmanach* 1796), which Novalis had undoubtedly read.

Chapter 6. The "Basic Schema" Completed or *"höhere Wissenschaftslehre"*

34. For background information pertaining to this document, see II, 299–309. The text may be found in II, 346–55; my discussion of it will concentrate on the last section, in particular excerpt 8 (II, 354, l. 34–355, l. 4). Friedrich Strack (*Im Schatten der Neugier*, 52–76, specifically 58) offers a most enlightening analysis of the significance this excerpt may have held for Novalis. I have profited greatly from his view in reaching my own conclusions, even though they point to different directions in a different context. However, I believe myself to be in general agreement, particularly since I shall later be in a position (part III, chapter 8) to support fully the argument he advances in this connection, namely that "Heinrich's dream is in all probability as perfect a transformation of Fichte's philosophy into a poetic statement as has ever been rendered" ("Wahrscheinlich ist Heinrichs Traum die vollkommenste dichterische Umsetzung, die Fichtes Philosophie je erfahren hat") (68).

35. Fichte establishes the entire *Wissenschaftslehre* on the unmediated principle of self-consciousness, which he expresses in his first axiomatic sentence (*erster Grundsatz*) as: *"Originally, the Self simply posits its own being" ("Das Ich setzt ursprünglich schlechthin sein eigenes Seyn")* (*SW*, 98). From this sentence, he derives a second axiomatic sentence, in which the nonego is posited, and finally a third one that comprises the following two sentences: (1)*"The Self posits itself as determined by the nonego,* [which also contains the sentence] *the nonego determines* (actively) *the self"* (*"Das Ich setzt sich, als bestimmt durch das Nicht-Ich,* [worin der Satz enthalten ist,] *das Nicht-Ich bestimmt* (thätig) *das Ich")* (*SW*, 127); this sentence furnishes the basis for the entire "Theoretical Part" of the *Wissenschftslehre*, and it is this "sentence" to which the word "Satz" refers in the eighth excerpt I cited from Novalis's collection. (2) "The Self posits the nonego as limited by the self" ("Das Ich setzt das Nicht-Ich als beschränkt durch das Ich") (*SW*, 125); this sentence furnishes the basis for the entire "Practical Part" of the *Wissenschaftslehre*.

36. Fichte's *Wissenschaftslehre* follows the pattern set by Kant who recognizes two human faculties: the faculty of cognition (*Erkenntnisvermögen*), which is analyzed in his first *Critique*, and the desirous faculty (*Begehrungsvermögen*), which is the subject of the *Critique of Practical Reason*.

37. Novalis refers to this particular aspect of Plato's philosophy a few months later (II, 573, ll. 23–24).

38. Novalis uses the term *Bildung* to explain his position to August Wilhelm Schlegel in a letter dated 12 January 1798; I shall refer to it in more detail later on.

39. Hans-Joachim Mähl discusses the simultaneity of practical and theoretical functions Novalis stipulates as transcending the theoretical and practical dimensions Kant and Fichte envision. He does so in connection with his introduction to the "Kant-Studies" (II, 335–40), a series of excerpts also made in late autumn of 1797 (II, 385–94). In the course of these studies, Novalis voices his suspicion that "practical" and "poetical" may be one and the same (II, 390, ll. 9–10), which Mähl considers to be the most telling formulation for characterizing the superior unity of practical and theoretical faculties (II, 339). It is, undoubtedly, true that Novalis does ultimately reassociate the practical and poetical — after all, he had already done so at the time of his correspondence with Schiller — but not as an equation in which moral agency is equated with, or even replaced by, free poetic "productivity that mediates a true knowledge of the produced" ("[jene schöpferische Erkenntnis, die im] Hervorbringen zugleich ein echtes Wissen um die Natur des Hervorgebrachten vermittelt") (Mähl, II, 339). Rather, I would argue, and this is the direction of my argument in this chapter, that Novalis comes to consider the capacity for moral agency to be also the capacity for receiving a revelation, just as he had experienced it in his encounter with Sophie. This moral capacity, which stays moral in the Kantian and Fichtean sense, must be developed, or rather the self must gain ever greater assurance in its freedom through practicing it, if the scope of revelation is to be expanded. Within such an expanded perspective, any object may assume the mediating function Novalis had once attributed exclusively to Sophie, and this is love no longer bound to a given earthly form but love for his beloved that goes beyond death; it is also the ability to behold the world in a poetic vision, which may be communicated to others because it is as objectively valid as the freedom that introduces moral value into the world. In short, Novalis poses his rhetorical question, "Is it possible that *practical* and poetical are one and the same — . . . ?" ("Sollte *practisch* und poetisch eins seyn — . . . ?") (II, 390, ll. 9–10) in order to deny it and conclude that the practical is not equivalent but rather prerequisite to the poetical. This difference needs to be emphasized since it puts Novalis's candidacy as a forerunner of symbolism and other forms of nonreferential art into serious question.

40. My quotations will pertain to the collections entitled "Logologische Fragmente" (II, 522–32) and "Vermischte Bemerkungen" (II, 412–70); most of the latter appeared, slightly altered at times, a few months later in the journal *Athenäum*, which the brothers Schlegel started in 1798. As for the contemporaneity of these two collections and their connection with the Hemsterhuis and Kant-Studies, see II, 342.

41. For information on the *Hymns* consult I, 115–28; more detailed information pertinent to conjectures concerning the dates of origin may be found in Heinz Ritter's "Die Datierung der *Hymnen an die Nacht*," *Euphorion* 52 (1958):114–41, and in his *Der unbekannte Novalis: Friedrich von Hardenberg im Spiegel seiner Dichtung*.

42. "Instead of dealing with cosmogonies and theogonies, our philosophers deal with anthropogonies" ("Statt Cosmogenien und Theogenien beschäftigen sich unsre Philosophen mit Anthropogenien") (II, 528, ll. 23–24). The term "anthropogonies" applies in an entirely positive sense to critical philosophy, particularly to Fichte's "science of science" (*Wissenschaft kat exoxin*), as will be clear later in my discussion.

43. Manfred Dick offers a thorough analysis of the same fragment in a similar context. He is of the opinion that Novalis substitutes the sentence "the self is determined" ("Ich wird bestimmt") for Fichte's primary axiomatic sentence of self-determination and thus denies the very foundation of the *Wissenschaftslehre* with his "*höhere Wissenschaftslehre*" (*Die Entwicklung des Gedankens der Poesie in den Fragmenten des Novalis*, 270–73). I believe my analysis has shown that this is not the case. With reference to this fragment's Fichtean lineage, I find myself entirely in agreement with Hugo Kuhn, who very definitely recognizes in Novalis's formulation a reversal of the axiomatic

principles from which the theoretical and practical parts of the *Wissenschaftslehre* are derived; since then, Friedrich Strack has made the same point (*Im Schatten der Neugier*, 147, note 238). Their views, however, differ from mine in that they emphasize the practical nature of Novalis's newly evolved concept of the theoretical to the exclusion of its passive element. When, for example, Hugo Kuhn does mention it, then only as the mutual cancellation of activity and passivity in Novalis's identification of "idealism" with the "active passivity" of "Quietism" ("Poetische Synthesis oder ein kritischer Versuch über romantische Philosophie und Poesie aus Novalis' Fragmenten," *Zeitschrift für philosophische Forschung* 5 [1951]:161–78, 358–84, in particular 362, note 3, and 375). Strack, on the other hand, considers it confusion and a "grave error" (188) to equate theoretical and practical reason, which, for Kant, stay quite separate, but not, he observes, for Fichte and even less so for Novalis, who is thought to add "poetic creativity" to the equation (189). I do not believe that this criticism is justified since Novalis's "*höhere Wissenschaftslehre*" only ascribes a theoretical dimension to the practical faculty and does not propose to substitute the latter for the former; nor does his concept of the poetic entail the kind of absolute free creativity that is entirely independent of theoretical stricture because it maintains a "passive" element to which he refers as "true Quietism." The question concerning the relationship of the theoretical and practical aspects of the *Wissenschaftslehre* has also been singled out by Hans-Joachim Mähl in his introductory essay to section 3 of *Romantik in Deutschland*, 331–40, where he specifies that this question is central to an understanding of Novalis's concepts of nature, religion, and the poetic (336). In this respect he points to the contributions by Friedrich Strack, "Die 'göttliche Kunst und ihre Sprache'" (369–91), and Hannelore Link, "Zur Fichte-Rezeption in der Frühromantik" (355–68). With the latter's basic thesis that Novalis's poetic theory and practice constitute a "*productive reception of Fichte's philosophy*" ("*produktive Rezeption der Fichteschen Philosophie*") (357), I am in full agreement.

44. The active passivity Novalis develops in his concept of a "*höhere Wissenschaftslehre*" has definite religious implications that have already surfaced in his theory of mediation. Here, the theoretical momentum that complements the practical one is very much akin to a concept of grace, as he states it a few months later, toward the end of the year 1798:

> Mystischer Dogmatism des Orients — (entstanden
> aus *Trägheit* und *Ahndung*) höhere Mittheilung der
> Erkenntniß -- intellectueller Quietismus — System
> des Wissens, wie System der Gnade — Bassives
> System — indirect thätiges System.
> Axiom: Wir *können von uns selbst nichts wissen*,
>   Alles ächte W[issen] muß uns gegeben seyn
> (Thätige Bearbeitung und *Erhebung der Trägheit*.)

> Mystical dogmatism of the Orient — (composed
> of *passivity* and *intuition*) higher
> impartation of knowledge — intellectual Quietism —
> system of knowledge, as a system of grace — passive
> system — indirectly active system.
> Axiom: We *cannot know anything on our own*,
>   All true knowledge must be given to us
> (Active cultivation and *elevation of passivity*.)

(III, 441, ll. 19–25)

Almost a year later, not quite two years after he had formulated his concept of a "*höhere Wissenschaftslehre*," he returns to the concept of "Quietism" just cited, equating the two with reference to the concept of art. In a marginal comment to one of Friedrich Schlegel's "Ideas" on religion he says:

(Thätige Unthätigkeit, ächter Quietismus ist der
kritische Idealism. Du wirst leicht einsehn, wie
sehr Fichtens W[issenschafts] L[ehre], nichts als
Schema des innern Künstlerwesens ist . . .)

(Active passivity, true Quietism, that is what
critical idealism [i.e., critical philosophy]
is. You will have no difficulty in realizing
that Fichte's *Wissenschaftslehre* is nothing else
but a systematic exposition of the mentality
required for being an artist).

(III, 492, ll. 1–6)

Actually, "mentality" would mean in this case consciousness of the self's free being brought about
in a manner that parallels the schematic pattern of the process traced out in the *Wissenschaftslehre*,
and this form of self-consciousness is the inner requisite for the self's entertaining an artistic relation-
ship to the world. In other words, Fichte's moralism is the active cultivation of passivity that makes
the self receptive to the impartation of higher knowledge, which is a gift that can be referred to as
"grace," or artistic vision.

Chapter 7. Poetic Statement and *"höhere Wissenschaftslehre"*

1. For a detailed analysis see my article, "The Composition of Novalis' *Die Lehrlinge zu Sais*:
A Reevaluation."

2. With reference to the symbolic significance of stones that appear in similar configurations
of centrality in Novalis's works, see Theodore Ziolkowski's historic study "Der Karfunkelstein,"
Euphorion 55 (1961):297–326.

3. *Heinrich von Oferdingen* has been the object of a great number of studies, some of which
have already been cited. In my discussion of the novel, which extends throughout the rest of part
III, I have refrained from extensive academic debate over areas of difference and agreement since
I do not seek to justify my reading of the text in these terms but rather in terms that arise from the
context of the "basic schema."

Chapter 8. Dreams and Fairy Tales

4. The concept is borrowed from William Blake's *The Marriage of Heaven and Hell*; also, in
this connection, my essay "Mysticism and a Romantic Concept of Art: Some Observations on Evelyn
Underhill's *Practical Mysticism* and Novalis' *Heinrich von Ofterdingen*," *Studia Mystica* 6.2
(Summer 1983):66–75.

5. I generally base my translation on Palmer Hilty's text, *Henry von Ofterdingen* (New York:
Frederick Ungar, 1964); to indicate this fact, the name Hilty and the page appear with every quotation,
unless I have substituted my own version instead.

6. "[als wäre ich] in eine andere Welt hinübergeschlummert" "([as though] slumber had
carried me into another world") (I, 195, ll. 14–15; Hilty, 15).

7. For the detailed record that substantiates this claim, see my article, "Another Glance at
Novalis' 'Blue Flower'," *Euphorion* 67 (December 1973):272–86.

8. Rupprecht Matthaei, *Goethe: Die Schriften zur Naturwissenschaft*, ser. 1, vol. III (Weimar,
1951), 15.

9. In this connection it is of interest to note that Novalis speaks of God as the "personified
x" or rather the personified "Fichtean nonego" ("das personificirte x — Fichtes N[icht] I[ch]"), a

concept that has its origin in a "moral revelation," which he calls "a miracle of centralization" ("mittelst einer moralischen Offenbarung, eines moralischen Zentrirwunders entstanden"). These thoughts were jotted down less than a year before his work on *Heinrich von Ofterdingen* (III, 448, ll. 9–12; for the approximate date, see the "Introduction" to "Das allgemeine Brouillon," III, 207–41, particularly 224).

10. I, 307, l. 13 refers to Sophie's blue veil; also, the liquid from her bowl turns into "blue haze" ("blauen Dunst") when it comes into contact with Ginnistan or either of the two children (I, 294, ll. 16–17).

11. For the background of scientific speculation and research that led to the association of galvanism with universal organicity see W. D. Wetzels's monograph on Novalis's friend, J. W. Ritter, *J. W. Ritter: Physik im Wirkungsfeld der Romantik* (Berlin: de Gruyter, 1973), and Maria M. Tatar's *Spellbound: Studies on Mesmerism and Literature* (Princeton: Princeton Univ. Press, 1978), particularly 64–67, and passim.

12. The pattern is one familiar since the time of Plato; it is based on the theme of love's inherently true orientation and the dangers of disorientation in a world of phenomena that are mistaken for reality. Quite untraditional is the perspective of Friedrich A. Kittler, who views the entire topic from a poststructuralist vantage point in his "Der Dichter, die Mutter, das Kind: Zur romantischen Erfindung der Sexualität," *Romantik in Deutschland*, 102–14, and also the discussion on 161–62. He considers romantic literature to be expressive of the psycho-socio-historic shift into a matrilinear familial constellation that took place from the seventeenth century onward; according to his view, *Heinrich von Ofterdingen* is the recording of this event and of its sexual implications along with the poetics arising from them. The story, so he argues, is most succinctly told in Klingsohr's tale, particularly in Eros's wanderings and the shifting panorama of sexual alliances that accompany them.

Chapter 9. The Journey

13. In his critical essay on the "poetic state" ("Der poetische Staat. Utopie und Utopiereflexion bei den Frühromantikern"), Hans-Joachim Mähl has pointed out that Novalis did not conceive his "mythic stylization" of the Middle Ages as a fictive state of primitive innocence, as paradise lost or the golden age that initiates the traditional triadic scheme within which the process of history is thought to extend from an absolute beginning, to an absolute goal; rather, his portrayal of the Middle Ages is meant to contrast with the divisive present for which he fashions the teleological image of "the new Church" in his essay "Christendom or Europe." Here, the Middle Ages have a similar function, one that shows them to be in contrast not only with the time that follows but also with the time that precedes them. They are truly central, and in this sense they are representative of the beginning and end of the triadic scheme simultaneously.

14. In his "The Movable Feast: The Role and Relevance of the *Feast* Motif in Novalis' *Heinrich von Ofterdigen*," *New German Studies* 7 (1979):23–40, David A. Scrase recognizes the theme of the feast as central to the novel, linking chapters 3, 6, and 9 as components of a "whole rhapsody, itself composed of the most disparate, yet unified and unifying elements," by which terminology he means to refer to the feast's being the occasion for recapturing and celebrating "an erstwhile universal harmony." His position is very well taken; except that I tend to view the festivity's function in chapter 6 more in the context of Schiller's definition of "play."

15. The best summary survey of pertinent issues in modern language theory that link it to transcendental philosophy is offered by Karl-Otto Apel in his *Transformation der Philosophie*, 2 vols. (Frankfurt: Suhrkamp, 1973).

16. Derrida is not entirely unaware of the confining aspect his position entails, when he employs the metaphor of an endless picture gallery in his essays on Husserl (Jacques Derrida, *Speech and Phenomena: And Other Essays on Husserl's Theory of Signs*, trans. David B. Allison [Evanston, Ill.: Northwestern Univ. Press, 1973], 104).

17. It has been generally acknowledged that romantic ideology played a notable role in the development of nationalistic and reactionary tendencies that were to prove disastrously compatible with Nazi mentality. The best and most comprehensive study of the subject in English is still, at this writing, George L. Mosse's *The Crisis of German Ideology* (New York: Grosset and Dunlap, 1964). The frontispiece of the paperback edition, which displays a contemporary and widely reproduced painting of Hitler in medieval armor, is particularly illustrative not only of the appeal romantic concepts of the hero held for the public but also to what political use that appeal could be put. See also in this connection Klaus Peter's instructive introductory essay to his volume on *Romantikforschung seit 1945* (Königstein/Taunus: Hain, 1980), 1–39, especially 1–8.

18. The decisive turn in the history of literature occurred with Erich Maria Remarque's *All Quiet on the Western Front* (1929). There had been doubts and questions before, particularly after 1918, but no literary statement of international acclaim had ever been as categorical as this novel in its refutation of the traditional hero image and its corollary, the glorification of war.

19. The difference between Novalis and ourselves is one of historical perspective and not one of moral judgment, I believe. Our heroes and their battles are measured by the same ethical standard Novalis would have us employ, only we have the advantage of being able to rely on different models that have developed since then. The heroic concept has undergone considerable differentiation over the years, and the traditional model of the warrior, on which Novalis had to rely, has been expanded to include those whose militancy does not demand that moral superiority be proved by force of arms. For example, the elimination of armed conflict from their respective programs of struggle allowed such personages as Gandhi and Martin Luther King to be far more effective than any medieval knight in demonstrating the very qualities of heroism to which Novalis subscribed. It seems to me that his inability to illustrate these qualities without compromise was entirely due to his use of traditional images, which had nurtured the misconception that heroes could only prove themselves in war. For a more extensive discussion of differing concepts of the heroic ideal in romantic literature, consult James D. Wilson's *The Romantic Heroic Ideal* (Baton Rouge: Louisiana State Univ. Press, 1982).

20. For a detailed analysis of this poem as well as the second one, see Gerhard Schulz " 'Der ist der Herr der Erde . . .': Betrachtungen zum ersten Bergmannslied in Novalis' *Heinrich von Ofterdingen*" and "Die Verklärung des Bergbaues bei Novalis: Betrachtungen zum zweiten Bergmannslied im *Heinrich von Oftendingen, Der Anschnitt* 11, no. 3, 10–13 and no. 4, 20–23, respectively (1959). Most pertinent for my interpretation is the first stanza whose initial line, slightly varied, also concludes the poem:

> Der ist der Herr der Erde
> Wer ihre Tiefen mißt,
> Und jeglicher Beschwerde
> In ihrem Schoß vergißt.

> He is lord of the world
> Who fathoms her depths
> And forgets in her lap
> All the weight of want.

(I, 247, ll. 5–8)

My translation of "Beschwerde" as "weight of want" may seem odd, at first glance; however, it is not quite as arbitrary as it may appear since the more common equivalents ("hardship" or "burden") are expressive of a condition that is confined or weighed down precisely because that which would alleviate it is absent and thus constitutes "want."

21. Such as the collection of fragments entitled, "Faith and Love" ("Glaube und Liebe," 1798) or the essay on Europe's history and future ("Die Christenheit oder Europa," 1799).

Chapter 10. Journey's End

22. More precisely, Schiller defines the "play-instinct" (*Spieltrieb*) as the coincidence of personal inclination and the ethical command of the categorical imperative, which is free of all inclination. See Friedrich Schiller, *On the Aesthetic Education of Man in a Series of Letters*, letter 14.

23. Klingsohr refers to war in this context as "truly poetic" ("echte Dichtungen") (I, 285 l. 17).

24. The concept of "romantic irony" is viewed from a contemporary perspective in David Simpson's extensive and insightful work, *Irony and Authority in Romantic Poetry* (London: Macmillan, 1979). For a broader background and more traditional analyses of the concept of irony, consult the classic works by Ernst Behler, *Klassische Ironie, romantische Ironie, tragische Ironie: Zum Ursprung dieser Begriffe* (Darmstadt: Wissenschaftliche Buchgesellschaft, 1972), and Ingrid Strohschneider-Kohrs, *Die romantische Ironie in Theorie und Gestaltung* (Tübingen: Max Niemeyer, 1960).

25. Among others, most specifically by Karl-Otto Apel, to whom I shall refer more precisely in the concluding chapter.

26. *Speech and Phenomenology*, 104.

27. My point is essentially that a theory of signs cannot be confined to epistemology but must be anchored in the philosophy of practical reason. The same point is made very eloquently by Jochen Schulte-Sasse in his "Foreword" to Peter Bürger's *Theory of the Avant-Garde*, trans. Michael Shaw (Minneapolis: Univ. of Minnesota Press, 1984), XXII–XXIII.

Chapter 11. Georges Poulet's *Metamorphoses of the Circle:* A Critical Reading

1. *Unendliche Sphäre und Allmittelpunkt. Beiträge zur Genealogie der mathematischen Mystik* (Halle: Max Niemeyer Verlag, 1937).

2. *Natural Supernaturalism: Tradition and Revolution in Romantic Literature* (New York: Norton, 1971). The concept of the circle is of importance throughout the book, particularly parts 3 and 4 (143–252). One of the mottos introducing part 4 happens to be taken from Novalis's *Heinrich von Ofterdingen*: "Wo gehn wir denn hin?" "Immer nach Hause." ("Where are we going?" "Home all the time.") The general theme of the book is similar to the one I am about to broach here since it deals essentially with the secularization of traditional metaphysics.

3. *The Shape of German Romanticism* (Ithaca, N.Y.: Cornell Univ. Press, 1979).

4. Georges Poulet, *Metamorphoses of the Circle* (Baltimore: Johns Hopkins Univ. Press, 1966).

5. Poulet, *Metamorphoses*, xi.

6. All references to *Faust* simply indicate line numbers, which pertain to the Hamburger Ausgabe of *Goethe's Werke*, vol. 3, ed. Erich Trunz (Hamburg: Christian Wegner Verlag, 1949) and to the English version, occasionally supplemented by my own translation, in the Norton Critical Edition of *Faust*, ed. Cyrus Hamlin, trans. Walter Arndt (New York: Norton, 1976).

7. Poulet, *Metamorphoses*, 95.

Chapter 12. A Short Survey of Western Mysticism's Principal Tenets

8. This chapter and some excerpts from the next one have been published as part of an article entitled "Aspects of Western Mystical Tradition and the Concept of 'Education' (*Bildung*) in German Literature," *Studia Mystica* 1, no. 3 (Fall 1978):3–22. I thank the editors for granting me permission to make use of this material here.

9. *Practical Mysticism: A Little Book for Normal People* (New York: E. P. Dutton, 1915), 3.

10. My contention that Socrates's speech ought to be understood as a description of the *via mystica* essentially reflects the view of Alfred E. Taylor, who states: "In spite of all differences in

precise outlook, the best comment on the whole narrative [i.e., the one told by Socrates] is furnished by the great writers who, in verse or prose, have described the stages of the 'mystic way' by which the soul 'goes out of herself,' to find herself again in finding God'' (*Plato: The Man and His Work* [1927; rpt. New York: Meridian Books, 1960], 225. The first edition is dated 1926). For further references to substantiate the fundamentally mystical doctrine of the *Symposium*, consult the entire chapter, 209–34.

11. *Symposium. The Collected Dialogues of Plato Including the Letters*, ed. Edith Hamilton and Huntington Cairns. Bollingen Series LXXXI (New York: Pantheon Books, 1961), 562, ll. 210e–211b. When the text does introduce positive terminology, the vocabulary pertains to modes of being quite beyond the range of human experience, all indicative of perfect unity with reference to time and space.

12. The principle of proportionality for the concept of beauty had been the standard of Greek aesthetics at least since the Pythagoreans. For that same principle's application to the motivational complex of the soul and to human interaction within the framework of social institutions, refer to Plato's *Republic*; the same dialogue also ascribes to the human rational faculty the unifying function of phenomenal reality's correct apportionment, which achieves its culmination and summary effect in the practice afforded reason by the "philosopher king."

13. Compare Evelyn Underhill's discussion of Dionysius in *Mysticism* (New York: Meridian Books, 1965), 456–57. Her book appeared first in 1910 and has remained a standard reference work of undiminished importance ever since.

14. "To [Dionysius] Christian literature owes the paradoxical concept of the Absolute Godhead . . . 'the negation of all that *is*' — *i.e.*, of all that surface consciousness perceives — and of the soul's attainment of the Absolute as a 'divine ignorance,' a way of negation'' (Underhill, *Mysticism*, 457). The idea is common to Greek and Indian philosophy. With Dionysius it enters the Catholic fold. For a more recent exemplary analysis of Dionysius's "negative theology" consult Josef Hochstaffl's *Negative Theologie* (Munich: Kösel-Verlag, 1976), in particular 120–55.

15. The concepts of "purgation, illumination and perfection" are to be found in Dionysius's treatises on the hierarchies, both celestial and ecclesiastic. Also: "Da Dionysius hierarchologisch denkt, lehrt er Mystagogie in den drei Stadien der Reinigung, der Erleuchtung und der Einigung'' ("Since Dionysius thinks in hierarchical terms, his doctrine of mystical ascent comprises the three stages of purification, illumination, and union'') (Hochstaffl, 149).

16. Already in Socrates's case, particularly with reference to his "Apology," "wisdom" consisted of knowing that he knew nothing, whereas commonly acknowledged wisdom proved to be mere self-deception resting on the belief that whatever limited knowledge one may possess — and all knowledge is limited — is not limited but all-inclusive and unsurpassed. From there, the tradition of "divine ignorance" continues, with the notable way stations of Dionysius's doctrine and, later, Nicolas of Cusa's *docta ignorantia*. For Dionysius, also see note 14.

17. Ernst von Bracken establishes the philosophical continuity from Meister Eckhart to German idealism in his book *Meister Eckhart und Fichte* (Würzburg: K. Triltsch Verlag, 1943). Hochstaffl recognizes in Meister Eckhart's mysticism the turning point for the history of negative theology from which its secularization becomes possible (157 and the discussion that follows). William A. Earle speaks of Meister Eckhart's identification of the self's essence with God as "not merely an exultant and extravagant *feeling* or metaphysical *euphoria*, but . . . a literal truth, a truth moreover which is the keystone to every rational system of metaphysics, particularly those prominent in the seventeenth century" ("Phenomenology of Mysticism," *The Monist* 59 [1976]:527).

18. Dionysius is, of course, quite conscious of God's immanence; however the stress lies on divine transcendence, particularly in his book *The Divine Names and the Mystical Theology*, trans. C. E. Rolt (1920; rpt. London: Lewis Reprints, 1971).

19. *Meister Eckhart: A Modern Translation*, ed. and trans. Raymond Bernard Blakney (New York: Harper & Row, 1941), 210 and 326.

20. *Eckhart*, 210–11.

21. That is the topic of an entire sermon entitled "This Is Meister Eckhart from Whom God Hid Nothing," 95–102.

22. *Eckhart*, 168.

23. The English translations of the Greek terms *Poros* and *Penia* vary; however, the general significance remains the same: they stand for the polar contrast of plenitude and lack. Also, see Taylor, *Plato*, 226.

24. For contemporary versions of "negative theology," particularly with reference to critical philosophy, Hegelian dialectics, and the philosophy of language, see Hochstaffl, *Negative Theologie*, 157ff. Even Derrida, despite his expressed denial that his philosophy is "negative theology," circumscribes nothing else but the dynamics of the *via negativa* with his key concept of "*différance.*"

Chapter 13. Mysticism in a Secular Context and Goethe's Metamorphoses of the Circle: An Illustration with Reference to *Faust*

25. H. A. Korff summarized the entire era under the title of *Goethezeit*, to which he devoted a comprehensive study comprising four volumes: *Geist der Goethezeit*, 4th ed. (Leipzig: Koehler und Amelang, 1958).

26. This remark applies in particular to Schiller's aesthetic theory as formulated in his *Aesthetic Letters*.

27. This reference applies primarily to the function Kant ascribes to "ideas" (*Ideen* or *Vernunftbegriffe*) as opposed to "rational concepts" (*Verstandesbegriffe*); however, it applies also to Fichte's dichotomy of absolute and relative ego, to Schelling's "philosophy of identity" (*Identitätsphilosophie*) within which the dualism of nature and spirit is resolved, and to Hegel's Absolute as origin and end of the infinite process of becoming that constitutes our reality.

28. See my essay "Wilhelm Meister's Apprenticeship as an Alternative to Werther's Fate," *Goethe Proceedings*, ed. Clifford A. Bernd et al. (Columbia, S.C.: Camden House, 1984), 77–91.

29. For a most rewarding discourse on the problem of inwardness and the related topic of *Bildung*, consult W. H. Bruford's *The German Tradition of Self-Cultivation* (Cambridge: Cambridge Univ. Press, 1975).

30. Refer to Meyer H. Abram's penetrating discussion of the "Circuitous Journey" as the typically romantic topos in *Natural Supernaturalism*, 141–252, particularly 190–95.

31. Whether Faust's "salvation" is traditional in the Christian sense is debatable; there is no question, however, that he is transported into the presence of Eros's final goal, into Reality, as the last lines of the drama, chanted by the *Chorus Mysticus*, proclaim.

32. For the Kantian aspects of *Wilhelm Meister*, see my essay "Goethe's Reading of the 'Critique of Esthetic Judgment': A Referential Guide for Wilhelm Meister's Esthetic Education," *Eighteenth-Century Studies* 15, no. 4 (1982):404–20.

33. For example, much of Act II in the second part of *Faust* relies for its symbolism on the positions maintained by Vulcanists and Neptunists respectively.

34. Poulet very astutely recognized Fichte as the one most keenly aware of the self's punctual centricity from the perspective of its being the center of an absolutely reduced sphere or, rather a point that is potentially the absolute sphere; 98–100.

35. (Engel schwebend in der höheren Atmosphäre, FAUSTENS UNSTERBLICHES TRAGEND.)

> Gerettet ist das edle Glied
> Der Geisterwelt vom Bösen,
> Wer immer strebend sich bemüht,
> Den können wir erlösen.
> Und hat an ihm die Liebe gar

Von oben teilgenommen,
Begegnet ihm die selige Schar
Mit herzlichem Willkommen.

(Angels floating in the higher atmosphere, bearing FAUST'S IMMORTAL ESSENCE)
Pure spirits' peer, from evil coil
He was vouchsafed exemption;
"Whoever strives in ceaseless toil,
Him we may grant redemption."
And when on high, transfigured love
Has added intercession,
The blest will throng to him above
With welcoming compassion.

(ll. 11934–41)

36. The last lines:

Alles Vergängliche
Ist nur ein Gleichnis;
Das Unzulängliche,
Hier wird's Ereignis;
Das Unbeschreibliche,
Hier ist's getan;
Das Ewig-Weibliche
Zieht uns hinan.

All that is transitory
Is merely symbolic;
The unattainable
Is realized here;
The indescribable
Is enacted here;
The eternally feminine
Draws us toward this ultimate Reality.
[i.e., love is our guide to the perspective of
ultimate Reality Faust's soul is about to attain.]

(ll. 12104–12111; my translation)

37. "Noch hab' ich mich ins Freie nicht gekämpft" ("I have not yet fought my way into freedom"). Line 11403, from which these words were taken, is followed by statements that leave no doubt the free space, or freedom, in question is the same his last words acknowledge.

38. Faust's opinion of Mephistopheles's wares is exactly this, that they can do nothing but tantalize (ll. 1675–1687).

Chapter 14. Goethe and Novalis

39. For further substantiation of this argument, see my articles, "The Conditions of Faust's Wager and Its Resolution in the Light of Kantian Ethics," *Publications of the English Goethe Society* 51 (1981):48–80, and "Conceptual Affinities Between Kant's *Critique of Judgment* and Goethe's *Faust*," *Lessing Yearbook* 14 (1982):23–41.

40. Harold Jantz, *Goethe's Faust as a Renaissance Man* (Princeton, N.J.: Princeton Univ. Press, 1951).

41.Goethe's acquaintance dates back to 1790, when he studied the *Critique of Judgment* and the *Critique of Pure Reason*; he held Kant's contribution in high regard all his life. For further details see Karl Vorländer, *Kant. Schiller. Goethe* (Leipzig: Verlag der Dürr'schen Buchhandlung, 1907), and my article, "Goethes Studium der *Kritik der Urteilskraft*: Eine Zusammenstellung nach den Eintragungen in seinem Handexamplar," *Goethe Yearbook* 2 (1984):137–222.

Chapter 15. Novalis in Contemporary Context

1. *Novalis und die französischen Symbolisten.*

2. Most notable in this respect is John Neubauer's penetrating historical study, *Symbolismus und symbolische Logik: Die Idee der "ars combinatoria" in der Entwicklung der modernen Dichtung* (Munich: Wilhelm Fink Verlag, 1978). Similarly, Walter Moser ("Translating Discourse: Inter-Discursive Mobility and the Early Romantic Encyclopedia," *The Eighteenth Century: Theory and Interpretation* 22 [1981]:3–20) draws the line of intellectual relationship from Novalis's concept of "interdiscursive translation" (6) to the semiology of Charles S. Peirce, Roman Jakobson, and Roland Barthes. The element of difference that persists between Novalis's point of view and any theory based even remotely on a concept of literary or linguistic autonomy is stated most astutely by Strack, who maintains that Novalis's "poetic fictions continue to refer to reality," which is, to be sure, a "potential reality" equivalent to Fichte's concept of "practical purposes" (*Im Schatten der Neugier*, 190). The "potential reality" Strack refers to is one produced by "poetic creativity" (*Welterzeugungskraft*) but there, I believe, he overlooks the decisive element of passivity that is essential to Novalis's concept of the poetic vision. His "potential reality" is not poetically "created" but rather, I maintain, poetically or creatively interpreted.

3. Gerald Graff, *Literature Against Itself: Literary Ideas in Modern Society* (Chicago: Univ. of Chicago Press, 1979), 39, passim. From an affirmative rather than critical perspective, and with specific reference to Novalis, the link to poststructuralism is also established by Friedrich A. Kittler (Foucault, Lacan) in his "Der Dichter, die Mutter, das Kind: Zur romantischen Erfindung der Sexualität," already cited, and by Jochen Hörisch (Derrida, Lacan, Foucault, Kristeva, 408–9) who proposes a shared opposition to transcendental philosophy and its axiomatic concept of self-identity as the factor linking Novalis, Adorno, and "French poststructuralists" ("Herrscherwort, Geld und geltende Sätze. Adornos Aktualisierung der Frühromantik und ihre Affinität zur poststrukturalistischen Kritik des Subjekts," *Materialien zur ästhetischen Theorie Th. W. Adornos: Konstruktion der Moderne*, ed. Burkhardt Lindner and W. Martin Lüdke [Frankfurt: Suhrkamp, 1979], 397–414). However, prior to Hörisch, Ulrich Stadler, in "Die Auffassung vom Gelde bei Friedrich von Hardenberg (Novalis)," *Romantik in Deutschland*, 147–56, had already pointed out with reference to Ernst Bloch that Novalis's concept of money, which Hörisch uses to support his position, cannot be viewed as "a form of pre-capitalistic anti-capitalism" (151), so that the link to Adorno seems as questionable on this basis as it is on the basis of the supposition that Novalis rejected the fundamental tenets of transcendental philosophy.

4. Abrams, *Natural Supernaturalism*, 428–29, passim.

5. René Wellek, *The Attack on Literature and Other Essays* (Chapel Hill: Univ. of North Carolina Press, 1982), 9.

6. Gilles Deleuze, *Kant's Critical Philosophy. The Doctrine of the Faculties*, trans. Hugh Tomlinson and Barbara Habberjam (Minneapolis: Univ. of Minnesota Press, 1984).

7. The term is meant to connote a regression to pre-Kantian dogmatic realism, no matter how modern its garb and how thoroughly undogmatic it may seem. The epistemological fallacy consists of the erroneous assumption that epistemology furnishes the horizon for practice rather than that

practical reason proceeds according to a law that furnishes the horizon for all that may be known. In this regard, one of the most significant conclusions Deleuze presents his readers is the statement "that the final relationship between Nature and man is the result of a *human* practical activity" (*Kant's Critical Philosophy*, 69).

8. Jean-François Lyotard and Jean-Loup Thébaud, *Just Gaming*, trans. Wlad Godzich (Minneapolis: Univ. of Minnesota Press, 1985).

9. This has become evident throughout their work; in Habermas's case within recent years, in Apel's from the very beginning, as his concentration on C. S. Peirce indicates. Most explicit in this connection seems to me the volume entitled *Sprachpragmatik und Philosophie*, ed. Karl-Otto Apel (1976; rpt. Frankfurt: Suhrkamp, 1982), to which Habermas contributed his essay "Was heißt Universalpragmatik?" (174-272) and Apel his even more extensive article, with the revealing title "Sprechakttheorie und transzendentale Sprachpragmatik zur Frage ethischer Normen" (10-173). With reference to Habermas, Detlef Horster is quite specific in pointing out his Kantian background and his reliance on language philosophy from the Anglo-American sphere, particularly speech-act theory, in his attempt to deal with phenomena not accounted for in Marxist theory: *Habermas: Zur Einführung* Hannover: SOAK Verlag, 1980), 15-16, passim; for further substantiation, consult the outstanding and comprehensive study by Thomas McCarthy, *The Critical Theory of Jürgen Habermas* (1978; rpt. Cambridge, Mass.: MIT Press, 1981), 272-357, passim.

10. His position is best summarized in his *Transformation der Philosophie*, 2 vols.; all future references to this work will simply be made by volume and page numbers.

11. Cited according to Apel, II, 173. From Peirce's concept of community, Apel draws the line to Royce, Mead, Morris, Austin, Searle, and Chomsky, to whose concept of generative linguistics he devotes an entire chapter in II, 264-310.

12. II, 223, passim.

13. I, 28, passim.

14. I, 24.

15. See, for example, the arguments that inspired the collective volume to which Apel, von Bormann, Bubner, Gadamer, Giegel, and Habermas contributed in the spirit of a "discussion of theory": "Theorie — Diskussion": *Hermeneutik und Ideologiekritik* (1971; rpt. Frankfurt: Suhrkamp, 1981). In this country, E. D. Hirsch has leveled the same attack from a different perspective in his *Validity in Interpretation* (New Haven, Conn.: Yale Univ. Press, 1967), 245-64. Aside from Apel's essay "Szientistik, Hermeneutik, Ideologiekritik: Entwurf einer Wissenschaftslehre in erkenntnisanthropologische Sicht" in *Hermeneutik und Ideologiekritik*, 7-44, his remarks in I, 28 and 35-52 make his position quite clear; since his aim is to go beyond Heidegger and Gadamer, he refers to them throughout his work in a tone that frequently admixes appreciation to his criticism, particularly in the former's case.

16. II, 403.

17. "Die Sprache ist das Haus des Seins. In ihrer Behausung wohnt der Mensch" ("Language is the house of being. In it man is housed") ("Brief über den Humanismus," *Martin Heidegger: Gesamtausgabe*, ed. Friedrich-Wilhelm von Herrmann et al., vol. 9, [Frankfurt: Vittorio Klostermann, 1976], 313). Aside from Derrida's own references to Heidegger, the ground Derrideans and he hold in common is made evident in Herbert Spiegelberg's apt contrast between Husserl's position and Heidegger's. The former's straightforward call, "zu den Sachen" ("to the things themselves") becomes for the latter, "zu den Sachen über den Text" ("to the things by way of classical texts") (*The Phenomenological Movement: A Historical Introduction*, 2 vols., 2nd ed. vol. 1 [The Hague: Martinus Nijhoff, 1971], 352). Derrideans would have no difficulty in agreeing with the formulation Spiegelberg attributes to Heidegger, but they would also categorically deny that its promise can ever be realized, so that the path supposedly leading "to the things" remains caught up in an infinitely self-referential textuality. If one were to extend the comparison to Novalis, his variation of the theme would have to be stated as, "zu den Sachen über das Prinzip des gemeinmenschlich Verbindenden,

worauf alles Sprechen und Handeln fundiert'' (''to the things by way of the principle that characterizes all speech and action as communal or socially oriented.'') With this principle, which he derives from the Fichtean moral imperative, Novalis is able to furnish the basis for the very possibility of any communication, or textuality, at all; this principle stipulates the reality of things as a reality affecting all selves in common and furnishes the referential ground for any form of communication, whether it intends that reality as its referent or whether it does not.

18. Heidegger conceives of language as the ''house of the truth of being'' (''das Haus der Wahrheit des Seins'') (318) that must be thought of ''as the abode of human being'' (''als Behausung des Menschenwesens'') (333). These and similar remarks throughout this essay and his other publications are meant to characterize language as the phenomenon that accommodates the specifically human capability for being receptive to ''being'' (*Sein*) rather than ''beings'' (*Seiendes*) a state which he also calls ''jutting into being'' (''Hin-aus-stehen in die Wahrheit des Seins'') (326) or simply ''ek-sistence'' (*Ek-sistenz*). In other words, language completes the hermeneutical circle from being to being (''das vom Sein ereignete und aus ihm durchfügte Haus,'' 333), which guarantees the bond of communicative authority. It is quite evident that in this particular context humanity exists — no matter what manner of spelling is employed — as a function of being, whereas the relationship is reversed for Novalis, because if being is to mean anything, it can do so only as a function of humanity. In both contexts the house of language is indeed the same and stands revealed as humanity's abode; the decisive difference is that its contemporary inhabitants have either forgotten or intentionally deny that they are also the landlords, and this is a crucial difference with fatal ethical implications. The efforts of such thinkers as Habermas and Apel tend, in my opinion, to correct this flaw by calling the inhabitants of the house of language back to the responsibility of citizenship in the community of all human beings in whose name that house is built and maintained.

Bibliography

Bibliography

Works by Novalis

Schriften. Die Werke Friedrich von Hardenbergs. Ed. Paul Kluckhohn and Richard Samuel. Zweite, nach den Handschriften ergänzte, erweiterte und verbesserte Auflage in vier Bänden und einem Begleitband. Stuttgart: Kohlhammer Verlag.

Vol. 1. *Das Dichterische Werk.* Ed. Paul Kluckhohn and Richard Samuel together with Heinz Ritter and Gerhard Schulz. 1960; 3rd enlarged and revised edition, 1977.

Vol. 2. *Das philosophische Werk I.* Ed. Richard Samuel, Hans-Joachim Mähl, and Gerhard Schulz, 1965; 3rd edition, 1981.

Vol. 3. *Das philosophisches Werk II.* Ed. Richard Samuel, Hans-Joachim Mähl, and Gerhard Schulz, 1968; 3rd edition, 1983.

Vol. 4. *Tagebücher, Briefwechsel, Zeitgenössische Zeugnisse.* Ed. Richard Samuel, Hans-Joachim Mähl, and Gerhard Schulz. 1975.

(Standard historical-critical edition; supersedes all previous editions. Hans-Joachim Mähl has very recently gained access to new material that is to be published in a sixth volume, which will extend the edition beyond the index volume that was to be the fifth and final one of the series.)

Novalis Werke. Ed. Gerhard Schulz. 2nd ed. Munich: Beck, 1981. (Exemplary one-volume annotated edition of all important texts, with an extensive selection of theoretical works; newly revised, and based on the new historical-critical edition.)

Recent English Translations

The Novices of Sais. Trans. Ralph Manheim. Preface Stephen Spender. Sixty drawings by Paul Klee. New York: C. Valentin, 1949.

Hymns to the Night and Other Selected Writings (including "Klingsohr's Fairy Tale," "Christendom or Europe," and "Selected Aphorisms"). Trans. Charles E. Passage. New York: Liberal Arts, 1960.

Henry von Ofterdingen. Trans. Palmer Hilty. New York: Ungar, 1964.

Works Cited

Abrams, Meyer H. *Natural Supernaturalism: Tradition and Revolution in Romantic Literature*. New York: Norton Library, 1971.

Albertsen, Leif Ludwig. "Novalismus." *Germanisch-Romanische Monatsschrift* 48 (1967):272–85.

Apel, Karl-Otto. "Sprechakttheorie und transzendentale Sprachpragmatik zur Frage ethischer Normen." *Sprachpragmatik und Philosophie*. Ed. Karl-Otto Apel. 1976; rpt. Frankfurt: Suhrkamp, 1982, 10–173.

_____. "Szientistik, Hermeneutik, Ideologiekritik: Entwurf einer Wissenschaftslehre in erkenntnisanthropologischer Sicht." *Hermeneutik und Ideologiekritik*. Karl-Otto Apel, Claus v. Bormann, Rüdiger Bubner, Hans-Georg Gadamer, Hans Joachim Giegel, and Jürgen Habermas. 1971; rpt. Frankfurt: Suhrkamp, 1980.

_____. *Towards a Transformation of Philosophy*. Trans. Glyn Adey and David Frisby. London, Boston: Routledge and Kegan Paul, 1980.

_____. *Transformation der Philosophie*. 2 vols. Frankfurt; Suhrkamp, 1973.

Arendt, Dieter. *Der "poetische Nihilismus" in der Romantik*. 2 vols. Tübingen: Max Niemeyer Verlag, 1972.

Barrack, Charles W. "Conscience in *Heinrich von Ofterdingen:* Novalis' Metaphysic of the Poet." *Germanic Review* 46 (1971):257–84.

Behler, Ernst. *Klassische Ironie, romantische Ironie, tragische Ironie; Zum Ursprung dieser Begriffe*. Darmstadt: Wissenschaftliche Buchgesellschaft, 1972.

_____. "*Wilhelm Meisters Lehrjahre* and the Poetic Unity of the Novel in Early German Romanticism." *Goethe's Narrative Fiction*. Ed. William J. Lillyman. Berlin: Walter de Gruyter, 1983, 110–27.

Berglar, Peter. "Geschichte und Staat bei Novalis." *Jahrbuch des Freien Deutschen Hochstifts* (1974), 143–208.

Bracken, Ernst von. *Meister Eckhart und Fichte*. Würzburg: K. Triltsch Verlag, 1943.

Brown, Marshall. *The Shape of German Romanticism*. Ithaca, N.Y.: Cornell Univ. Press, 1979.

Bruford, W. H. *The German Tradition of Self-Cultivation*. Cambridge: Cambridge Univ. Press, 1975.

Deleuze, Gilles. *Kant's Critical Philosophy: The Doctrine of the Faculties*. Trans. Hugh Tomlinson and Barbara Habberjam. Minneapolis: Univ. of Minnesota Press, 1984.

Derrida, Jacques. *Of Grammatology*. Trans. Gayatri Chakravorty Spivak. Baltimore: Johns Hopkins Univ. Press, 1976.

_____. *Speech and Phenomena: And Other Essays on Husserl's Theory of Signs*. Trans. David B. Allison. Evanston, Ill.: Northwestern Univ. Press, 1973.

Dick, Manfred. *Die Entwicklung des Gedankens der Poesie in den Fragmenten des Novalis*. Mainzer Philosophische Forschungen 7. Ed. Gerhard Funke. Bonn: Bouvier, 1967.

Dionysius the Areopagite. *The Divine Names and the Mystical Theology*. Trans. C. E. Rolt. 1920; rpt. London: Lewis Reprints, 1971.

Earle, William A. "Phenomenology of Mysticism." *The Monist* 59 (1976):519–31.

Faber, Richard. *Die Phantasie an die Macht*. Stuttgart: Metzler, 1970.

Fichte, Johann Gottlieb. *Fichte's Sämmtliche Werke*. Ed. I. H. Fichte. 11 vols. Berlin: Veit, 1845–46.

_____. *Science of Knowledge (Wissenschaftslehre)*. Ed. and trans. Peter Heath and John Lachs. New York: Appleton-Century-Crofts, 1970.

_____. *The Vocation of Man*. Trans. Roderick M. Chisholm. New York: Liberal Arts Press, 1956.

Fish, Stanley. *Is There a Text in This Class? Authority of Interpretive Communities*. Cambridge, Mass.: Harvard Univ. Press, 1980.

Frank, Manfred. "Die Philosophie des sogennannten 'magischen Idealismus'." *Euphorion* 63 (1969):88–116.

————. *Das Problem "Zeit" in der deutschen Romantik*. Munich: Winkler, 1972.

Frye, Lawrence. "Prometheus Under a Romantic Veil: Goethe and Novalis' 'Hymnen an die Nacht'." *Euphorion* 61 (1967):318–36.

————. "Spatial Imagery in Novalis' 'Hymnen an die Nacht'." *DVLG* 41 (1967):568–91.

Furst, Lilian. "Novalis' 'Hymnen an die Nacht' and Nerval's 'Aurélia'." *Comparative Literature* 21 (1969):31–46.

Gäde, Ernst-Georg. *Eros und Identität: Zur Grundstruktur der Dichtungen Friedrich von Hardenbergs*. Marburg: Elwert Verlag, 1974.

Gaier, Ulrich. *Krumme Regel: Novalis' "Konstruktionslehre des schaffenden Geistes" und ihre Tradition*. Untersuchungen zur deutschen Literaturgeschichte 4. Tübingen: Max Niemeyer, 1970.

Geppert, Klaus. *Die Theorie der Bildung im Werk des Novalis*. Frankfurt/Bern: Peter Lang, 1977.

Goethe, J. W. *Faust*. Norton Critical Edition. Ed. Cyrus Hamlin. Trans. Walter Arndt. New York: Norton, 1976.

————. *Goethes Werke*. Ed. Erich Trunz. 14 vols. Hamburg: Christian Wegner Verlag, 1948–64.

Graff, Gerald. *Literature Against Itself: Literary Ideas in Modern Society*. Chicago: Univ. of Chicago Press, 1979.

Habermas, Jürgen. "Was heißt Universalpragmatik?" *Sprachpragmatik und Philosophie*. Ed. Karl-Otto Apel. 1976; rpt. Frankfurt, Suhrkamp, 1982, 174–272.

Haering, Theodor. *Novalis als Philosoph*. Stuttgart: Kohlhammer Verlag, 1954.

Hannah, Richard W. *The Fichtean Dynamic of Novalis' Poetics*. Bern/Las Vegas: P. Lang, 1981.

Haslinger, Josef. *Die Ästhetik des Novalis*. Königstein/Taunus: Hain, 1981.

Haywood, Bruce. *Novalis: The Veil of Imagery*. Cambridge, Mass.: Harvard Univ. Press, 1959.

Heftrich, Eckhard. *Novalis. Vom Logos der Poesie*. Studien zur Philosophie und Literatur des neunzehnten Jahrhunderts 4. Frankfurt: Vittorio Klostermann, 1969.

Heidegger, Martin. "Brief über den Humanismus." *Martin Heidegger: Gesamtausgabe*. Vol. 9. Ed. Friedrich-Wilhelm von Herrmann et al. Frankfurt: Vittorio Klostermann, 1976.

Hiebel, Friedrich. *Novalis: Deutscher Dichter, europäischer Denker, christlicher Seher*. Munich/ Bern: Francke Verlag, 1972.

————. *Novalis: German Poet, European Thinker, Christian Mystic*. Univ. of North Carolina Studies in Germanic Languages and Literatures, no. 10. Chapel Hill: Univ. of North Carolina Press, 1954.

Hirsch, E. D. *Validity in Interpretation*. New Haven, Conn.: Yale Univ. Press, 1967.

Hochstaffl, Josef. *Negative Theologie*. Munich: Kösel-Verlag, 1976.

Hörisch, Jochen. "Herrscherwort, Geld und geltende Sätze. Adornos Aktualisierung der Frühromantik und ihre Affinität zur poststrukturalistischen Kritik des Subjekts." *Materialien zur ästhetischen Theorie Th. W. Adornos: Konstruktion der Moderne*. Ed. Burkhardt Lindner and W. Martin Lüdke. Frankfurt: Suhrkamp, 1979, 397–414.

Horster, Detlef. *Habermas: Einführung*. Hanover: SOAK Verlag, 1980.

Jantz, Harold. *Goethe's Faust as a Renaissance Man*. Princeton, N.J.: Princeton Univ. Press, 1951.

Kant, Immanuel. *Critique of Judgment*. Trans., with an introduction by J. H. Bernard. New York: Hafner Publishing, 1951.

————. *Critique of Practical Reason*. Trans., with an introduction by Lewis White Beck. New York: Liberal Arts Press, 1956.

————. *Critique of Pure Reason*. Trans. Norman Kemp Smith. 1929; rpt. New York: St. Martin's Press, 1965.

————. *Kants Werke. Akademie Textausgabe*. 9 vols. Berlin: Walter de Gruyter, 1968.

Kittler, Friedrich A. "Der Dichter, die Mutter, das Kind: Zur romantischen Erfindung der Sexualität." *Romantik in Deutschland: Ein interdisziplinäres Symposion*. Ed. Richard Brinkmann. Stuttgart: Metzler, 1978, 102–14.

Korff, H. A. *Geist der Goethezeit*. 4th ed. Leipzig: Koehler und Amelang, 1958.

Kudszus, Winfried. "Geschichtsverlust und Sprachproblematik in den 'Hymnen an die Nacht'." *Euphorion* 65 (1971):298–311.

Kuhn, Hans Wolfgang, *Der Apokalyptiker und die Politik. Studien zur Staatsphilosophie des Novalis*. Freiburg im Breisgau: Rombach Verlag, 1961.

Kuhn, Hugo. "Poetische Synthesis oder ein kritischer Versuch über romantische Philosophie und Poesie aus Novalis' 'Fragmenten'." *Zeitschrift für philosophische Forschung* 5, nos. 2–3 (1951):161–78; 358–84.

Link, Hannelore. *Abstraktion und Poesie im Werk des Novalis*. Studien zur Poetik und Geschichte der Literatur 15. Stuttgart: Kohlhammer Verlag, 1971.

_____. "Zur Fichte-Rezeption in der Frühromantik." *Romantik in Deutschland. Ein interdisziplinäres Symposion*. Ed. Richard Brinkmann. Stuttgart: Metzler, 1978, 355–68.

Lyotard, Jean-François and Jean-Loup Thébaud. *Just Gaming*. Trans. Wlad Godzich. Afterword by Samuel Weber, trans. Brian Massumi. Minneapolis: Univ. of Minnesota Press, 1985.

Mähl, Hans-Joachim. "Einführendes Referat." *Romantik in Deutschland. Ein interdisziplinäres Symposion*. Ed. Richard Brinkmann. Stuttgart: Metzler, 1978, 331—40.

_____. "Friedrich von Hardenberg (Novalis)." *Deutsche Dichter der Romantik*. Ed. Benno von Wiese. Berlin: Erich Schmidt Verlag, 1971, 190–224.

_____. "Goethes Urteil über Novalis. Ein Beitrag zur Geschichte der Kritik an der deutschen Romantik." *Jahrbuch des Freien Deutschen Hochstifts* (1967), 130–270.

_____. *Die Idee des goldenen Zeitalters im Werk des Novalis*. Heidelberg: Carl Winter, 1965.

_____. "Novalis' Wilhelm-Meister-Studien des Jahres 1797." *Neophilologus* 47. 4 (1963):286–305.

_____."Der poetische Staat. Utopie und Utopiereflexion bei den Frühromantikern." Utopieforschung 3. Stuttgart: Metzler, 1981, 273–302.

Mahnke, Dietrich. *Unendliche Sphäre und Allmittelpunkt. Beiträge zur Genealogie der mathematischen Mystik*. Halle: Max Niemeyer Verlag, 1937.

Mahoney, Dennis F. *Die Poetisierung der Natur bei Novalis*. Bonn: Bouvier, 1980.

Mahr, Johannes. *Übergang zum Endlichen. Der Weg des Dichters in Novalis' "Heinrich von Ofterdingen."* Munich: Fink, 1970.

McCarthy, Thomas. *The Critical Theory of Jürgen Habermas*. 1978; rpt. Cambridge, Mass.: MIT Press, 1981.

Malsch, Wilfried. *"Europa" Poetische Rede des Novalis*. Stuttgart: Metzler, 1965.

Mangoldt, Ursula von. *Novalis: Europa oder die Christenheit: Utopie oder Wirklichkeit: Versuch einer Antwort*. Weilheim: Otto Wilhelm Barth-Verlag, 1964.

Matthaei, Rupprecht. *Goethe: Die Schriften zur Naturwissenschaft*. Ser. 1, vol. III. Weimar: Hermann Böhlaus Nachfolger, 1951.

Mein, Margaret. "Novalis a Precursor of Proust." *Comparative Literature* 23 (1971):217–32.

Meister Eckhart: A Modern Translation. Ed. and trans. Raymond Bernard Blakney. New York: Harper & Row, 1941.

Molnár, Géza von. "Another Glance at Novalis' 'Blue Flower'." *Euphorion* 67 (1973):272–86.

_____. "Aspects of Western Mystical Tradition and the Concept of 'Education' (*Bildung*) in German Literature." *Studia Mystica* 1, no. 3 (Fall 1978):3–22.

_____. "The Composition of Novalis' *Die Lehrlinge zu Sais*: A Reevaluation," *PMLA* 85 (1970):1002–14.

_____. "Conceptual Affinities Between Kant's *Critique of Judgment* and Goethe's *Faust*." Lessing Yearbook 14 (1982):23–41.

_____. "The Conditions of Faust's Wager and Its Resolution in the Light of Kantian Ethics." *Publications of the English Goethe Society* 51 (1981):48–80.

_____. "Goethe's Reading of the 'Critique of Esthetic Judgment': A Referential Guide for Wilhelm Meister's Esthetic Education." *Eighteenth-Century Studies* 15, no. 4 (1982):404–20.

_____. "Goethes Studium der *Kritik der Urteilskraft*: Eine Zusammenstellung nach den Eintragungen in seinem Handexemplar." *Goethe Yearbook* 2 (1984):137–222.

_____. "Mysticism and a Romantic Concept of Art: Some Observations on Evelyn Underhill's *Practical Mysticism* and Novalis' *Heinrich von Ofterdingen.*" *Studia Mystica* 6, no. 2 (Summer 1983):66–75.

_____. *Novalis' "Fichte Studies." The Foundations of His Aesthetics.* The Hague: Mouton, 1970.

_____. "Die Umwertung des moralischen Freiheitsbegriffs im kunsttheoretischen Denken des Novalis." *Erkennen und Deuten: Essays zur Literatur und Literaturtheorie: Edgar Lohner in memoriam.* Ed. Martha Woodmansee and Walter F. W. Lohnes. Berlin: Erich Schmidt Verlag, 1983.

_____. "Wilhelm Meister's Apprenticeship as an Alternative to Werther's Fate." *Goethe Proceedings at Davis.* Ed. Clifford A. Bernd et al. Columbia, S.C.: Camden House, 1984, 77–91.

Moser, Walter. "Translating Discourse: Inter-discursive Mobility and the Early Romantic Encyclopedia." *The Eighteenth Century: Theory and Interpretation* 22 (1981):3–20.

Mosse, George L. *The Crisis of German Ideology.* New York: Grosset and Dunlap, 1964.

Mueller-Vollmer, Kurt. "Fichte und die romantische Sprachtheorie." *Der transzendentale Gedanke: Die gegenwärtige Darstellung der Philosophie Fichtes.* Ed. Klaus Hammacher. Hamburg: Felix Meiner Verlag, 1981, 442–61.

_____. "Von der Poetik zur Linguistik — Wilhelm von Humboldt und der romantische Sprachbegriff." *Universalismus und Wissenschaft im Werk und Wirken der Brüder Humboldt.* Ed. Klaus Hammacher. Frankfurt: Klostermann, 1976, 224–40.

Neubauer, John. *Novalis.* Twayne World Series 556. Boston: Twayne, 1979.

_____. *Symbolismus und symbolische Logik: Die Idee der "ars combinatoria" in der Entwicklung der modernen Dichtung.* Munich: Wilhelm Fink Verlag, 1978.

Nivelle, Armand. *Frühromantische Dichtungstheorie.* Berlin: Walter de Gruyter, 1970.

Peter, Klaus. *Stadien der Aufklärung: Moral und Politik bei Lessing, Novalis und Friedrich Schlegel.* Wiesbaden: Akademische Verlagsgesellschaft Athenaion, 1980.

_____, ed. "Einleitung." *Romantikforschung seit 1945.* Königstein/Taunus: Hain, 1–39.

Pickar, Gertrude B. "Elements of the Enlightenment in Novalis' Poetics." *Rice University Studies* 55. Houston: Rice Univ. Press, 1969, 185–95.

Plato. *Symposium. The Collected Dialogues of Plato Including the Letters.* Ed. Edith Hamilton and Huntington Cairns. Bollingen Series 71. New York: Pantheon Books, 1961, 526–74.

Poulet, Georges. *Metamorphoses of the Circle.* Trans. Corley Dawson and Elliott Coleman in collaboration with the author. Baltimore: Johns Hopkins Univ. Press, 1966.

Preitz, Max, ed. *Friedrich Schlegel und Novalis: Biographie einer Romantikerfreundschaft.* Darmstadt: Gentner, 1957.

Ritter, Heinz. "Die Datierung der 'Hymnen an die Nacht'." *Euphorion* 52 (1958):114–41.

_____. *Der unbekannte Novalis.* Göttingen: Sachse & Pohl, 1967.

Ruder, Klaus. *Zur Symboltheorie des Novalis.* Marburg: Elwert Verlag, 1974.

Schanze, Helmut. *Index zu Novalis' Heinrich von Ofterdingen.* Frankfurt: Athenäum, 1968.

_____. "Zur Interpretation von Novalis' *Heinrich von Ofterdingen:* Theorie und Praxis eines vollständigen Wortindex." *Wirkendes Wort* 20 (1970):19–33.

_____. *Romantik und Aufklärung. Untersuchungen zu Friedrich Schlegel und Novalis.* Erlanger Beiträge zur Sprach-und Kunstwissenschaft 27. Nürnberg: Hans Carl, 1966.

Schiller, Friedrich. *On the Aesthetic Education of Man in a Series of Letters.* Ed. and trans. Elizabeth M. Wilkinson and L. A. Willoughby. Oxford: Clarendon Press, 1967.

_____. *Schillers Werke: Nationalausgabe* 22. Ed. Julius Petersen and Hermann Schneider. Weimar: Hermann Böhlaus Nachfolger, 1958.

Schings, Hans-Jürgen. "Agathon — Anton Reiser — Wilhelm Meister. Zur Pathogenese des modernen Subjekts im Bildungsroman." *Goethe im Kontext*. Ed. Wolfgang Wittkowski. Tübingen: Max Niemeyer Verlag, 1984, 42–68.

Schulte-Sasse, Jochen, introd. *Theory of the Avant-Garde*. By Peter Bürger. Minneapolis: Univ. of Minnesota Press, 1984.

Schulz, Gerhard. "'Der ist der Herr der Erde . . .': Betrachtungen zum ersten Bergmannslied in Novalis' *Heinrich von Ofterdingen*." *Der Anschnitt* 11, no. 3 (1959):10–13.

_____. "Die Verklärung des Bergbaues bei Novalis: Betrachtungen zum zweiten Bergmannslied im *Heinrich von Ofterdingen*." *Der Anschnitt* 11, no. 4 (1959):20–23.

_____. "Die Poetik des Romans bei Novalis." *Jahrbuch des Freien Deutschen Hochstifts*. Tübingen, 1964, 120–57.

_____. *Novalis in Selbstzeugnissen und Bilddokumenten*. Rowohlts Monographien 154. Reinbek bei Hamburg: Rowohlt, 1969.

Scrase, David A. "The Movable Feast; The Role and Relevance of the *Feast* Motif in Novalis' *Heinrich von Ofterdingen*." *New German Studies* 7 (1979):23–40.

Simpson, David. *Irony and Authority in Romantic Poetry*. London: Macmillan, 1979.

Spiegelberg, Herbert. *The Phenomenological Movement: A Historical Introduction*. 2 vols., 2nd ed. The Hague: Martinus Nijhoff, 1971.

Spring, Powell. *Novalis, Pioneer of the Spirit*. Winter Park, Fl.: Orange Press, 1946.

Stadler, Ulrich. "Die Auffassung vom Gelde bei Friedrich von Hardenberg (Novalis)." *Romantik in Deutschland. Ein interdisziplinäres Symposion*. Ed. Richard Brinkmann. Stuttgart: Metzler, 1978, 147–56.

Stopp, Elizabeth. "'Übergang vom Roman zur Mythologie.' Formal Aspects of the Opening Chapter of Hardenberg's *Heinrich von Ofterdingen*, Part II." *DVLG* 48 (1974):318–41.

Strack, Friedrich. "Die 'göttliche Kunst und ihre Sprache'." *Romantik in Deutschland. Ein interdisziplinäres Symposion*. Ed. Richard Brinkmann. Stuttgart: Metzler, 1978, 369–91.

_____. *Im Schatten der Neugier*. Tübingen: Max Niemeyer Verlag, 1982.

Strohschneider-Kohrs, Ingrid. *Die romantische Ironie in Theorie und Gestaltung*. Tübingen: Max Niemeyer, 1960.

Summerer, Stefan. *Wirkliche Sittlichkeit und ästhetische Illusion: Die Fichterezeption in den Fragmenten Friedrich Schlegels und Hardenbergs*. Bonn: Bouvier, 1974.

Tatar, Maria M. *Spellbound: Studies on Mesmerism and Literature*. Princeton, N.J.: Princeton Univ. Press, 1978.

Taylor, Alfred E. *Plato: The Man and His Work*. 1927; rpt. New York: Meridian Books, 1960.

Thalmann, Marianne. *Zeichensprache der Romantik*. Heidelberg: Lothar Stiehm, 1967.

Underhill, Evelyn. *Mysticism: A Study in the Nature and Development of Man's Spiritual Consciousness*. London, 1910; rpt. New York: Meridian Books, 1965.

_____. *Practical Mysticism: A Little Book for Normal People*. New York: E. P. Dutton, 1915.

Unger, Rudolf. *Herder, Novalis und Kleist*. 1922; rpt. Darmstadt: Wissenschaftslehre Buchgesellschaft, 1973.

Vietta, Silvio. *Sprache und Sprachreflexion in der modernen Lyrik*. Literatur und Reflexion 3 (1970).

Vordtriede, Werner. *Novalis und die französischen Symbolisten*. Stuttgart: Kohlhammer Verlag, 1963.

Vorländer, Karl. *Kant. Schiller. Goethe*. Leipzig: Verlag der Dürr'-schen Buchhandlung, 1907.

Wellek, René. *The Attack on Literature and Other Essays*. Chapel Hill, N.C.: Univ. of North Carolina Press, 1982.

Wetzels, W. D. *J. W. Ritter: Physik im Wirkungsfeld der Romantik*. Berlin: Walter de Gruyter, 1973.

White, J. J. "Novalis's *Heinrich von Ofterdingen* and the Aesthetics of 'Offenbarung'." *Publications of the English Goethe Society* 52 (1983):90–119.

Wilson, James D. *The Romantic Heroic Ideal*. Baton Rouge: Louisiana State Univ. Press, 1982.

Ziolkowski, Theodore. "Der Karfunkelstein." *Euphorion* 55 (1961):297–326.

Index

Index

Prepared by Hassan Melehy

Géza von Molnár is professor of German language and literature at Northwestern University. He is the author of *Novalis' "Fichte Studies": The Foundations of his Aesthetics* and co-editor of *Versuche zu Goethe.* His essays on Novalis, Goethe, and Kant have appeared in *PMLA, Goethe Jahrbuch, Lessing Yearbook, Goethe Yearbook,* and other scholarly publications.

Jochen Schulte-Sasse is professor of German and comparative literature at the University of Minnesota and is co-editor with Wlad Godzich of the series Theory and History of Literature.